Talking
with
Psychopaths
and Savages

Born in 1948 in Winchester, Hampshire, **Christopher Berry-Dee** is a direct descendant of Dr John Dee, Court Astrologer to Queen Elizabeth I. A former HM Royal Marines 'Green Beret' Commando, he is the founder and former Director of The Criminology Research Institute (CRI), and the former publisher and Editor-in-Chief of *The Criminologist* – the world's most respected and oldest journal on matters concerning: law enforcement; penology; forensic psychiatry/psychology; penal reform; the judiciary, and all criminology subjects.

Christopher has interviewed and interrogated more than thirty of the world's most notorious serial killers and mass murderers. He has appeared on TV as a consultant on serial homicide, and was co-producer/interviewer for the acclaimed 12-part documentary series *The Serial Killers*, as well as consulting on the cases of: Fred and Rose West; Ian Brady and Myra Hindley; and Dr Harold Shipman in the Twofour-produced TV series *Born to Kill*.

Notable book successes include: *Monster* – the book that formatted the movie about the US serial killer, Aileen 'Lee' Carol Wuornos; *Dad Help Me Please* – concerning the tragic case of Derek Bentley who was hanged for a murder he did not commit, and was subsequently detailed in the film *Let Him Have It*, starring Christopher Ecclestone – and *Talking with Serial Killers 1*, his 2003 bestselling true-crime book.

Christopher Berry-Dee

Talking
with
Psychopaths
and Savages

A journey into the evil mind

JOHN BLAKE

Published by
John Blake Publishing Limited,
3 Bramber Court, 2 Bramber Road,
London W14 9PB, England

www.johnblakebooks.com

www.facebook.com/johnblakebooks ![f]
twitter.com/jblakebooks ![t]

First published in paperback in 2017

ISBN: 978-1-78606-122-5

British Library Cataloguing-in-Publication Data:
A catalogue record for this book is available from the British Library.

Design by www.envydesign.co.uk

Printed in Great Britain by CPI Group (UK) Ltd

3 5 7 9 10 8 6 4

Papers used by John Blake Publishing are natural, recyclable products
made from wood grown in sustainable forests. The manufacturing processes
conform to the environmental regulations of the country of origin.

Every attempt has been made to contact the relevant copyright-holders,
but some were unobtainable. We would be grateful if the appropriate people
could contact us.

*For Claire, who I sensed sat on my shoulder
throughout the research and writing of this book,
and for my son, Jack. God bless you both.*

Contents

Acknowledgements

The naïve person believes every word but the shrewd
one ponders each step. The wise one is cautious and
turns away from evil but the stupid one is reckless and
over-confident.

Proverbs 14: 15–16

I realise that upon reflecting over the many years of research for
this book and also during the time I spent writing *Talking with
Psychopaths and Savages*, I almost entered an abyss of darkness;
most often a distressing place to be, as the reader will soon
realise – a world of incalculable heartbreak, broken bodies, and
families ruined when precious lives are lost forever.

How does one submit oneself to such a task, you may rightly
ask, without the German philosopher Friedrich Nietzsche's
dire warning being taken into account:

Whoever fights monsters should see to it that in the
process he does not become a monster. And when you
look into the abyss, the abyss looks into you.

Well, the answer is straightforward enough to explain, for I have enjoyed the support of countless people, organisations and institutions along my journey and they have given up their valuable time without a single complaint along the way. Indeed, were I to list everyone, that is all the law enforcement officers and respective agencies serving many jurisdictions, to include the FBI, FDLE, U.S. Marshals Service and British Police (from as far away as Singapore, Malaysia, the Russian Federation, Ukraine and India); correctional staff; judges; attorneys from both defence and prosecution, occasionally psychiatrists – more frequently psychologists; court officials and Public Records Departments; all those grimly associated with some of the offenders featured throughout this book; next-of-kin and the killers themselves I could easily have compiled 4,000 words of 'with thanks' to many of them, some of whom you will find mentioned in this book and the other books I have had published by John Blake (London), Virgin Books (London), WH Allen (London) and Ulysses Press (Berkeley, California).

I have also enjoyed immense assistance from the media: accredited newspaper journalists and well-respected investigative reporters, to include Stephen Wright (*Daily Mail*), from both sides of 'The Pond', along with TV producers who have taken my work to heart, to include my long-time buddy Frazer Ashford (formerly Crystal Vision), TwoFour Group and ITV.

Where I have mentioned the monster Neville Heath, I drew material from the *Murder Casebook* series of magazines, for Heath set the historic 'Gold Standard' for the aggressive narcissistic/ homicidal psychopathic personality. In this respect what applied to him before his neck was slipped into the hangman's halter in the mid-1940s still holds good today.

Although I have never met Professor Robert Hare, who formulated his PCL-R Checklist (maybe I will bump into

ACKNOWLEDGEMENTS

him someday), I am also pleased to recommend the author of *The Psychopath Test*, Jon Ronson. It's a most insightful, laid-back read; one that gives a balanced peek into Robert Hare's internationally renowned, groundbreaking work. Ronson has also visited the edge of the abyss. Like me, he stepped back and I think that he even questions why he, too, didn't fall in. Very humorous the book is too, says British novelist and journalist Will Self, and I agree. Conversely, the subjects of aggressive narcissism, psychopathy, and savagery are not funny at all, something that I trust this book addresses.

Fortunately for me, I have *not* fallen into the abyss that constitutes the psychopathic or savage mind, thus I thank everyone for pulling me back when I might have done just that.

CHRISTOPHER BERRY-DEE
former editor-in-chief, *The New Criminologist*, and director of
the Criminology Research Institute (CRI)

A Letter from Professor Annabel Leigh

Christopher.

In trying to get inside the heads of serial killers, any attempt to appeal to the better side of a psychopath's better nature will be judged by these master manipulators as a sign of weakness, for conscience is something they do not possess, and one's efforts will fail. While every case is different, in some instances the only key to success is recognising their own perversions and needs, for these people never learn from their mistakes.

You should be using their 'victimology' against them. It is the strongest weapon of all. You would have achieved much greater success with the serial sex-killer, homosexual John Wayne Gacy, had you presented yourself as an attractive young man when you wrote to him – falsified a 'pretty' photo if need be – so that Gacy could have sexually identified with you; in his subconscious you becoming a possible victim, and photographic image that he could masturbate over while locked up in [his] prison cell.

You, like so many criminologists and psychologists, often miss the obvious. With respect, you guys fail to think outside of the box. If you are writing to a female killer, you should use a multi-sensory approach: the written word which has to appeal to the inmate's way of thinking; photographic visual stimuli that will conform to their victim type and, finally smell – the latter being the most important. A spray of expensive cologne will linger in her cell long after the written word has been absorbed, making your letter stand out, and bring back memories of better days long past.

The same approach works even better with men. A sexy photograph, a splash of perfume, and they have to reply, and this is why I am adopting this approach with Mr John 'JR' Robinson.

While this may seem very unprofessional of me, I think that your thousands of dedicated readers will appreciate my no-nonsense statement, being: Mr Robinson's thought-processing system seems, for the better part of his life, to have been hung between his legs. For my part, I see no reason why nothing much would have changed today. Therefore, I hope that you, and your readers, will find the results of my correspondence with JR of some interest.

In the meanwhile, I look forward to collaborating with you in your own approach to Mr Robinson. Let's see where this leads us.

A LETTER FROM PROFESSOR ANNABEL LEIGH

Finally, on behalf of us here at Quantico, I wish you every success.

FBI Supervisory Special Agent, professor of criminal justice Annabel Leigh [name changed to protect her identity] to the author

Whoever Fights Monsters

HERE ARE A FEW EXTRACTS FROM
MY CONTACTS:

'Dear Dee. Thank you for your letter. For the last 8-months I have been busy. Watching football on TV takes up much of my time. I will be happy to put you in touch with my solicitor and wife, Teena. She has been instructed to hand over the car and scooter used in alleged murder of Julie Dart and kidnap of Stephanie Slater. I can arrange a prison visit because the security arrangements here [HM Prison Full Sutton] are slack.'
From: Inmate # HP2510 Michael Benniman Sams – letter to the author, January 1995

'The lies being told about me, about things I'm meant to have said and done are too numerous for me to care about... now you are really getting my back up.'
From: British serial killer, Inmate # A0616A Joanne Christine Dennehy – letter to the author, 8 June 2014

5

'Christopher, you are certainly pushing her [Dennehy's] buttons.'

From: DCI Martin Brunning, Bedfordshire,
Cambridgeshire & Hertfordshire Major Crime Unit –
email to the author, 2014

'I know where your house is. You have a silver Mercedes car. But I will make sure nothing an' no one hurts you or your family as I have friends in your country who look after me.'

US serial killer Harvey Louis Carignan's chilling welcome to the author at the Minnesota Correctional Facility (MCF), Stillwater, MN, 1996

'I've been fuckin' waiting for two hours for you. Who'd do ya think I am? I got better things to do.'

From: Inmate #75-A-4053, Ronald 'Butch' DeFeo Jr
(subject of *The Amityville Horror* movie, 2005), Drawer B,
Green Haven Correctional Facility, Stormville, NY – to the
author and film crew, 23 September 1994

'On behalf of all US police agencies you have assisted over the years, please accept the enclosed gift as a small token of our collective appreciation.'

From: Lieutenant Glenn R. Miner, New York State Police –
letter to the author, 21 August 2013

'Thank you for the copies of your books [*Talking with Serial Killers I* and *II*]. They will go into our students' library. Enclosed are a few items as a gift to you for your kindness.'

From: Gregory M. Vecchi, Ph.D., Unit Chief, FBI
Behavioral Science Unit, Quantico, VA 22135 –
letter to the author, 26 October 2009

'Following your letter to HM Coroner for West London, I made an immediate search for the Muriel Maitland papers you are seeking. As luck would have it the documents were about to be destroyed so your application is most timely.'

From: Louise Hall, Clerk to HM Coroner, West London –
phone call to the author, 2 January 2012

'Thank you for your Application for Notes of Evidence (Photocopies) r.57 Coroners Rules 1984 [Evidence of Muriel Maitland on May 1957]. Enclosed are 47 pages.'

From: Louise Hall, Clerk to HM Coroner, West London – letter
to the author, 5 January 2012

'I am in receipt of the copies of HM Coroner's inquest you have sent to us, which we assumed were now destroyed. I would be very grateful for any other information that you discover during your own research that may assist our [cold case] review [Muriel Maitland, murdered Cranford Park, London, 1957] of this case. We have assigned a forensic scientist to search for the documents and physical evidence you require. Please let me know how you get on... I will inform as soon as we make any significant progress, including recovery of case papers and exhibits. Thank you for all of your assistance and good luck.'

From: MetPol SCDI – Homicide and Serious Crime
Command (Special Casework Investigations Team),
New Scotland Yard – correspondence to the author, circa
January 2012

'He's a Brit [this author] and he's nuts. I've been working homicide for twenty years but he scares the crap outta me. He got me to hand over the Carignan files... I got deep shit from my supervisor. Then Chris opened up Harv's mind as easy as a tin of beans and pissed all over the shrinks trying to rehabilitate him.

'Harvey Carignan? The guy's the fuckin' Devil. They should have fried him years ago, period, an' they would have queued up to pull the switch. When he was dead, they should have driven a stake through his heart and buried him, digging him up a week later to ram another stake in, just to make sure he was fuckin' dead.'

From: Detective Russell J. Kruger, Chief Investigator, Minneapolis PD, 15 June 1966

Introduction

Welcome to 'Christopher's World', with a gilt-edged invitation to take you on a journey for, dare I say that I am your 'tour guide' on a road trip into the deeply disturbing and darkest recesses, the abyss of the minds of psychopaths and savages, because now that you are reading this book, you are coming with me, like it or not!

For decades I have been interviewing homicidal psychopaths and savages, at once clearing up several cold-case murders during the process, so it came as no surprise when my long-time publisher, John Blake, asked me to write *Talking with Psychopaths and Savages*. John's stipulation was that I bring you along with me. No 'ifs' and 'buts', period. Excuse 'period', but I do love this Americanism, much as I love, 'Ya'll have a nice day', which this book will *not* bring you as you read through the pages. Period!

This book's title – it occurred to John – would follow my bestselling series of books *Talking with Serial Killers* and the two sequels. I do have thousands of unpublished letters, documents and other unused material in my library so maybe I thought I could blow off the cobwebs and use this valuable, unique resource for creating the book you are about to read.

Oh, how wrong could I have been.

Marching steadily along to the point where I had completed some 45,000 words of the contracted 75,000-word typescript (you'll find it now runs to circa 80,000 words), I suddenly received an email from my executive editor, Toby Buchan. To paraphrase Toby, it went something like this: 'Ah! Yes, Christopher... but we are thinking about *all types* of psychopaths and savages. Not just the killers you have been working with.'

I was back to page one!

For years I have been maintaining that the offenders I have interviewed, and those I still communicate with today, live in a world where elephants fly, lead balls bounce and fairies reign supreme. Actually, I didn't invent that description – my dear friend and consultant on several of my TV documentaries did. Former Judge Stuart Namm, out of Suffolk County, Long Island, dropped it into a conversation while we were swimming in his pool in 2000. However, following up on John and Toby's somewhat belated instructions the penny dropped, for it seems we are *all* living in a world where elephants fly, lead balls bounce and fairies reign supreme.

Indeed, we are surrounded by sociopathic, expenses-fiddling politicians who 'lie and treat us like idiots', writes Max Hastings, *Daily Mail*, 9 December 2015. Money-grabbing corporate fat cats and bloated swindlers such as the late publishing tycoon and arch-swindler Robert Maxwell (who was probably bumped off by MOSSAD), who may be described as a bombastic, psychopathic megalomaniac bully if ever there was any doubt as to the meaning of those terms.

INTRODUCTION

Then we have religious leaders, mad doctors, psychiatrists and the thousands upon thousands of nobodies who are given almost unlimited power, and make everyone else's life a damned misery, simply because they have been presented with a hi-viz jacket and a set of kit that would turn any SWAT team cop green with envy.

'Killer breed' criminal psychopaths and savages get locked up. Some are even executed and in my opinion, good riddance, too. However, the punishment for a conscienceless chief executive of a failed bank, whose alleged criminal negligence has financially ruined the lives of tens of thousands of its customers, leaving them 'potless', with many to commit suicide – is a multi-million-pound payoff in the form of a pension larger than the economy of, let's say, Greece, topped off by elevation to the House of Lords.

To paraphrase Anthony Trollope writing in his 1875 literary masterpiece *The Way We Live Now*, the whole lot of them (politicians) are 'false from head to toe... and should be horsewhipped.' While psychopathic and savage killers rot behind bars, these sociopathic pinstriped 'suits' who have ripped off society, causing incalculable damage, sit on fancy yachts and buy properties around the world, all the while sniggering over their successes and excesses, completely incapable of being able to say 'sorry'. It's a case of 'How do you spell "sorry"' methinks? But I digress.

For those who hold an interest in murder most foul, this book will not disappoint. Indeed, for the first time in criminal history I have asked one of the world's most savage serial killers to review two of my books; requesting his 'professional' opinion on the cases detailed within.

Keith Hunter Jesperson, aka the 'Happy Face Killer', is presently incarcerated within the grim walls of the Oregon

State Penitentiary (OSP). I sent him hardback copies of *Talking with Serial Killers I* and *II* (the same books that are now required reading for students at the FBI's Behavioral Science Unit, Quantico, VA) and I was curious to learn how this boastful man – a person without any conscience, or even a shred of remorse for his terrible sex-related crimes, a six-foot-six giant of disgusting humanity – would analyse men and women who include psychopaths and savages. I have included a few extracts from Jesperson's critique in this book. It will blow your mind, as it blew the minds of my friends at the FBI.

At one point, Keith sent me an outline trace of his right hand. 'To strangle someone,' he wrote, 'you need big hands like mine.' Boasting that 'murder groupies' still wanted to marry him, he also posted a letter from an admiring woman, upon which was a red lip imprint, which was, however, not cosmetic in any sense. 'That's menstrual blood,' he claimed.

It goes without saying that my publisher's lawyers absolutely forbid me from naming the woman who sent Jesperson this mark of affection. But I want to go even further in writing *Talking with Psychopaths and Savages*. Years ago I wrote a well-received paper for *The Justice of the Peace* journal – its subscribers being, quite obviously, magistrates and judges – the latter empowered to take into consideration mitigation presented by defence psychiatrists, who were paid mostly, if not always, from public funds.

Of course, you'll already know that prosecution psychiatrists – also earning a small fortune paid out of public funds – will always disagree with their colleagues on the opposite side of the court. Put half a dozen 'shrinks' in a room and they will have as much chance of agreeing with one another as you or I have of winning the National Lottery.

This book documents just a few of the most tragic cases

where killers are set free, only to kill and kill again. The mass killer Paul Beecham, whom I interviewed in Broadmoor, is such a case. A kindly League of Friends visitor of his, Rita Riddlesworth, fell in love with him and then campaigned for his release, which was granted in 1985. He went on to kill her and then blew his own brains out. We'll return to Paul shortly.

Surprisingly there are also those of religious faith who support the parole of monsters such as Kenneth Alessio Bianchi (the notorious US sexual serial killer of women and schoolgirls, aka the 'Hillside Strangler'). Indeed, Father Frederick Ellsworth, a priest from the Christ the Healer Orthodox Mission, Washington State, wrote in a parole recommendation in support of this creature:

Ken is open, willing to share and quite responsive. I have two young daughters, and I would even welcome him into my home. He would fit in well with my family and his writing has been a high lit [sic].

In addition tax consultant Bruce Zicari from Penfield, New York, declared:

I would certainly like to reiterate my confidence and high regard for Kenneth Bianchi, and I am certain that he has the capabilities to be successful at whatever field of endeavour as he might choose.

Bianchi is a savage sado-sexual serial homicide (with at least 15 women and child victims). However he did go on to complete a ministerial training programme given by the Evangelical Theological Seminary and was then blessed to be ordained by a full Catholic Church in 1986, to become the 'Reverend

K. Bianchi'. He completed independent studies in Eastern religions, Earth religions, Judaism and Biblical archeology, going on to write a homily entitled *Word on the Word…* before suing an American playing card company for millions of dollars because 'they breached my copyright' and 'used my picture in the pack without permission', as he railed in a letter to me in 1966.

'My husband and I divorced because of the stress,' Katherine Yronwode, former owner of Eclipse Enterprises Inc, of Forestville, California, told me during a phone call in 1965, adding, 'everything we had worked for all of twenty years to achieve came to nothing. I cannot say what I think of Bianchi. I just can't say in case he sues me again. I am bankrupt. All of our dreams, the future financial security for our children, their college education, watching them grow up to become homemakers, has been shit canned and sent in a hand basket to Hell.'

While in prison child-murdering Kenneth Bianchi (who now no longer likes me at all) became a Member of the American Bar Association. Supported and funded in this 'Improvement Programme' by the Washington State Department of Corrections, he went on to sue the aforementioned Katherine Yronwode. Then he had a pop at Washington State for allowing me to infringe upon his private life – he had gone crazy when I visited his cell without making a prior appointment. Indeed, he has even tried to sue me. Fortunately he made an error. As I reside in England, I was well clear of his legal jurisdiction. You really could not make this up if you tried, but the very threat of litigation, hollow as it transpired to be, certainly put the wind up John Blake Publishing Limited, believe me!

So, welcome to the edge of the abyss of this insidious world of psychopaths and savages. Fall into this hellhole and your life will never be the same again.

Psychopathy

Over the past few decades it has been thought that the label 'Psychopathy' was a politically incorrect term and those with a liberal bent sought to change things to 'Sociopathy'. Actually, the two concepts are so entwined it is almost impossible to determine the difference. However, more recently it has become *de rigueur* to revert back to psychopathy.

Jon Ronson, author of *The Psychopath Test: A Journey Through the Madness Industry*, would never have considered replacing 'psychopath' with 'sociopath'. I dare say Channel 5's three-part series *Meet the Psychopaths* would have lost thousands of viewers had it been advertised as *Meet the Sociopaths* for a very good reason. 'Sociopath' has a clean PC ring about it. It gives a nod to 'social', meaning living, or preferring to live in a community rather than to live alone, with 'sociability' inferring the subject might be friendly or companionable. However, I can assure the reader that there is nothing 'social' about the characters featured throughout this book and were I

15

to give the term any leeway at all, it would be to add 'Anti', as in 'Antisocial', but that would not make for a very good book title, either.

What *is* good about the label 'psychopath' is that it can be added to and disassembled to one's heart's content:'psychopathic', 'psychopathological', 'psychopathy', or stripped down to the basic 'psycho', with the latter's immediate cinematic association being with the gruesome 1960 motion picture *Psycho*, directed by Alfred Hitchcock and starring Anthony Perkins and Janet Leigh. Many of you will remember the iconic shower scene, where Janet is taking a shower and Anthony creeps in and stabs her to death. Then, considering more aspects of word association, you can also think of 'Silence' then 'Lambs', and we instantly recall the 1991 thriller *The Silence of the Lambs*, involving our bloodthirsty psychopath, Dr Hannibal Lecter (Anthony Hopkins).

'Psychopath' is not a glittering sounding name either; it is one that sends shivers down our spines and makes the hairs on the napes of necks rise – a common physiological occurrence to many people immediately prior to natural death, or upon execution.

There are hundreds of books, articles and professional papers published on the subject of psychopathy; to include titles such as: *Are you a Psychopath?* and *Psychopaths – How Can You Spot One?* Therefore, I was intrigued when my publisher asked me to consider the working title of *Talking with Psychopaths and Savages*, concluding surely this subject had been thoroughly dealt with before. However I was soon to learn, excepting only very few such books, perhaps another one is due. But, I wondered, why would they ask me to set out on this task?

For those readers who have not already read at least one of my books, I confirm that I have interviewed face-to-face some thirty serial killers, plus mass murderers with a couple of spree killers and one-off offenders thrown in for good measure. I will also say that most of the offenders I talked to suffered a murderous psychopathic compulsion to seek out innocent people and visit upon them terrible, ungodly destruction.

While I have every admiration for those who make it their lifetime's work to study the subject of psychopathy, we might perhaps all agree that our understanding of the workings of the 'machine' we call the human brain is still in its infancy. There are differing opinions concerning psychopathy's causation, depending on which side of the fence one sits, with forensic psychiatrists and psychologists often at odds with one another when it comes down to giving 'expert' testimony in court or anywhere else come to that. Furthermore, at the present time the answer to the question comes down to the scenario where just as one believes the cause of psychopathy may be discovered, we find that the stable door has been left open, the horse having bolted.

Recent investigations show that the amygdala part of the brain often comes into conflict with the frontal lobe. A lack of serotonin may also be a cause of psychopathy and could be the reason why killers do what they do. We get terms like 'displacement' and 'misinterpreted needs', 'hemispheric oscillation', 'faulty, and repetitious lack of emotional control' thrown at us. It seems the amygdala has a lot to answer for when our wires short out en route to the frontal cortex, with our axons and dendrites not enjoying a good day.

I vividly recall the US psychiatrist, Dr Dennis Philander, throwing up his hands in frustration during the trial of serial killer Harvey Carignan (a man I spent years corresponding with and interviewing face-to-face). After leaving a court hearing, Dr. Philander shouted, 'Why can't at least two of my colleagues agree at least once on a mental diagnosis?' He added before he stormed off: 'and the trouble with *all of us* is we never seem to agree on anything. Screw his amygdala. If my client turns up in court next time wearing a white robe and leather sandals, I shall advise his attorney that as God didn't help him out last time, I'll follow suit.'

> Their [psychopathic] robotic cruelty reflected dehumanization, stunted conscience, and ability to empathize. They are usually smooth, verbose, glossy, neat, and artificial – both controlled and controlling. Behind a 'mask of insanity', they live superficial and often destructive lives.
>
> – Dr Richard Kraus

And here is a fact that will have you leaning forward in your chair. Did you know that there are a hundred million brain cells in the average person and the presence of one extra chromosome in each cell equates to the presence of an additional one hundred million chromosomes in the XYY male? Studies conducted by world-respected Dr Arthur Robinson were aligned with work carried out by Dr Richard Kraus, who commented: 'Studies report that the XYY male has a 20-fold increase in his lifetime risk, as compared to their incidence in the population, of being institutionalized in a mental hospital or prison – a risk that is not trivial.'

This conclusion seems to be supported by Dr John Money, who gives weight to this debate. Writing in an article entitled 'Human Behavior Cytogenetics', published in the *Journal of Sex Research*, he says: 'It seems perfectly obvious that an extra chromosome in the nucleus of every cell of the brain, somehow or other makes the individual more vulnerable to the risk of developing mental behavioral disabilities or abnormalities, possibly one of the causes of violent psychopathy.'

During my research into the case history of the American serial killer Arthur John Shawcross (since deceased), I found Superman – or at least I almost did! Apart from having the aforementioned alleged XYY problem, Shawcross had a biochemical imbalance as well. Many of us have experienced such a chemical imbalance after a heavy night's drinking followed by a curry, but Arthur's concern was one of the little known inconveniences revolving around a substance called kryptopyrrole. Indeed, so little was known about kryptopyrrole that half of the authorities Dr Kraus consulted for advice had never heard of it and the biochemistry laboratory at the University of Rochester didn't know how to spell the word, replying: 'it sounds like something out of a *Superman* movie, doesn't it?' Of course this all seems a little far-fetched, however, like it or not, if one has a lot of this kryptopyrrole washing around inside then there is a problem – a very *serious* problem indeed.

When considering the case of Arthur Shawcross, during laboratory examinations of Shawcross's blood and urine, Dr Kraus found that while the copper, zinc, iron and histamines were well within the normal range expected to be found in a healthy person, one of the results from an analysis of urine showed unexpected findings. Kryptopyrrole showed 'H 200.66mcg/100cc' against an expected value of 0-20. The 'H' was laboratory shorthand for 'High'.

The term 'Kryptopyrrole' comes *kryptos*, the Greek word for 'hidden', while *pyre* is a prefix for 'fire'. The derivation is both Greek and Latin, and *pyrrole* is a combination word meaning 'fiery oil'. Thus kryptopyrrole becomes 'hidden fiery oil', the chemical structure of which resembles other chemicals known to be toxic to brain function, such as LSD (the 'psychedelic' drug lysergic acid diethylamide). The presence of kryptopyrrole in elevated amounts, although not regarded as a sign of a particular, or, specific disease entity, is, in abnormal amounts, considered a biochemical marker of psychiatric dysfunction akin to the reading of an elevated clinical thermometer being an indicator of physical illness. This biochemical metabolite (5 hydroxyl [l]-kryptopyrrole lactam) is normally present in humans in either very low amounts, or not at all, and its presence can be detected in a person's urine, which may have a mauve-coloured appearance.

Feeling now that he was finally on to something, the indefatigable Dr Klaus burned his own midnight oil and, in so doing, learned that any kryptopyrrole reading of 20mcg/100cc was cause for concern. Shawcross's readings were ballistic, at up to 200mcg/100cc.

Kryptopyrrole is also related to bile and when excessive amounts are present, it can combine with vitamin B6 and zinc to cause a metabolic defect called 'pyroluria'. This proved to be another clue to understanding Shawcross's psychopathy, for pyrolurics function well in controlled settings of low stress, proper diet and predictability. Apart from the initial settling down periods, which are common to all prison inductees, Shawcross, as with most of the serial offenders I have interviewed, was always quite at home within the structured correctional system, where he enjoyed a balanced diet.

Conversely, pyrolurics appear to suffer when living in poorly controlled conditions, such as outside a prison environment. Being unable to control anger, once provoked, these sufferers have mood swings, cannot tolerate sudden loud noises, are sensitive to bright lights, and tend to be 'night people'. They usually skip breakfast, have trouble recalling night dreams, and suffer poor short-term memory, meaning they are likely to be bad liars. Sometimes they lack pigment in the skin and therefore appear unnaturally pale. Their hair is prone to be prematurely grey and they have a diminished ability to handle stress. As such, they may be very dangerous individuals and can constitute a grave risk to the public.

Having myself studied Shawcross over many years, and having interviewed him several times, I viewed his personality in an interesting light, for as Dr Kraus agrees, it seems the symptoms manifested by Arthur Shawcross correlated in every way with those of a person suffering from abnormally elevated levels of this toxic 'chemical invasion'. Having burrowed deep into Shawcross's entire history, literally from cradle to grave, encompassing his parental disorientation, abnormal ECGs, general nervousness, progressive loss of ambition, poor schooling performance and decreased sexual potency, I found that these problems were all embedded in his past.

The abnormality, while being no mitigation for his awful crimes, also correlated with marked irritability, rages, inability to control anger once provoked, mood swings, terrible problems with stress control, violence and psychopathic behaviour. All of these characteristics aligned with the high risk of him becoming violent at the drop of a hat were evident in this man's behaviour. In truth, he was a 'human time bomb'. I have dedicated a full chapter to Shawcross in my best selling *Talking with Serial Killers*, published by John Blake.

Another of my subjects was Kenneth Alessio Bianchi, who is what I'd describe as evil – by which I mean he has a lack of empathy for anybody else. Indeed, if one were to look up 'evil' in the dictionary, you'd find Bianchi's unblinking, ink-black eyes staring straight back at you. Ken is one of the coldest characters I have ever interviewed, and that is saying something, believe me. But he is not a psychopath, as the term is medically and legally defined.

During the 1979 Washington State trial of this heinous, sexually sadistic serial killer, a handful of North America's most eminent psychiatrists could not, *and still cannot*, agree on this offender's state of mind. One experienced, hard-as-nails detective told me, and his conclusion may appear hard to swallow: 'After Lucifer tossed himself off over a shithouse wall, Bianchi hatched out in the sun.'

> It seemed that whenever Ken had a fight with a girlfriend, or had a problem, he went out and killed someone. That's why I am convinced he killed the three schoolgirls way back in 1971 thru 1973. I even told the police the same thing.
>
> – Frances Bianchi, Kenneth's adoptive mother
> to the author at interview in 1964

Telling lies was Bianchi's way of making himself seem cleverer than he actually was: he could not allow himself to be seen as inferior in the eyes of his peers, who were all succeeding when he was failing. Ken needed to be admired for something he was not. He performed dismally at all of his college studies, applied to join the police and was duly rejected only to be offered the menial job of jail deputy, which he declined. He *had* to excel in everything he undertook.

Looking back through Bianchi's history one can see his goal setting was unreasonably high, for he saw himself as 'exceptional'.

The women who fell for this good-looking, plausible liar were soon disabused of his phoney grandiose façade after he cheated on them, so they dumped Bianchi. He had an impaired ability to recognise or identify with the feelings and needs of others – including his own mother, Frances, and later, his common-law wife, Kellie Kay Boyd (now deceased). He had feelings of entitlement. Haughty and self-centred, he was firmly holding the belief that he was better than anyone else and condescending to others whom he deemed to be beneath him. However, Bianchi *did* fail, and we can see that his interpersonal, superficial relationships and efforts to succeed, indeed, his entire ego, hung in the air on a very fine thread, like a balloon about to pop. His self-esteem, grandiosity, arrogance and exploitation of others had come to naught. Like wet cement ultimately disintegrating his vanity crumbled away.

After this savage monster was sent to prison for life in October 2979, the Church became involved and concluded: 'Ken is a good man who has found the Lord.' As mentioned previously, one priest even argued that he would support any parole application, adding, 'and if Ken were to be released, we would welcome him into our home. I would certainly have faith trusting him with my wife and two daughters.'

Bianchi later received a Bachelor of Science in Law degree, followed by a Juris Doctor degree to become a Member of the National Bar Association. In 1988, in a letter to me he claimed that he had received his Associate in Arts degree.

Bianchi exhibited signs of multiple-personality disorder with his 'Steve' and 'Billy', which the psychiatrists had to probe after his arrest. More recently his quest for alternative identities has flourished. In short order he legally adopted a couple of squeaky clean new alter egos that have a good old-fashioned Italian ring about them: 'Anthony D'Amato' (meaning 'of the beloved') and 'Nicholas Fontana'. This heavily pock-marked creature has a hoard of female admirers who hope to marry him.

TALKING WITH PSYCHOPATHS AND SAVAGES

Forget it, girls! At the last count he has wed three women in as many years only to promptly divorce them.

During his killing days Kenneth invented several other false identities too. While in Los Angeles he was a phoney psychiatric counsellor called 'Dr Bianchi', but clients failed to materialise.

Thereafter he emerged as a pseudo cop, to later cook up 'Captain Bianchi' while working as a security guard in the small seaport town of Bellingham, Washington State, where he killed two co-eds. His final tally added up to at least eleven murdered women plus two schoolgirls. Incidentally, he is still the prime suspect for raping and killing three young girls at Rochester, New York, in the early 1970s. Aficionados of true crime will know these incidents were dubbed by the media 'The Double Initial Murders' and 'The Alphabet Murders' because each victim's Christian name began with the same letter as the surname: Carmen COLON (10), Wanda WALKOWITZ (11) and Michelle MAENZA (11).

'Chris, I have genuinely lost the seven pages you require.'
– Bianchi in a 1965 letter to the author regarding
his movements and his blood grouping concerning
the murders of Karen Mandic and Diana Wilder,
Bellingham, Thursday, 11 January 1979.
(The documents were later found hidden in his cell
after this author instigated a search.)

Detective Terry Wight, one of the cops who arrested Bianchi in Bellingham, told me this: 'We couldn't give a fuck whether he's a psycho or not. What we can say is Bianchi is either a damned good actor or he has a degree in bullshit. Now look at those crime photos and tell me that the dead girls' parents give a shit about his brain.'

Detective Wight has a good point. I liked this cop very much.

Later, while in a Bellingham bar eating a slab of steak with ranch fries, principal scenes-of-crime detective Robert Knudsen went even further, saying: 'He [Bianchi] is about as honest as a politician. Chris, I told him flat out: "We got a make on your truck, an' we know you were down that house when the two girls got wasted. We got witnesses, motorhead... we got prints... we got DNA off your fuckin' pants. LabTech is gonna tell us that you're a murdering scumbag. My supervisor wants you on that rope. Now, you wanna talk serious stuff, or be proactive an' commit suicide by jackin' us around?" Hey, Chris, buddy, you want another cold beer?'

I accepted the drink because I liked Bob Knudsen, too.

Detective Richard Crotsley (LAPD Homicide) went even further with his opinion: 'If Bianchi had kept his mouth shut, even a halfwit public defender could have blown enough smoke to have his client back walking the streets within hours. If the judicial train had managed to haul itself into the wrong station, the shrinks would have argued that Bianchi's scrambled brains had been left behind and, at the very least, it would have taken a fistful of psychiatrists a decade to agree on his state of mind. Then, it would be a merry-go-round of appeals, a trip to the State mental institution for more evaluation, back to jail, back to the nut house, and on and on. With the justice system now creaking at the seams, by the time of sentencing civilisation would be eating at a Wendy's on Mars. The bastard should hang!'

I also liked this sentiment *very* much because it resonated with me. Therefore, it is important for the reader to understand that I write merely with the limited experience of having corresponded with and interviewed many of these killers, and others of their ilk, first hand. Like the police, who have to clear up all of the God-awful mess and heartbreak left behind, I speak my mind; I say what I say. I write what I write not in an attempt to conform to the opinions of the professionals who lecture and hold forth on matters of criminal psychopathy, never having met one of these twisted individuals. In a nutshell, I am just like you. Forget the jargon; the fancy labels doctors attached to these terrible people. Some people are very good while others are terribly evil, we just have to live with it.

As another example, here is one much closer to home. None of Dr Harold Shipman's patients, his wife, his closest friends nor any of his medical colleagues (many of whom were psychiatrists) with whom he worked over decades ever considered the good family doctor to be anything but a caring GP. Gosh, didn't we all get a wake-up call when Shipman was exposed as one of the most notorious serial killers the world has ever known? Tragically, after Harold's home visits two hundred plus trusting patients were given a lethal injection, never to wake up again.

Can you imagine anything like this in your wildest dreams? For example, perhaps it is your mother who, apart from 'her feet', is otherwise in good health. She excitedly phones to say that Dr Shipman is popping round that afternoon. 'He's such a nice man,' she purrs. 'He has a beard, you know. Always dresses like your late dad, bless his soul. Tweed jacket, corduroy trousers, a Clydella checked shirt and brogues... um, oh, Dad was one of Dr Shipman's patients, too.'

That evening you get another call informing you that your nearest and dearest is down at the morgue, toe-tagged as a 'natural death'. Five and twenty minutes after the cremation you discover that the old dear's £350,000 estate, including everything you hoped to inherit has been bequeathed to Dr Shipman, who is secretly about to up sticks for Spain.

Fuck that!

So, when I read anything that claims that after studying a book, perusing a press article or browsing through papers on the Internet, or even watching a TV programme you can spot a homicidal psychopath and extend your life, I would ask you to think again. In most of the cases featured in *Talking with Psychopaths and Savages* the victim only discovers the fact s/he is going to become a dead person when it is far too late, with Shipman's victims losing all they had ever been, all they were, all they ever would be, while inconveniently discovering nothing at all about their killer's mindset.

Consider the case of Syed Farook and Tashfeen Malik to take this argument a step further. I think that I'm on firm ground here, for this husband-and-wife team from Redlands, California, planned and carried out the deadliest Islamist attack in the US since 9/11, in which 14 people were killed and 21 seriously injured.

These parents of a six-month-old baby, wearing body armour and combat clothing, were US green-card carrying citizens. Farook (twenty-eight) and Malik (twenty-seven), carried out their massacre at the Inland Regional Centre, San Bernardino, on Wednesday, 2 December 2015. Following a 'shoot out amidst a hail of red-hot lead', the couple were killed by law enforcement officers. Among the items seized by the FBI were 5,000 rounds of ammunition, 12 pipe bombs and tools to make improvised devices, along with a prayer mat, all found in the garage of their home.

Psychopaths Farook and Malik harboured terrorism intent. They enjoyed all of the benefits of living in a free society; they sponged off the State yet decided to commit the most atrocious cold-blooded mass murder without any qualms. This callousness extended to their own toddler, whose future they did not consider.

TALKING WITH PSYCHOPATHS AND SAVAGES

Did their nearest and dearest suspect that Farook and Malik were utterly and irretrievably psychopathic? Mohammad Abuershaid, one of the Farook family's lawyers, said: 'She [Malik] was very conservative. She was a stay-at-home mum (they call them "Homemakers" in the US) and the family was just in shock when they found out. This wasn't something we saw developing.' Farook's sister, Saira, said that she was shocked by her family member's murderous action: 'I can never imagine my brother or sister-in-law doing something like this.'

Homemaker, indeed. Bomb maker more like!

We do not live in a Utopian world: a place where the late crime writer, Joel Norris, advocated we should learn to spot a psychopath, even inform on them to the authorities if the label seems to fit. However, there *are* predictors in a person's behaviour that you may observe but by no means does this mean that people with these characteristics are all killers, who care little whether you live or die. With at least 1 per cent of the population having some form of psychopathic trait – yes, and one of them could be your partner, wife, a dentist, even a gun-toting, power-crazed American cop – you'd be extremely unlucky to fall foul of a psychopathic killer.

> 'Society makes rules we should all conform to. Most of us know the rules and abide by them, for the penalty for breaking them can be severe. Sadly, there are those who transgress and in some US States can face execution. That is their choice and they have no one else to blame but themselves.'
>
> – Suffolk County, Long Island, District Judge Stuart Namm talking to the author, 1975

PSYCHOPATHY

In general, psychopathic murderers on both sides of the Atlantic – or pretty much most places elsewhere for that matter – while they have frequently sought refuge in pleas of insanity, have seldom succeeded. This comes from the understanding that ordinary men and women now have of psychopaths who demonstrate their apparent normality so graphically in the sense that even those closest to them – family, friends and workmates – are unaware of their secret and perverted excesses.

American legal psychiatrist Dr Martin Blinder put it succinctly when he wrote in his 1973 book *Psychiatry in the everyday practice of Law*, 'The psychopath at first glance seems quite well put together.' He went on to enumerate the qualities of personality involved: 'There are no delusions or hallucinations, no memory loss and a solid grasp of reality. His defects, the signs of wayward behaviour, are chronic inability to conform to social norms, to defer gratification, tolerate frustration, control impulses or to form relationships.'

And what motivates the psychopath is the desire to take what he, or she, wants regardless of the consequences. He is insensitive to all but his own needs; his inability to recognise the needs or rights of others means that he sweeps them casually aside or simply uses them for his own ends. Of course, not all individuals with psychopathic tendencies commit murder, though they may at times be violent or extreme in their behaviour as an outlet for bottled-up emotions and inner tensions.

Many psychopathic personalities have an essentially antisocial character usually originating, then developing, throughout childhood. A psychopath does not suddenly wake up one morning and find himself metamorphosed into something evil, for there has to be an incubation period before a full-blown, murderous psychopathy emerges. In the cases of the sexually-motivated serial killers whom I have observed, there is most certainly an incubation process, almost a 'graduation process', where a person's crimes start with 'minor crimes' such as becoming a petty thief, then maybe a 'Peeping Tom' from which he gains some sexual gratification. This may evolve into stalking, then a physical sexual assault, before a rape, then on to serial rape, before stepping over the threshold into murder and onto serial homicide, with all too many of these types of offenders being fantasy-driven by pornography into an increasingly downward spiral into violence from which even they cannot escape.

And this is why trying to find love on the Internet can also be such a dangerous place for the unwitting. The World Wide Web, its chat rooms and 'Love Heart' forums are where thousands of men like modern-day Neville Heaths hunt for prey. But, don't just take my word for it: not a month passes when we do not learn that a woman has been fleeced of her life's savings by a merciless conman, a child abducted by a paedophile, or someone has been raped, or even murdered by a psychopathic human predator – a wolf in sheep's clothing – who has carefully set his web that one person, maybe several people innocently fly into.

It has also been established that psychopaths suffer feelings of deprivation that tend to alienate them from the rest of humanity and they grow up as individuals without a social conscience. Hence the term 'psychopath', described by one authority as the 'supreme con-artist', one who acts out of self-interest. The murderous psychopath is characterised by his lack of guilt or remorse and lacking any inhibitions or restraints, such a person is likely to kill again and again. The mainspring for his killing is not mental disability, but to profit by the sexual gratification from which he gets his kicks.

But for all his lack of social conscience, his disregard for the feelings of others, his inability to feel guilt and capacity for violence, the psychopath knows when he is committing a wrongful act. He understands the rules by which society operates but elects to override them, at whatever cost, to satisfy his private passions. Perverted but sane, his ethos is: 'I don't care – I'll have what I want, when I want, so fuck you!'

On Savages and
Savagery

Throughout this book, I have been at pains to distinguish between true psychopaths, as defined by expert opinion, and savages, so it seems only sensible to attempt a definition of the latter. For while 'psychopath' features heavily in criminal justice systems, and relates to clinical concepts, considering a 'savage' is just as important in cases in which no medical diagnosis of psychopathy can be made.

'Savage' is a tricky word, historically loaded with connotations. Its origin is the Latin *silvaticus*, or 'of the woods' through the Old French *sauvage* for 'wild'. These origins relate strongly to the *Oxford English Dictionary*'s first definition as '*1) a member of a people regarded as primitive and uncivilised*'. This significance is colonial, and it is one which must be largely ignored in the context of contemporary savages. It is the word that Westerners have historically used for peoples whom they considered less developed, and works on the assumption that Westerners are superior to those they colonise. This has nothing to do with savages as I deal with in this book.

More useful in the area of killers, is the general and blunt '*2) a brutal or violent person.*' This is undeniable of the killers I discuss in this book, considering the actions for which they were convicted. They might therefore be referred to as savages. But there is one more useful definition in the dictionary: *A cruel or fierce person. Also, one who is destitute of culture, or who is ignorant or neglectful of the rules of good behaviour.*' This last element is important in placing the concept of a savage in the context of killers.

The idea of savagery has been explored in relation to this lack of 'good behaviour' extensively in fiction. For example, William Golding's classic novel from 1954, *Lord of the Flies*, follows a group of schoolboys who are stranded on an island after a plane crash. The island life means that any lawful interaction between the traditionally 'civilised' boys descends into brutality and violence. Two of the boys are killed, the first (Simon) in an uncontrolled group frenzy and the second (Piggy) in a cold, calculated event in which another boy drops a rock on his head from a cliff. The very same Piggy asks of the group before his death 'What are we? Humans? Or animals? Or savages?'

It seems that savage behaviour here exists somewhere between humans and animals. In *Lord of the Flies* the boys personify this savage behaviour in 'the Beast', a shared myth that represents nothing more than the cruel and violent impulses they each have within them as humans. To use a more recent example from pop culture, there is an interesting exploration of the theme in Disney's Academy Award-winning animated film *Zootopia*. In the film, predatory animals – upstanding citizens of a thriving utopian society – turn 'savage' after being poisoned by the film's villains. They become violent, brutal and murderous, and are cast out by their fellows, creatures that, in a less idealistic world, would have been their prey. The predators revert to their animalistic instincts of flight or fight, and chaos ensues as a community based on mutual respect, the rule of law and social framework begins to fall apart. The film's protagonists eventually resolve the issue, and the predators are given back their 'human' characteristics: they revert to controlled, rational and lawful behaviour within their social framework. It is the defiance of the written and the unwritten rules of behaviour that defines them as savages.

The fact that savage humans' behaviour might be considered animalistic makes a similar assumption to the colonial sense of the word: that animals are less civilised than humans. Of course, if we judge a great white shark on its ability to discuss the weather over afternoon tea and scones, it will fail spectacularly. The difference, then, is that the human savage exists in the context of social human interaction, and acts willingly or unwillingly against this framework. An animal, on the other hand, would display the 'savage' behaviour of unrestrained violence only for food or self-defence. An animal's primary intention is not to hurt another being, but to survive – and if this means harming or killing another living thing, then so be it.

This is where the killers differ from animals. The savages I discuss in this book are not in life-or-death situations when they commit their crimes, nor do they need to harm another person in order to survive. The animal acts purely on instinct, and does not have the concept of its actions having social consequences – for it has no social framework on which to base these consequences. The savage has instead rejected, wittingly or unwittingly, the laws and social constructs of modern society.

Perhaps the best-known writer who deals with the theme of savagery is Joseph Conrad, who in his 1904 novella *Heart of Darkness* paints a picture of the 'savage' Congo Free State in which the colonial definition of the word is still pertinent. However, the entire novel is a contemplation of the different implications of the word, featuring references to violence as well as the breakdown of social order. The latter is done as subtly as in this passage: 'I interrupted him again. Being hungry, you know, and kept on my feet too. I was getting savage.' Even the simple fact that Marlow (the narrator) is hungry is enough to make him break a social rule: the rudeness of interrupting somebody's speech. And this too is a display of savagery in his own mind – the animalistic impulse of hunger makes him violate the rules of modern society.

The greatest irony in Conrad's novel is that the most savage character used to be an embodiment of Western civilisation, a man named Kurtz. He was formerly a writer, entrepreneur, budding politician and well-known artist, but he turns to such unrestrained violence when he travels to Congo to be an ivory trader that the book's protagonist Marlow is sent to find out what has happened. Kurtz has set up a society in which he rules as a demigod, in which his followers torture and kill locals for no clear reason. In a pamphlet composed of scrawlings by Kurtz, the words 'exterminate all the brutes' can be found. It is a sentiment of indiscriminate violence, and senseless violence at that – and this confirms his savagery.

But violence is by no means restricted to fiction – in fact, as the killers discussed in this book demonstrate, humans are very capable of performing the sort of violent acts that writers have imagined. One of the most important and cited experiments on people's capability to carry out acts of unrestrained violence was performed by Stanley Milgram in 1961. Members of the public were asked by Milgram's team to administer an increasingly powerful electric shock to a 'volunteer' each time the volunteer got an answer wrong on a multiple-choice test. The volunteer was unseen but audible. Two-thirds of the subjects were prepared to deliver the most powerful shock, which, although they were not told that it would kill the volunteer, supposedly caused exactly this result. Of course, what the subjects did not know is that the volunteers were actors, and that their switches delivered no real shocks. It was enough for subjects to receive orders from figures in authority (scientists in lab coats) for them to commit terrible acts of violence.

Milgram thus revealed that many more people were capable of violence than had been previously thought. Could all these people be described as savages? I would argue that the difference is that the subjects were acting within the framework that was given to them, that they were following rules. The experiment showed a conflict between two sets of rules; the first that you should listen to authority figures like scientists, and the second that you shouldn't kill other humans. While the experiment proves that people are capable of unrestrained violence in the right contexts, it does not mean that they have abandoned the rules of society in the way that a convicted killer has.

These are the two elements that come together to form the modern savage; brutal and unrestrained violence, and the incapacity to understand; overall, a wilful transgression of the laws and rules of society. And evidence from the trials of each of the killers that I describe as a savage suggests that they meet both these criteria.

For example, Justice Eric Leach, responsible for overturning Oscar Pistorius's manslaughter conviction, converting it to one of murder, highlights the brutal and violent aspect of Reeva Steenkamp's killing: 'Although he [Pistorius] may have been anxious, it is inconceivable that a rational person could have believed he was entitled to fire at this person with a heavy-calibre firearm, without taking even that most elementary precaution of firing a warning shot, which the accused said he elected not to fire as he thought the ricochet might harm him.'

The judge highlights the violence of the act and therefore Pistorius's savagery. It is also clear that the judge does not consider that Pistorius thought rationally about his actions and their consequences, and this is a clear ignorance of the social rules that govern modern society.

Middlesex County Superior Court Judge Frederick de Vesa stated at the end of Melanie McGuire's homicide trial in 2007, while convicting her to thirty years for first-degree murder: 'The depravity of this murder simply shocks the conscience of this Court. One who callously destroys a family to accomplish her own selfish ends must face the most severe consequences that the Law can provide.' The two elements of savagery come together once again: great violence with the word 'depravity', and total disregard for the laws of what is acceptable. The word 'conscience' is particularly revealing in displaying savagery; the online edition of the *Oxford English Dictionary* defines it as '*a moral sense of right and wrong, viewed as acting as a guide to one's behaviour.*' The incompatibility with the state's idea of good behaviour and McGuire's disregard for these rules points to her savagery.

When confirming the death penalty for John Edward 'JR' Robinson in 2015, the Kansas Supreme Court ruled that 'The state presented ample evidence that Robinson lured his victims with promises of financial gain, employment, or travel; exploited them sexually or financially; used similar methods to murder and dispose of their bodies; and used deception to conceal the crimes, including phoney letters and e-mails to victims' friends and family members.' The two elements that define a savage reoccur in the judge's statement: the brutality of the killings

– further evidenced by the fact that Robinson disposed of the bodies – and the killer's total abandonment of the laws of society. The rules of good behaviour that Robinson broke are not only shown in his murders, but also in his forgeries and identity thefts. These additional transgressions further show his incompatibility with modern society.

While the majority of humanity is capable of violence, our awareness of the written and unwritten laws of modern society stop us from performing these acts. Likewise, we are all capable of little transgressions of the laws that make society tick – like lying or being rude. It is only those who combine brutal violence with an animalistic disregard for any rules of human behaviour who can be called savages. You will meet many in my conversations with them, and I will explore what brings out their savagery.

As I said at the beginning of this chapter, the psychopath is defined by clinical concepts, and therefore may be said to be suffering from a condition that is beyond his overall control. The savage has no such excuse.

But first, we must return to psychopathy.

Professor Robert Hare
PCL-R Checklist

It stuns me, as much as it did forty years ago, that it is possible to have people who are so emotionally disconnected that they can function as if other people are objects to be manipulated and destroyed without any concern.

– Professor Robert 'Bob' D. Hare

Born in 1934, in Calgary, Alberta, Canada, Professor Robert Hare is a researcher in the field of criminal psychology. Among his many notable achievements, he is also the creator of the Psychopathy Checklist (PCL-R) – a psychological assessment used to determine whether someone is a psychopath/sociopath. Bob Hare advises the FBI's Child Abduction and Serial Murder Investigative Resources Center (CASMIRC) and acts as a consultant for various British and North America prison services. He is at pains to point out that his is *not* a test to be applied by non-professionals. In other words, don't try this at home for it is an eminently dangerous business, as I'll clarify later.

1. Glibness/superficial charm
2. Grandiose sense of self-worth
3. Need for stimulation/proneness to boredom
4. Pathological lying
5. Cunning/manipulative
6. Lack of remorse or guilt
7. Shallow affect
8. Callous/lack of empathy
9. Parasitic lifestyle
10. Poor behavioral controls
11. Promiscuous sexual behavior
12. Early behavior problems
13. Lack of realistic long-term goals
14. Impulsivity
15. Irresponsibility
16. Failure to accept responsibility for own actions
17. Many short-term marital relationships
18. Juvenile delinquency
19. Revocation of conditional release
20. Criminal versatility.

There are many of us who have watched the 2002 sci-fi film *Minority Report* in which people who are likely to commit crimes are locked up before they actually step over the line. Debunking Joel Norris, the crime writer, Professor Hare says: 'Many people in the population have high levels of psychopathy – about 1 per cent, but not all of them become criminals. In fact many of them, because of their glibness and charm and willingness to ride roughshod over the people in their way, become quite successful. They become company bosses, professional athletes, soldiers, politicians, moreover, these people are revered for their courage and their straight talk and their willingness to crush obstacles in their way.'

Professor Hare adds: 'Merely having psychopathy doesn't tell us that a person will go off and commit a crime. It is central to the justice system, both in Britain and America, that you can't pre-emptively punish someone.'

And that won't ever change, not just for moral, philosophical reasons, but also for practical ones, and here's why. The *Minority Report* scenario is a fantasy because it is impossible to predict what someone will do, even given their personality type (or their star sign if you are into that sort of thing), because life is complicated and crime is contextual. Once someone has committed a crime, once someone has stepped over a societal boundary, then there's a lot more statistical information about what they are likely to do in the future. However, until that happens you can't ever know. That is, with the proviso that one doesn't unwittingly advertise one's self as a gullible victim in a chat room or some other dark place on the Internet, for this is where psychopaths shoal like piranha, endlessly trawling for their next meal – to steal your pension pot, rob, rape, or even kill you.

I ordered the DSM book through the prison library. It's bullshit from the bullshit and none of it applies to me. I am not a fuckin' psychopath. While I'm at it, please pay more attention to your grammar. Inappropriate use of commas really annoys me. And victims don't always pee when they are about to die. I can testify to that so get your fuckin' facts straight. I expect perfection from you. Not bullshit.

> – Serial killer Keith Hunter Jesperson –
> 2011 letter to this author

The American Psychiatric Association now publishes its 5th Edition of the *Diagnostic and Statistical Manual of Mental Disorders* (DSM-1V-TR). This 886-page textbook is not one for the layperson, and certainly not an easy bedtime read. But if you insist, and you are honest with yourself, you will probably find at least several of the listed 374 mental disorders apply to the reasons for early years' enuresis (wetting oneself), insomnia, and why your partner is now slumbering in the spare room with a silver-plated .32 calibre 'Saturday Night Special' pistol under her pillow. However, DSM-1V-TR *is* a must-read for psychiatrists who may have a latent axe-murderer with a particular dislike for shrinks reclining on their couch.

I suggested to Keith Jesperson that he read DSM-1V-TR. My very suggestion to him that he is a sexually motivated serial killer, or even that he is antisocial, was alien to him, with his response being: 'Who are you and any of your doctor pals to judge who is normal and who is not? You sit in London enjoying cream teas. I enjoyed killing. I am just like you, it's just our personal preferences that differ.'

I was, however, also inclined to refer The American Psychiatric Association's book to, among others, Kenneth Bianchi. However, I thought better of it. Perhaps Dr R. Joseph's *The Right Brain and the Unconscious: Discovering the Stranger Within* might interest Ken, however? With Ken's apparent alter egos and his convincing multiple-personality disorders, Dr Joseph's book might have been something he could have really got his teeth into.

PROFESSOR ROBERT HARE PCL-R CHECKLIST

I am filing this reference on behalf of Ken. He is a member in good standing of my church. I have baptised Ken myself and, after extensive interviews, I have satisfied my mind as to his sincerity. He is an active member and regular attendee at our services on the prison campus. His attitude and conduct at the present time is exemplary.

– Letter dated 17 December 1958, from Pastor Dick Jewett, Stateline Seventh-Day Adventist Church, Milton-Freewater, Oregon, supporting Kenneth Bianchi's parole

It is clear to me that Ken lives in a world where elephants fly. However, many of the psychiatrists who visit with Mr Bianchi today disagree.

I have interviewed more heinous psychopathic serial killers, savages, spree killers, mass murderers and out-and-out nut balls than Stephen King could ever invent. I have heard psychiatric defence mitigation which has included everything from bad potty training to 'forced to wear a nappy until the Defendant was sixteen'. Other explanations for their behaviour include a bump on the head, or a fall from a playground slide, or maybe: 'As a toddler my client was forced to drink green-top milk instead of blue-capped full cream.' And that's before Our Lord enters the picture.

I have lost count of how many times Jesus gets the blame for a killer running amok, abducting young women, torturing them for hours, even days – and for the cutting, the raping and the killing, as was the case with Harvey 'The Hammer' Carignan. 'It was God's calling', according to Harvey, much like the defence of former gravedigger Peter Sutcliffe, aka 'The

Yorkshire Ripper', who self-allegedly received a 'message' while digging a hole in the ground.

More often than not, the problem is that psychiatrists, like lawyers, seek to put the best spin on their client's case.

LEE BAKER AKA 'THE BOURNEMOUTH CROSSBOW KILLER'

Way back in 1987, I attended the murder trial held at Winchester Assizes of twenty-year-old Lee Baker, whose mental competence, or lack of it, demanded furious debate between psychiatrists employed by both defence and prosecution. The *prima facie* substance of the murders for which Lee was arraigned was beyond doubt – he had pleaded guilty.

Baker was a handsome young man and it transpired that he had been dating a young woman since October 1983 but they broke up in April 1986, after he broke her nose during a fight. Understandably, the girl's mother, Alida, ordered her daughter to break off the relationship, which she did, and this caused Lee Baker to flip.

On Monday, 28 July 1986, Baker called upon Alida Johanna Maria Goode at her home at 6 Shelton Road, Bournemouth. There, he decapitated her, placed her body in her bed, shot the family dog – which was cowering under a kitchen table – with a crossbow, and set the place ablaze. Shortly thereafter, Lee spotted his former girlfriend cycling home. 'See those fire engines,' he told her, 'they're going to your house. Byeee!'

However, Baker was not yet finished. In Castle Lane he fired a bolt from his crossbow into one Arthur Rattue and then stabbed him. Rattue managed to stagger to a house, where he rang the bell before collapsing on the doorstep. An ambulance was called and the intended murder victim survived. Lee was arrested the following day, shortly after he visited a petrol station where he filled up several canisters. He was intending to firebomb unspecified targets.

By way of mitigation, the defence psychiatrist argued that Baker was of 'unsound mind' when he committed his crimes and this warranted some form of leniency on behalf of the judge when he considered sentencing. For their part, the prosecution produced two psychiatrists who countered this view, stating that the man standing in the dock was completely sane and therefore fully responsible for his actions. They described Baker as a 'cold-blooded psychopath, a man incapable of any feelings, emotion nor remorse'. And told how they had based their 'professional opinion' on many hours extensively interviewing the remanded defendant in the hospital wing of HM Prison Winchester.

Under cross-examination it was revealed through inmate visitation records that while one prosecution psychiatrist had indeed spoken to Lee for 60 minutes, his female colleague had merely popped in to say 'hello'. She had based all of her 'corroborating expert testimony' on what her associate had told her. Lee Baker is presently serving a life term at HM Prison Oakwood, Staffordshire, and I have been led to understand he hasn't shot anyone with a crossbow or decapitated anyone else since. For the purposes of researching this book, I did write to Baker but failed to get a reply.

For over three decades I have been interviewing sexual psychopaths – many of whom are serial murderers – in the human warehouses called 'Correctional Facilities' throughout America, Russia, India and the Far East. These are scary places, where the sweet stench of disinfectant and stale urine permeates every brick. I have sat with these men and women while they sometimes gleefully recounted their terrible crimes, only then to protest their innocence, so it has been a difficult task to select the few examples of extreme psychopathy, given the word count allocated to me for this book.

'You can't straighten out a crooked tree.'
— Suffolk County Long Island Asst District Attorney
Gerald Sullivan to the author in 1967

'The shrinks say that you cannot cure a murderous psychopath. What do they know? Down here we've got the perfect cure. That mean ole gurney through that door. Strap 'em down. Job done!'
— Neil Hodges, Asst Warden-in-Charge of
Executions, The Walls Prison, Huntsville, Texas —
to the author, concerning serial killer
Kenneth McDuff in March 1969.

Gruesome as Hodges's observation may be, I think he does have a point because I experienced the 'strap-down' protocol from Death Cell to gurney myself. Even though there were no tubes (the executioner was on vacation) it put the fear of God into me. Indeed, one could be suffering every illness known to mankind yet just a cocktail of three injections administered one after the other will cure the lot in seven minutes flat.

Aside from Warden Hodges's professional experience, it will soon become apparent that psychopathy is untreatable. Furthermore, its causes remain a matter of debate, an issue best left for others more qualified than me to include within the word count allocated me in this book. But, once a person is so afflicted he remains this way for life, for there are no drugs available — with the exception of Warden Hodges's 'cure': 8cc

PROFESSOR ROBERT HARE PCL-R CHECKLIST

2 per cent sodium thiopental, 15cc normal saline, 50mg/50cc pancuronium bromide, another 15cc normal saline and 1.50–2.70mEq/kg potassium chloride – to remove or suppress this specific condition.

In bygone days, electrocompulsive therapy (ECT) was used in futile attempts to cure all manner of mental ills. (In fact, up until recently in most US States electricity was also used to cure all manner of ills. It was called the 'Electric Chair' – 'Ole Sparky' to you and me. Inmates call it 'Riding the Lightning'.)

In Victorian times, immersion in ice-cold baths and the application of leeches were tried as experimental cure-alls for many of the mental illnesses, but none of these worked and often left the patients far worse off than before, to dribble and stumble around an asylum's well-manicured grounds dressed in white gowns in a state of utter bewilderment, as one might expect.

I used to live in the sleepy Hampshire village of Wickham and just a quarter-mile walk along a narrow lane led me to what was then Knowle Asylum, but has since been demolished to make way for a housing estate. Back in those old days, many of the patients were allowed to amble freely around the locality, to peer through the local pub window or knock on a pensioner's front door wearing nothing more than pyjamas – in warmer weather, nothing at all. They also used to commit suicide by hanging themselves in a local copse or by jumping over a railway bridge, which didn't do much for the mental state of the train drivers, either.

So, if psychopathy is untreatable, why bother to write a a large part of this book about psychopaths at all? Well, it occurs to me that there is one solid answer: by studying these incarcerated miscreants, law enforcement can learn how their dysfunctional minds tick. This knowledge is certainly valuable when trying to profile other offenders, who will almost certainly strike again before they are arrested. In a nutshell, this work becomes yet another tool in the homicide investigator's box. One cannot prevent a psychopath from starting his killing career – no one can do that – however, studies of other convicted psychopaths can hopefully nip in the bud another psychopath's killing spree.

PAUL BEECHAM

Before I bring this chapter to its conclusion, please allow me to briefly return to Paul Beecham, whom I mentioned earlier because I can hear you asking why this psychopathic mass murderer was released from Broadmoor after spending just 16 years behind bars.

From what scant details are available, it transpires that his father, Jim, and mother, Margaret, ran a boatbuilding yard in Bredon Road, Tewksbury, Gloucestershire. One evening in 1968, while Jim and Margaret were entertaining the latter's parents in their onsite bungalow, Paul, then aged twenty-six, arrived and shot his father with a semi-automatic rifle because 'I was annoyed with him,' as he told police. He shot his mother and grandmother because they wouldn't stop screaming and then, when his grandfather returned to the property, he too was shot, 'because he was the only one left,' Paul explained in a monotone sort of way.

Accepting that Beecham was suffering a form of mental illness, in 1969 the judge at Gloucester Assizes had him sent to the secure Broadmoor Hospital (formerly known as the Broadmoor Lunatic Asylum), where he was placed under the supervision of the then Superintendent, Dr Pat McGrath. It was here that Paul met an attractive League of Friends visitor called Rita Riddlesworth. The divorced mother of two sons was particularly taken by the quality of Beecham's oil paintings. (I was equally impressed – indeed I bought one, a near-perfect copy of Vladimir Tretchikoff's *Chinese Girl* aka *The Green Lady*.) Over time, Rita and Paul fell in love.

Considered 'Unlikely to kill again' by Superintendent Pat McGrath, Beecham was released from Broadmoor in 1985. The couple then moved into Rita's £250,000 house in Grange Road, Bracknell, just 10 miles from Broadmoor, and from where he started a very successful signwriting firm. In 1995, Rita had a mental breakdown from which she recovered, but in 1996 she had a recurrence and went back to hospital. It was during this second stay that she confided to her sons the details of Paul's background – specifically that he had been a mass murderer. And that's not the sort of thing one learns every day, is it?

They questioned Paul, who assured them that this was past history. Besides, they both considered him to be a loving father, a loyal husband to their mother and a hard-working man. However, it appeared that something *was* wrong and this problem was linked to the reason why Rita had suffered a nervous breakdown in the first instance.

After conducting quite a bit of research, despite hearing local rumours that Rita was a neurotic, over-possessive woman, I learned that she was anything but such a person. The truth of this entirely tragic matter is that Paul was reverting to his former, mentally unbalanced state of mind: that of a psychopath with paranoid schizophrenic tendencies that were accompanied by a whole raft of other psychiatric issues too complex to detail here.

Throughout the period following Beecham's release from Broadmoor until three months before he killed Rita, then himself, he and I enjoyed sporadic communication, mostly concerning his artwork; this was a mutual interest, as I am a painter in oils, too. Several times he explained to me over the telephone that he considered his work was no longer up to scratch; that he spent too much time alone and fretting in his studio workshop. And that people had discovered who he really was, that they were talking about him behind his back, and that Rita was behind this whispering campaign.

I asked him if he had spoken to Rita about this and he said that he had, that it was becoming almost a daily issue of discussion. Then, in one ominous statement he volunteered: 'All of them are looking at me... pointing fingers... and she *is* the cause of it all. She wants to leave me because she is scared.'

To break the ice, I asked: 'Shall we hook up and talk about painting?'

'Sure, why not?' he replied, so we arranged to meet up near Winchester and go for a stroll along the river by the college, which we did.

As any artist will testify, just as any trainspotter will agree, if you put two guys with similar interests together, they'll chat for hours, or until Hell freezes over. Paul and I talked about canvas supports, whether one preferred neat linseed oil or a proprietary substitute. That using student-quality oil paint was false economy, considering the higher concentration of pigment in artist's quality products meaning they lasted for longer. We bickered over Daler-Rowney, Winsor & Newton and the Rembrandt brands of paint while he laughed as my two dogs, William and Whisky, chased the ducks.

That night Paul stayed at my Wickham home. He left early without saying goodbye, however, while I slept soundly during the early hours he had quietly moved around the place and meticulously cleaned the kitchen from top to bottom. He left me this note:

Chris, seeing my painting on your wall tells me that you are the only person who understands me. I did my best [painting] work in hospital because I was left alone. I have tried hard to make good but the voices never stop. Now I have to go.

Rita was last seen alive on Tuesday, 21 October 1997, when the couple enjoyed a meal with friends.

On a chilly Wednesday, 12 November 1997, Paul Beecham finally cracked. He took up a 12-gauge shotgun and blasted Rita to death before burying her body three feet under their patio. The following day a friend contacted Beecham to arrange delivery of duty-free cigarettes ordered by Rita, only to be told that she had 'gone away'. When son Scott phoned later, Paul explained that his mother was returning that night and that Scott could bring his girlfriend round for supper. They found Beecham lying dead on the double bed, having been shot with a shotgun, whose barrels had both been discharged. A police sniffer dog found Rita's body under the patio five days later.

Paul was an accomplished artist. Upon release from Broadmoor his new enterprise as a signwriter could have been entirely successful had he not mentally 'rebooted' so that he had manifest delusions that fellow members of the Berkshire Rotary Club, customers at his local pub, along with most of the residents in his village, including tradesmen and his own clients, were plotting to kill him. If you ask me, these are all signs of paranoid schizophrenia.

Perhaps it had been somewhat remiss of the panel of 'experts', who gave Paul the green light to be freed after serving a mere sixteen years, not to have consulted me beforehand. Fully aware that Paul had shot dead his mother, father, grandmother and grandmother during one incident, I had spent many hours walking around the lush Broadmoor gardens with him. His main bone of contention during our discussions was that the doctors and nurses were metamorphosing into rats and flies and spying on him in his room. During one of our illuminating talks, he decided to amble over to another patient, who was quietly raking up leaves perhaps one hundred yards away. After tipping over the wheelbarrow and giving the old guy a good thwack, he came back to me, saying: 'He's actually a psychiatrist watching us. He sits on my bedside lamp when the lights go out.'

Using the great benefit of hindsight, it would be all too easy to point a finger at the competence of the professionals who determined that the utterly psychopathic, schizophrenic Paul Beecham was mentally fit to be released back into society, for clearly they were proven to be wrong. According to Dr McGrath's son, Patrick, writing in the *Mail Online* on 7 September 2012:

> My father, Dr Pat McGrath, was appointed the tenth and last medical superintendent of what was then called Broadmoor Lunatic Asylum. In 1957, the place was in bad shape. It was in many respects obsolete, and chronically overcrowded: 800 mentally ill men and women confined in a top-security institution designed for 500. Patients slept in corridors and day rooms. The staff comprised a corps of custodial attendants in black uniforms and peaked caps and, according to my father, just one-and-a-half-psychiatrists.

I highly recommend anyone to read Patrick McGrath's moving, yet shocking account of his father's work and the conditions inside a shockingly underfunded Broadmoor, for this dedicated, 'robust, forceful man, broad-shouldered, stocky man with a fine high forehead, thick black hair and a quick clear mind' suffered from his own demons too. How he must have felt upon learning that Paul had 'gone bad' after his release is anyone's guess.

In the Beginning

It is interesting to note that the great phrenologist Franz Joseph Gall, who lived between 1758 and 1828, was active during a period in history when there was turmoil and stress in the world with events like the French Revolution taking place, so that when he embarked on his discoveries, he attracted very little attention. Perhaps it could be said he received the greatest opposition and the most scathing criticism, although it might also be considered that he made the greatest discovery of all: that of the pattern in the physical brain – this 'machine' – its anatomy and physiology, which ultimately revealed for us the pattern of the brain centres.

In other words, Gall came to the belief that people's understanding was conditioned by the activity of their own mental faculties as they manifested through the particular pattern of the brain vis-à-vis 'what is going on inside their heads', while, as no coincidence, King XVI and Marie Antoinette were about to lose theirs.

Around the same time as Gall made his discovery, author Jon Ronson points out in his remarkable book, *The Psychopath Test*, that it was the French psychiatrist Philippe Pinel who suggested there was a madness that didn't involve mania or depression or psychosis. He called it *'manie sans délire'*, 'insanity without delusions'. Pinel claimed that sufferers appeared normal on the surface but they lacked impulse controls and were prone to outbursts of violence.

Time slipped by, and it was just after the era of Edinburgh's notorious body snatchers, William Burke and William Hare, who provided corpses for the city's nineteenth-century medical schools, that James Cowles Prichard, an English physician and one of the first Commissioners in Lunacy, described a type of madness, one lacking the characteristics of insanity. In 1835, he wrote about 'a morbid perversion of the natural feelings accompanied by no observable disorder or defect'. He was talking about the psychopathic condition in which an individual, who is to all intents and purposes normal and capable of distinguishing between good and evil, nevertheless acts without restraint. Thereafter, Victorians continued to mutter about 'moral insanity', a condition that Prichard acknowledged was 'as numerous as the modifications of feelings or passion in the human mind' – a kind of moral 'black hole', if you will?

Nevertheless, there was a surge of interest in the study of insanity in the 1840s, as gentlemen doctors, wearing top hats, tails and spats, sought and fought over ways to explain and define the aberrant aspects of human behaviour, often coming to blows when they disagreed. During one lecture, a member of the distinguished audience rose to his feet, rudely shouting: 'And you are suggesting, sir, that we are the descendants of apes.' The reply was cutting: 'Perhaps, sir, your parents might have been, but *not* mine,' leaving the heckler – a noted, somewhat parsimonious physician – to storm out in a huff.

However, it would be a Dr John Connolly, a London practitioner, who would eventually play a leading role in establishing what was to become, in 1865, the Medico-Psychological Association. Prior to this, doctors who studied and treated mental disorders were known as 'alienists'. John Connolly pioneered a more scientific approach to the subject, describing individuals who were extremely 'selfish, cruel and alcoholic and prone to indulge in illegal activity such as fraud, forgery and even murder, perpetrated as a sudden homicidal impulse.'

Connolly understood the significance of a long history of disordered behaviour as a prerequisite for diagnosing what is today called 'psychopathic disorder' and his use of the term 'morbidly intense perception' was particularly interesting, with: 'Psychopaths are unduly vulnerable emotionally and often take unwarranted offence at the words, actions or attitudes of others. Their reactions to stress are frequently exaggerated and abnormal, owing to the strong feelings of inferiority and compensatory arrogance which exist side by side.' According to Jon Ronson in *The Psychopath Test*: 'It wasn't until 1891, when the German doctor J. L. A. Koch published his book, *Die Psychopathischen Minderwertigkeiten*, that psychopathy eventually got its name.'

During my many years of interviewing murderous psychopaths, I have noted all of them have over-inflated egos. They are narcissists, pumped full of self-esteem, but that self-esteem is always hanging by a thread and once pricked, their egos burst like a balloon. As psychotherapist Dr Alice Miller has written in her book, *The Drama of Being a Child: The Search for the True Self*: 'The grandiose person is never really free. First, because he is so excessively dependent on admiration from others; and second, because his self-respect is dependent on qualities, functions and achievements that can suddenly fail with far-reaching consequences.'

By the 1880s, a decade that acknowledged murder for sexual motives in the anonymous shape of Jack the Ripper, doctors began to recognise a condition that was not a psychosis, and neither was it due to insanity. John B. Martin, in his book, *Break Down The Walls*, gave a pen portrait of the psychopath as an individual whose emotions 'are out of kilter – he is cold, remote, indifferent to the plight of others, hostile even.'

The American neuro-scientist Professor H. Cleckley defined this type of personality as one who 'can perceive consequences, formulate in theory a wise course of conduct, name and phrase what is desirable or admirable; but his disorder is, apparently, such that he does not feel sufficiently about these things to be moved and to act accordingly.'

> Women? They're weak and stupid. Basically crooked.
> That's why they're always attracted to rascals like me.
> They have the morals of alley cats and minds like sewers.
> They respond to flattery like a duck responds to water.
> Put me down as 'Not guilty', old boy.
> – Neville Heath, to his solicitor, Ian Near
> during his 1946 trial.

Neville George Clevely Heath was a murderer whose personality precisely fitted Professor Cleckley and Dr Alice Miller's definition of a psychopath. He was a twenty-eight-year-old former Royal Air Force Officer, a sado-masochist who mutilated, then murdered two women with terrifying brutality. An out-and-out cad, he was a womanising social misfit, a swindler and a plausible, intelligent man who disappointed family and friends because of his lack of effort in pursuing a promising career. The police knew Heath for he enjoyed a criminal and Borstal record. Court martialled twice, as well as being fined for unlawfully wearing a uniform and decorations to which he was not entitled, he was intolerant of discipline and social obligations, and developed cruel and antisocial traits that ended up with him committing murder. Well groomed, he was a snappy dresser whose appearance gave no hint of the violence and sexual perversion beneath the surface of his apparent true character.

When he was tried, in September 1946, at the Old Bailey (the Central Criminal Court, London), a defence plea of insanity did not dissuade the jury from finding him guilty and he was duly hanged by the long-serving Albert Pierrepoint at Pentonville Prison on 16 October 1946. When asked if he would like the traditional brandy to steady his nerves before he stood on the scaffold, Heath cockily replied, 'Come on, boys, let's get on with it. While you are about it, you might make that a double!'

But it is worth comparing Heath's state of mind with the unravelling mentality of defence psychiatrist Dr William de Bargue Hubert BA, MRCS, MRCP, who had diagnosed Heath as suffering from 'periods of insanity' rather than a fully emerged psychopathy. For his part, Dr Hubert was evidently incompetent, for he was suffering from severe depression caused by an addiction to morphine. Indeed the doctor's thinking was so befuddled that he badly contradicted himself in the witness box. Anthony Hawke, for the prosecution, required only a few exchanges to destroy Hubert's credibility. A year later Hubert killed himself by taking a drug overdose.

So, it is this outward plausibility, often combined with an impressive personality that so bewitches the psychopath's victims. Heath literally charmed his prey to death and a new generation of serial killers has since repeated much of the same formula of techniques. You will find several such criminals featured throughout this book.

> 'I felt an inner compulsion to kill a prostitute. I knew from the outset that I didn't want intercourse with her, I just wanted to get rid of her.'
>
> — Peter Sutcliffe, to police after his arrest in January 1981.

Lorry driver Peter William Sutcliffe, aka Peter Coonan aka 'The Yorkshire Ripper', who murdered at least thirteen women, attempted to kill seven others and was tried for his crimes in 1981. Unlike Heath, Sutcliffe was a crude, working-class individual, with no pretentions above his station in life. He certainly didn't court his victims into their graves, for he targeted prostitutes as well as decent young women out walking during the late hours, and stabbed them with a screwdriver or beat them to death with a ball-peen hammer. And, like Harvey Carignan, who blamed some of his crimes on messages from Our Lord, Peter also claimed that he 'heard the word of God'.

However, the jury roundly rejected Sutcliffe's defence plea of insanity, with Mr Justice Morris summing up, with: 'You will see that insanity is not to be found merely because some conduct might be regarded as so outrageous as to be wholly unexpected from the generality of men. Strong sexual instinct is not of itself insanity; a mere love of bloodshed, or mere recklessness, are not in themselves insanity; an inability to resist temptation is not itself insanity; equally, the satisfaction of some invented impulse is not, without more, to be excused on the grounds of insanity.'

The key question in Peter Sutcliffe's trial was his state of mind when he carried out the attacks. Was he mentally ill, suffering from the rare but clearly definable paranoid schizophrenia? Or was he a clear-thinking sadist who was fully aware of what he had done? In short, was he mad or sane and as guilty as sin – with the term 'psychopath' never entering the trial?

Sutcliffe's defence, represented by James Chadwin QC, maintained that his client was suffering from paranoid schizophrenia. This diagnosis was based on the evidence of three forensic psychiatrists: Dr Hugo Milne of Bradford, Dr Malcolm McCulloch of Liverpool and Dr Terrence Key of Leeds – each of whom had interviewed the defendant.

What Doctors Milne, McCulloch and Kay believed to be crucial was Sutcliffe's claim that, since the age of twenty, he had been following 'instructions from God'. This was the defendant's account to the psychiatrists. Sutcliffe subsequently contradicted himself at trial by saying that he had first heard the voice of God seemingly coming from a gravestone in Bingley Cemetery, when he worked there as a gravedigger. The voice, according to Sutcliffe, told him to clean the streets of prostitutes. It seems that God had even helped him by preventing the police from capturing him until his arrest on Friday, 2 January 1981. He conceded that he had been planning to do the 'Lord's work' on Olivia Reivers when police, more by fluke than good detective work, took him into custody.

But the Crown Prosecution Service, led by the former Attorney General Sir Michael Havers, would have none of it. Havers countered that Sutcliffe's tale of a divine mission was a lie and that he was 'a clever callous murderer who deliberately set out to create a cock and bull story to avoid conviction for murder.' Firstly, there was the evidence of a prison officer at Armley, West Yorkshire, who had overheard Sutcliffe telling his wife, Sonia, that he was planning to deceive the doctors about his mental state. He had told her that if he could convince people he was mad, he might only get ten years 'in the loony bin', aka Broadmoor. This scenario was supported by the fact that during his original interviews with police, Sutcliffe never once mentioned a divine mission. Indeed, he had not mentioned a divine mission until one of his defence psychiatrists innocently asked him if had ever heard the 'Word of Our Lord'.

> 'Well, it was me all along. I would have killed and kept on killing. It was a miracle that they didn't apprehend me earlier. They had all the facts and now even the psychiatrists have got it all wrong.'
> – Peter Sutcliffe at trial after his arrest (Source *Murder Casebook*, Marshall Cavendish, 1991)

Doctors Milne, McCulloch and Kay concluded Sutcliffe was indeed suffering from schizophrenia. He had at least one confirmed personal experience of schizophrenia. According to the professionally written Marshall Cavendish's weekly publication *The Murder Casebook*, Vol. 1, 1989, and not legally challenged, the consultants David Jessel, Dr Susan Blake MB, ChB, MRC Psych, James Morten MA and Bill Waddell (then Curator of the Black Museum) confirm that in 1971, his wife, Sonia, had allegedly suffered a nervous breakdown while doing a teacher-training course at the Rachel McMillan College, Greenwich, south-east London.

That Sonia went off the rails in 1971 mattered little and the jury's distrust was reinforced when Dr McCulloch testified that he had taken 30 minutes acquainting himself with Sutcliffe to reach his professional diagnosis and that he had not interviewed Sutcliffe and looked at Sutcliffe's own statement the day before the trial.

Late in the afternoon of Friday, 22 May 1981, Justice Boreham sentenced Peter Sutcliffe to life imprisonment, with a recommendation that he should serve at least thirty years. He was incarcerated in the special top-security wing at HMP Parkhurst on the Isle of Wight after being brought down to Portsmouth under the tightest security for the short ferry crossing.

During his stay at Parkhurst Sutcliffe was attacked by another inmate, who slashed his face with a broken coffee jar and caused him to lose his left eye. Three years later, in March 1984, Sutcliffe was moved to Broadmoor to occupy a room in 'Ward One' of Somerset House.

Throughout the time that Peter Sutcliffe was being diagnosed by medical staff as 'totally incoherent', he was typing well-written letters to me about his interest in watercolour painting. Like the late Paul Beecham, Sutcliffe knows a thing or two about painting, although his artistic skills of dexterity and knowledge do not come close to Beecham's abilities in any respect. Nevertheless, Sutcliffe's correspondence was without a grammatical error. All of the 'dots' and 'commas' were well placed – his use of English grammar was almost perfect, even controlled. He was courteous, without a hint of manipulation, and we did not discuss his crimes. Indeed his correspondence was lucid and did not support the conclusion that he was 'totally incoherent'.

Sutcliffe's younger brother, Carl, believes that Peter has been faking mental illness for years in order to avoid serving time in a tough, maximum-security jail.

> 'He's cooking his own goose for Christmas. Staff just want to make sure Christmas passes off OK inside and we'll let them cook their own goose if they can.'
>
> – Officer at Broadmoor (*Mail Online*, Peter McKay, 7 December 2015)

And perhaps Sutcliffe *has* finally cooked his own goose. Along with Kenneth Erskine – between them responsible for twenty-three murders – they requested a goose instead of a turkey for their 2015 Christmas dinner at the NHS-run Broadmoor. They also demanded that the potatoes be roasted in goose fat – as you do!

'Like in every NHS hospital, patients at Broadmoor Hospital are offered a festive meal,' was the somewhat disingenuous comment, issued by an official spokesperson.

This might partly explain why Sutcliffe resisted moves by the Home Secretary, to move him to prison which, according to press reports, is said to have happened in August 2016. If so, he'll now spend the rest of his days watching his back with his one remaining eye. His present custody location within the Home Office Prison Estate has not been made public for security reasons.

Dennis Nilsen was a mild-mannered civil servant who slaughtered fifteen young down-and-outs in London in the early 1980s. Mr Justice Croom-Johnson said of him: 'A mind can be evil without being abnormal.' He added, 'There are evil people who do evil things. Committing murder is one of them.'

Nilsen, with whom I also corresponded while he was at HM Prison Parkhurst, had been a former Metropolitan Police Special Constable (like necrophiliac serial killer John Reginald Halliday Christie, who was hanged at HM Prison Pentonville on Wednesday, 15 July 1953). While he was killing, Nilsen was employed as a local authority social worker (I will amend this to 'local authority *anti*social worker') and his employers never suspected a thing.

The Mental Health Act (1983) defines a psychopathic disorder as 'a persistent disorder or disability of mind, whether or not including significant impairment of intelligence, which results in abnormally aggressive or seriously irresponsible conduct'. Dr Denis Power, writing in *The Criminologist*, commented on the difficulties involved in attempting to define the psychopathic type. He emphasised there was no objective test for any form of psychopathic disorder, but that there were a number of comparative criteria which distinguished the psychopath from the non-psychopath. Persistently abnormal behaviour was an important characteristic: a single antisocial act, no matter how violent, would not solely merit a psychopathic label. Inability to learn from experience was a behavioural trait in psychopaths, so that their bad conduct tended to be repeated and performed with an increasing scale of violence.

Again, in general, the criminal psychopath tends to be a person who carries out crimes when there is no material need and often makes scant use of his gains anyway. While acknowledging the rule of law and order, he does not stop to consider the consequences of his heinous actions even though in the US they might warrant a death sentence. He is essentially a loner with no loyalties or allegiances, and although his lack of anxiety and guilty feelings will deflect suspicion, he ultimately ceases to worry about protecting his interests and lays himself open to incrimination.

However, murders committed by sexual psychopaths are often the most difficult to trace back to their perpetrators. The predictability and patterns, which often emerge with their motive in other crimes, are missing here, for sex killers are totally unpredictable, with the knack of conducting themselves without creating the least suspicion. They are often cloaked with a protective cunning, sufficiently aware that they have offended against society to exhibit intelligence and cool-headedness in covering up their tracks. Completely lacking emotion and devoid of guilt, they can commit the most odious acts of violence and return home physically spent to fall into a deep sleep, or as some cases have proven, to take their kids shopping on Saturday and then to church on a Sunday morning to entertaining neighbours during the afternoon.

Perhaps the most terrifying thing regarding serial sex murderers is that while law enforcement may know such a person is on the loose, no one has a clue who that individual is, or where and when he will strike again.

And that character could be living next door to you!

Aggressive Narcissism and Psychopathy

Throughout the decades of interviewing psychopaths I found myself constantly drawn to the subject of narcissistic personality disorder (NPD), which I have concluded is inextricably linked to psychopathy, although this link is rarely mentioned in medical papers or among the psychiatric profession generally.

As with psychopathy, people with NPD make up approximately 1 per cent of the population with rates greater in men. Another direct comparison between those suffering with NPD and psychopathy/sociopathy is that both types are characterised by exaggerated feelings of self-importance. In its moderate to extreme forms these people are excessively preoccupied with personal adequacy, power, prestige and vanity; mentally unable to see the destructive damage they are causing themselves and others. Symptoms of the NPD disorder include seeking constant approval from others who are successful in positions of power in whatever form it may be. Many are selfish, grandiose pathological liars; their egos and sense of self-esteem over-inflated, while at once they are torn between exaggerated self-appraisal and the reality that they might never amount to much.

I encountered this while studying the life and crimes of US serial murderer sado-sexual Kenneth Bianchi and other killers of his ilk. His adoptive mother, Frances, had never talked to anyone about her son's crimes until I interviewed her for a 1994 radio interview. 'Ken was a blatant liar,' she explained. 'You'd catch him doing something wrong, ask him why he did it, he'd tell you "I didn't do it." I'd catch him [in his] lies, and he would deny everything. And, in the end, you felt like you were the crazy one, not him. He is such a smooth liar. He tells such lies that you believe him. You really believe what he says until you prove it for yourself.'

Perhaps you have witnessed this type of behaviour in a partner whom you know is having an affair behind your back. We see this in TV series such as *Cheaters*, where a man, caught with his trousers down, still blatantly denies he is doing anything wrong. Of course women do this too.

> 'It seemed that whenever Ken had a fight with a girlfriend, or had a problem, he went out and killed someone.'
>
> – Frances Bianchi, to the author at interview in 1994.

Telling lies was Bianchi's way of making himself seem cleverer than he actually was. He could not allow himself to be seen as inferior in the eyes of his peers, who were all succeeding where he was failing. Ken needed to be admired for something he was not. He performed dismally at all of his college studies, applied to join the police and was rejected only to be offered the menial job of jail deputy, which he declined. He *had* to excel in everything he undertook. When, in someone like Bianchi, that fails to happen, a bout of severe depression is imminent – catastrophe is most often immediate and sometimes lethal. This psychopathic misogynist obviously had impairments in interpersonal self-functioning

As Dr Alice Miller says: 'the grandiose narcissists are never really free. First, because they are so totally dependent on admiration from others, and second, because their self-respect is dependent on qualities, functions and achievements that can suddenly fail.'

People who are diagnosed with narcissistic personality disorder, indeed most if not all psychopaths, use 'splitting' as a central defence mechanism. This merging of the inflated self-concept of one's 'ideal self' and the 'actual self': it is a confused internal struggle between one's fantastical dreams of unlimited success and an even greater fear of failure.

It is this conscious, ever-revolving door of magical dreams and dread that enables people to achieve great things, much in the same way as those who seek to attain great power and influence in politics and in business; ultimately leading them to the self-belief that they are superior to anyone else. Like so many showbiz stars and famous TV personalities, they become preoccupied with dreams of unlimited success, power, brilliance and beauty and ideal love from a partner or the masses. They come to believe that they have a *right* to entitlement, favourable treatment or automatic compliance with his, or her, expectations and demands.

We most often see these psychological traits in the movie business – for instance where some previously unknown person from an extremely poor upbringing becomes a prima donna international movie star, or singer, only to treat their entourage, hotel and airline staff like dirt. Can such people now stand criticism? Of course not, for they are obsessively megalomaniac; they are too absorbed with personal adequacy, the power, prestige and vanity and public acclaim, while simultaneously mentally unable to see the destructive damage they are causing to others, and ultimately themselves.

CASE STUDY: SAVAGE
Oscar Pistorius – Shots in the Dark

Oscar Leonard Carl Pistorius, aka 'Blade Runner' and also dubbed by the media as 'The Fastest Man On No Legs' requires not much by way of introduction to the reader, for the entire world knows who he is, and that he is now serving a lengthy prison term for the savage murder of his beautiful girlfriend, Reeva Steenkamp, in his Pretoria, South Africa, home, on Valentine's Day, 2013.

Born with fibular hemimelia (congenital absence of the fibula) in both legs, which were amputated halfway between his knees and ankles when he was eleven years old, through sheer guts Oscar Pistorius went on to become one of the greatest, the richest and publicly feted Paralympic champions to date. Never before has a man with such a dreadful physical disability attained such international fame.

Despite all of the well-deserved adoration lavished on Pistorius by sports fans and worldwide media alike – and we must take off our hats to him for his sponsorship and charitable efforts too – we can never take away from him his sporting achievements and his various desires for success either. If only he had not had that fatal flaw that resulted in the shooting to death of the woman who loved and adored him.

The mechanical nuts and bolts in this case of murder are gruesome yet simple to understand. In the early hours of Thursday, 14 February 2015, Pistorius shot his girlfriend, young model Reeva Steenkamp, with a heavy-calibre firearm, following an argument at his upmarket home in Pretoria. The weapon, a silver-plated 9mm semi-automatic pistol, was loaded with the 'Black Talon' brand of hollow-point bullets, also known as 'Dum-Dums' or, as Pistorius called them, 'Zombie-Stoppers'. Exiting the muzzle at 280 metres a second, the four high-velocity rounds tore into Reeva – the head shot, according to the autopsy report, split her skull in two.

Pistorius's trial began on 20 May 2014. His mitigation was that it was all a terrible mistake. He testified that he believed the person he'd blasted to death in his tiny bathroom was an intruder; that he thought Reeva was downstairs at the time. He explained that he had heard a noise. He climbed out of the bed he shared with Reeva and, on his stumps, tentatively edged his way along the passage and entered the bathroom before firing through the closed closet door. According to his own testimony, he gave no warning before he discharged the pistol – an admission of guilt that should in any event have warranted a first-degree murder charge under South African law. The trial proceedings were adjourned until 30 June to enable Pistorius to undergo psychiatric evaluation to establish whether he was criminally responsible for the death of Miss Steenkamp. Enter the psychiatrists. Once again we find that the learned professionals from both sides could not agree.

Psychiatrist Dr Merryll Vorster appeared for the defence,

testifying she had diagnosed Pistorius as suffering from a 'Generalised Anxiety Disorder', as if that was sufficient mitigation to remove criminal intention for the killing. For the prosecution's part, after consulting with his psychiatrist expert, the tenacious Gerrie Nel held that the accused 'did not suffer from a mental illness or defect that would have rendered him criminally not responsible for the offence charged'.

Anyone watching the televised proceedings would have seen a bewildering mixture of Oscar Pistorius crying, exhibiting signs of remorse, lying his back teeth out and refusing to give straight answers to straightforward questions put to him by prosecutor Nel, who, at one point, was driven almost to distraction. Reeva's unwell father, Henke, and her mother, Sheila, stoically witnessed it all in despair. Sitting without a jury, Judge Thokosile Masipa completely accepted the evidence of psychiatrist Merryll Vorster and her assessment of Pistorius's state of mind.

On 12 September 2014, Judge Masipa found Pistorius guilty; not of intentional murder but of the lesser charge of culpable homicide, and an almost insignificant charge in the scheme of things: one firearm-related charge of reckless endangerment related to him discharging a weapon in a restaurant. He was found not guilty of a further two firearm-related charges: illegal possession of ammunition and firing a gun through the sunroof of a car.

On 21 October 2014, Oscar Pistorius received a prison sentence of five years with a further concurrent term of three years, suspended. In a world where elephants fly, lead balls bounce and fairies reign supreme, he had received a slap on the wrist for blasting an innocent woman to her death. After serving just a handful of months in jail – approximately one-sixth of his sentence – the following August he was released from the

Kgosi Mampuru II prison under 'correctional supervision'. His release was based on his 'good behaviour' and that 'he was not considered a danger to the community' as South African Commissioner of Correction Services, Modise, told the BBC. This was notwithstanding that Pistorius had spent his short time behind bars lodging complaint after complaint; that he did not have a private bathroom – one he had obviously denied Reeva Steenkamp – and that he was denied the use of a stool in the communal shower room. He added, in his vain way, that he was denied the opportunity to advise inmates held in the hospital wing about exercise and was not granted his wish to initiate a prison basketball programme.

An appeal against the ridiculously light sentence was held on November 2015 in the Supreme Court of Appeal, Bloemfontein. The matter was heard before five Supreme Court judges, who, by unanimous decision, overturned Pistorius's culpable homicide conviction and found him guilty of first-degree murder.

No one will probably ever know exactly why Pistorius became so enraged during the late hours of 14 February 2014. But he became so completely out of control that a terrified Reeva rushed to the bathroom, where she locked the door in fear of her life. The couple had been out for dinner and had returned to Pistorius's home, where, after a short while, Reeva started talking to another man on her mobile phone. She was laughing and joking, and then suddenly the Olympian snapped and a heated argument ensued; one that close neighbours overheard prior to shots being fired.

In Pistorius we can see that his entire ego hung in the air on a very fine thread, like a balloon about to pop. When he wrongly imagined that the thoroughly decent and faithful Reeva was cheating on him – even though he had frequently cheated on her, he resorted to wilful murder.

CASE STUDY – SAVAGE: OSCAR PISTORIUS

It was revealed at trial that he and Reeva had a turbulent relationship. He frequently accused her of being unfaithful – when she was not – while he himself was playing around. She had confided in friends and her parents, who all advised her to distance herself.

Had he been a 'real man', Pistorius would undoubtedly have thrown himself on his sword and the mercy of the court. His mitigation should have been that he simply lost 'the plot' after a heated argument. That a 'Red Mist' had descended over his eyes, meaning he suffered some form of Intermittent Explosive Disorder (IED), which is characterised by extreme expressions of anger, often to the point of uncontrollable rage, that are disproportionate to the situation at hand.

In a nutshell, Intermittent Explosive Disorder is all about someone who exhibits symptoms more commonly found in 'Road Rage' incidents. Irritability causes an adrenalin rush and increased energy, racing thoughts, in some cases tingling, tremors, palpitations and chest tightening. The result can be temper tantrums, tirades, heated arguments, shouting, slapping, shoving, pushing, physical fights, property damage, threatening or assaulting people, even killing them, as evidenced by the 'Red Mist' – the 'Blowing of a Fuse' – that overcame Oscar Pistorius. Therefore, 'I am terribly sorry' would not have gone amiss and the court might have looked upon one of the world's greatest sporting achiever's awful crime in a more compassionate light. He now contemplates a much longer prison term in a facility where his former international status will cut no ice at all with his fellow inmates.

CASE STUDY: PSYCHOPATH
Harold Shipman –
The Doctor from Hell

Now let's take a look at one of the most prolific serial killers in world history – a family doctor called Harold Shipman.

On Thursday, 31 January 2000, Dr Harold Frederick 'Fred' Shipman, dubbed by the media 'Dr Death' aka 'The Angel of Death', was sentenced to natural life imprisonment for 15 murders, with 4 years added to his sentence for forgery. It is believed by police that he probably killed at least 215 of his trusting male and female patients during a medical career that spanned twenty-eight years. This gives a mean average of eight murders every twelve months.

Born on Monday, 14 January 1946, on Nottingham's Bestwood council housing estate, to lorry driver Harold Frederick Shipman and Vera *née* Brittan, 'Fred' was the second of four siblings; their parents were devout Methodists and snobs, although to be fair to them they wanted the very best for their brood. Young Fred was sent to Nottingham's High

Pavement Grammar School and did moderately well in his studies. After he was arrested for serial homicide, several of his former school pals described him as a friendly lad, although he was inclined to remain aloof, often looking down his nose at his contemporaries.

After his father died, Fred became very close to his mother, who passed away on Friday, 21 June 1963. She had suffered lung cancer and had been administered morphine to deaden the pain by her own GP, and the lad, aged just seventeen, was often present when the doctor called.

By now, Shipman was dating a religiously inclined young woman called Primrose 'Rose' May Oxtoby. The couple had four children, although after the first child was born Fred coldly remarked to a friend: 'Well, I didn't want a child, but she got pregnant and marrying Rose was the only thing I could do.'

After graduating in medicine at Leeds School of Medicine in 1970, Fred found a position at Pontefract General Infirmary in the West Riding of Yorkshire. In 1974, the Abraham Ormerod Medical Centre in Todmorden, West Yorkshire, advertised for a general practitioner. He was interviewed and offered the job; the practice would later wish that they hadn't done so, for, from almost the outset he became a 'Dr Know-All': bossy and arrogant, someone who thought he knew best. He was intolerant of advice given him by the senior doctors and staff, and, like all narcissists, the developing pathological Dr Shipman came to believe that he had a *right* to entitlement. He considered himself far superior to his colleagues, demanding favourable treatment or automatic compliance with his expectations and demands. However, this moral bigot had a fatal flaw: he was addicted to the cocaine-based painkiller pethidine (demerol), which he obtained by prescribing patients with the drug and effectively short-changing them on dosage. The remainder he injected into his inner thigh, or between his fingers, where no one would notice the syringe marks.

Whether Dr Shipman's medical colleagues ever suspected that Fred was a narcissist while he practised in Todmorden is still open for debate. He was most certainly displaying all of the psychological characteristics of a narcissist, something his former colleagues are now inclined to agree about – in not so many words, that is. However, the problem was that Dr Shipman was the most popular GP among all of Todmorden's residents, who'd prefer to wait a little longer for an appointment 'just to see Fred'.

To his loyal patients he was regarded as a 'saint'. As one woman described his professionalism: 'the other doctors at the practice had already written out a "script" (prescription) before one entered the room. It was like get us in and out as fast as possible. Dr Shipman was never like that. He was genuinely interested in us. He'd spend time asking about my personal life and seemed genuinely concerned. He was everything one wanted from a family doctor. If you can't trust your doctor, who can you trust?'

During his time at Todmorden it is now known that Shipman murdered at least two elderly patients by giving them lethal injections of diamorphine. There may have been other victims but we will never know. And here also we find the psychological 'splitting' of his character – a Dr Jekyll and Mr Hyde, if you will. Dr Shipman had become 'two people'. To his surgery colleagues he was a bullying megalomaniac who held forth on all the latest medical developments at staff meetings, where he presented professional papers and advised on the benefits of new drugs. Unable to stand criticism – another flaw in the narcissist's character – he would talk over anyone who questioned him, sneering at them, his eyes fixed upon them from behind his spectacles as if they were of much lower status than he was.

Yet, to his hundreds of patients, Fred was the polar opposite of this. Those whom he treated for all manner of ills respected and sought out only Dr Shipman when they were under the weather. It is this 'splitting' of character, this mask of sanity covering an entity of distilled evil, that is all too common in psychopaths.

Then Fred came unstuck.

In 1975 he was caught by Todmorden surgery staff forging demerol prescriptions for personal use; he was fired and fined £600. With the great benefit of hindsight he should have been struck off the Medical Register, never to be allowed to practice again. However, this cunning man attended a drug rehabilitation clinic in the City of York. Before two years had expired he had conned his peers into believing that he was 'clean' and therefore able to practice as a doctor once more.

Then in 1977, Fred found a situation at the Donneybrook Medical Centre in the small town of Hyde near Manchester. Here he worked as a GP throughout the 1980s, becoming so successful that he founded his own surgery at 21 Market Street in 1993. He was now aged forty-seven and, like so many narcissists and psychopaths, he sought out the approbation of his self-imagined peers to pump up his already over-inflated ego.

Any normal person would have been content with having the support of the hundreds of devoted patients, but not Fred Shipman. He wanted much more and to this end he promoted himself to the media as a respected member of the community – which, ironically he already was – to later give, in 1983, an interview on a Granada *World in Action* documentary. The subject of this was how the mentally ill should be treated in the community. Smiling into the camera after a 'runner' (make-up artist) had powdered his nose, Fred obviously felt it would have been remiss of him to mention that he was murdering scores of his patients; or that he'd killed someone a few days before the interview, and that he would be giving another dear old soul a lethal injection of diamorphine before the TV production company's cheque for his televised contribution even arrived in the post.

> As seen on TV. Your own Dr Fred Shipman who cares for You!
>> – a notice that might as well have been pinned to
>>> the wall of Shipman's surgery waiting room.

Dr Shipman made much out of his *World in Action* TV appearance. This was publicity that money couldn't buy. Indeed, the cold facts are such that he might as well have been given a licence to commit murder. Our bespectacled man-about-town – wearing his well-worn tweed jacket, frayed-collared Clydella shirt, cavalry twills and slightly tattered brown brogues – flaunted his credentials while attending local meetings, giving some little money to charitable causes, at the same time dragging his wife Rose along as a homely prop.

In every single respect he was the good doctor any elderly patient would identify with. Bearded and wearing glasses over a keen enquiring eyes, he was compassionate in tune with the patter: 'nothing is too much trouble... I can always call on you after surgery hours, even on a Sunday, if needs be'.

Drug addict, showman, extreme narcissist and homicidal psychopath, Shipman now enjoyed a licence to kill. Tragically, the last sight of life 200-plus patients experienced was the steady, penetrating gaze of their family doctor as he injected them with diamorphine, followed by a suffocating slowness of breath accompanied by his now distant, calming words. And they were never to wake again.

According to the NHS, diamorphine is one of the most dangerous of a class of drugs called opioids. 'It is in effect a cleaned-up version of heroin, and carries the same risk of overdose,' wrote Denis Campbell, health correspondent for the *Guardian*, on Thursday, 21 May 2009. Campbell says: 'opioids are strong painkillers used routinely across the NHS to relieve severe pain in a patient who has had an operation or accident, or who has cancer, for example.' History shows these drugs carry the risk of causing injury or death, so medical staff and doctors like Shipman are told to always exercise caution when using them.

The life and crimes of Dr Shipman are adequately covered in journalists Brian Whittle and Jean Ritchie's book *Prescription for Murder: The True Story of Harold Shipman* (2000). Nevertheless, in March 1998, Dr Linda Reynolds of The Brooke Surgery, in Hyde, with not a little prompting from Deborah and Frank Massey and Sons Funerals, raised concerns with John Pollard, the coroner for the South Manchester District. Specifically, Dr Reynolds drew Pollard's attention to the large number of cremation forms for elderly women that Shipman needed countersigned. There was also the matter of other doctors countersigning the death certificates drawn up by Shipman. Police were called in to investigate.

Later, in the following Shipman Inquiry, it was determined that other GPs had merely taken Shipman's word for 'Cause of Death' and not made any further examinations themselves. The inquiry also criticised the police's handling of the case, which had been dropped on 17 April 1998, for their use of inexperienced officers in this most sensitive of inquiries. Fred would go on to murder at least another three patients before he was arrested on Monday, 7 September 1998.

CASE STUDY – PSYCHOPATH: HAROLD SHIPMAN

Dr Shipman's trial started on Tuesday, 5 October 1999, His Honour Mr Justice Forbes presiding. Fred stood in the dock charged with the murders of Marie West, Irene Turner, Lillie Adams, Jean Lilley, Ivy Thomas, Muriel Grimshaw, Marie Quinn, Kathleen Wagstaff, Nianka Pomfret, Norah Nuttall, Pamela Hillier, Maureen Ward, Winifred Mellor, Joan Melia and his final victim, Kathleen Grundy – whose will he also forged in his favour to the tune of £386,000 (in today's money just over £610,000).

The evidence against Dr Shipman was incontestable. Exhumation of several of the bodies showed lethal doses of diamorphine. He had been backdating and falsifying medical records to show that his causes of death were 'natural' after the patients were suffering ill health. Added to that it was proven that he had used his own battered typewriter to forge Kathleen Grundy's will. Aside from this, the circumstantial evidence against him was also overwhelming.

The following are the headings under which the various factors of circumstantial evidence are usually analysed and we can see that Dr Shipman ticked every box:

1. Motive for committing the crime.
2. Acts indicative of guilty consciousness or intent.
3. Preparation for the crime.
4. Opportunity for committing the crime.
5. Recent possession of the fruits of the crime (the victims' jewellery).
6. Refusal to account for suspicious circumstances or unsatisfactory explanations.
7. Indirect admissions of guilt.
8. Tampering with or fabrication of evidence.
9. Certain statutory presumptions.
10. Scientific testimony.

On 31 January 2000, a jury found Dr Shipman guilty on all counts. He was sentenced to fifteen concurrent life terms with the recommendation that he should never be released but once again he cheated the system. At 06.20 am on Tuesday, 13 January 2004, he tied bed sheets to the bars of his HM Prison Wakefield cell and hanged himself – it was the eve of his fifty-eighth birthday.

I first became interested in the case of Dr Shipman after I was asked to consult, and then to appear, on the Twofour-produced television documentary series *Born to Kill*. My book with Steve Morris, *Born Killers: Childhood Secrets of the World's Deadliest Serial Killers*, published by John Blake in 2009 and endorsed by Twofour, included a chapter on Shipman.

The principal motive for my interest rested in Shipman's motive for committing serial homicide and, to be frank, we may never know his motive/s, probably not even the killer himself did. Journalists Brian Whittle and Jean Ritchie (the latter also appearing in the Twofour programme) report two of their own theories on why Shipman forged Kathleen Grundy's will in the book:

1. That he wanted to be caught because his life was out of control.
2. That he planned to retire aged fifty-five and then leave the United Kingdom.

However, I believe these two theories to be incorrect – Shipman's psychopathology is a lot more complicated than these suggested theories, making his true motive for committing fraud and serial homicide even more difficult to determine because at the root of this man's evil sits narcissism, a 'God Complex' where he could choose between life or death, one that graduated into a full-blown psychopathy.

CASE STUDY – PSYCHOPATH: HAROLD SHIPMAN

Perhaps one of the most enlightening articles on NPD can be found on the World Wide Web under *Narcissistic Personality Disorder*. Last reviewed on 17 February 2015, the sources are spot on.

- American Psychiatric Association. Diagnostic and Statistical Manual of Mental Disorders, Fourth Edition, Revised.
- Center for Substance Abuse Treatment, Assessment and Treatment of Patients with Coexisting Mental Illness and Alcohol and Other Drug Abuse. Treatment Improvement Protocol (TIP) Series, No. 9.
- National Institutes of Health – National Library of Medicine.
- BUSHMAN, Brad, CAMPBELL, W. Keith, PAULHUS, Del and ROBINS, Richard W.

I have read through these extensively written academic papers and have moreover considered all of my own hands-on experience interviewing and working with murderous psychopaths over decades. Bearing all this in mind, coupled with a careful study of my well-thumbed copy of *The Right Brain and the Unconscious: Discovering the Stranger Within* by Dr R. Joseph, a psychotherapist, neuropsychologist and neuroscientist (one of the world's handful of experts on both the brain *and* the mind who actually *does* know what he is talking about), I am pointed straightaway to Shipman's narcissistic parents as a starter for ten.

Narcissistic parents – which Frederick Sr and Vera most certainly were – often demand certain behaviours from their children because they see their offspring as extensions of themselves. This is called 'mirroring' for parents need to represent their children in a world in ways that meet the parents' emotional needs. In many of the cases I have been involved with, these 'expectations' have gone to the extreme of psychological child abuse. In a nutshell, the parents need their child to be more than they, themselves, could ever be – the mirror itself being flawed.

Of course, generally it is a good thing for parents to want their children to succeed when they themselves have not made their own mark in life. However, I am also mindful of Professor Elliott Leyton's observation to me years ago: 'Christopher, millions of kids have narcissistic parents, even brutal parents, but they don't all go on to commit serial murder, do they, so what?' Take it from me, read a few of Leyton's books; open the first page of his acclaimed *Hunting Humans: The Rise of the Modern Multiple Murderer* and you'll also realise that this chap knows what he is talking about!

Then, of course, the question arises as to why Harold Shipman turned out to be the only rotten apple in a basket of three other siblings who went on to live perfectly healthy, decent lives. We'll see more of this phenomenon later with other offenders and will see the simplistic answer being that we are not all 'wired up' quite the same. Mentally, we are psychologically different from our siblings, often as different as chalk is to cheese.

For my part, I see the young Shipman as being mentally 'split'. It is a well-documented fact that women are the favoured victims of male serial killers such as Fred. They claim to enjoy the company of females while, at once, hating them with a deep-seated passion. I believe that although Shipman superficially loved his ailing mother, he also detested her for demanding excellence (something she and her husband had never achieved) from him.

Putting myself inside Shipman's head, I can see this teenager watching as his mother suffered terrible pain, his mind somewhat detached, like a bystander – watching on as dispassionately as the scientist who studies under the microscope a blowfly preserved in amber – while the good family doctor gave Vera pain-killing relief. I think that this entire process morbidly fascinated Shipman; this fascination being echoed in the remark he made to a school friend the Monday following his mother's death. When Fred, out running, was asked 'Did you have a good weekend?' the cold reply, without a tear in his eye, was, 'My mother died.'

End of conversation.

To complicate matters further, Shipman murdered elderly men too, so I am also drawn to the suggested part motive, that of financial gain. Furthermore, what all of us who are interested in 'motive' will agree upon is succinctly documented in *Seven Murders*, first published by William Heinemann Limited in 1931. Written by Christmas Humphreys MA, LLB (Cantab) of the Inner Temple, Barrister-at-Law, who went on to become one of the greatest judges in British criminal history, who puts the most common motives down to:

- The desire of avenging some real or fancied wrong.
- Getting rid of a rival or an obnoxious connection.
- Of escaping from the pressure of pecuniary or other obligation.
- Obtaining plunder or other coveted objects.
- Preserving reputation, or of gratifying some other selfish or malignant passion.

'These may be summed up concisely,' as Christmas Humphreys says, 'as Money, Hatred and Women' – the latter term might be entirely unacceptable today, but I see *all* of these motives combined in Dr Shipman's reasons for killing.

I suggest that Shipman ticks all of the above, for notwithstanding that he had attempted to falsify Kathleen Grundy's will to the tune of £360,000, in 2005 it also came to light that he had stolen some jewellery worth over £10,000 from his victims. The booty was found by detectives in his garage, with Primrose Shipman soon pressing for it to be returned to the victims' next-of-kin where possible. Sixty-six pieces were returned to Primrose – mainly because the Assets Recovery Agency could not discover provenance – and 33 pieces, which were not hers, were auctioned for charitable causes. The outstanding item (a platinum–diamond ring) was returned to a murdered patient's family. Primrose Shipman denied any knowledge of her husband's murderous activity.

Serial killers often take 'trophies' from their victims in the form of underwear, jewellery, hair and even photographs and make video recordings of their victims as they suffer terrible torment, much in the same way as a big game hunter takes away the head of a shot animal for display on his wall or snaps pictures of his expedition. Many of the murderers I have interviewed kept gruesome mementos of their crimes. Sometimes they take them out just to relive the events. In many instances these deviants masturbate over their trophies. Michael Bruce Ross masturbated over his *memories* of killing – priapic Ross worked himself off at least 40 times a day to the degree that he developed sores on his penis. He has since ceased this practice because he has been executed – the auspicious time and date being precisely 2:25 a.m. 13 May 2005.

There is no suggestion from me that Shipman got a sexual thrill from the act of killing, or from the trophies he took away with him after his victims died. And I strongly dispute the suggested scenario put forward by journalists Whittle and Ritchie: *that he planned to retire aged fifty-five and leave the United Kingdom.* He was already aged fifty-two when he murdered his last victim, Kathleen Grundy, and had not exactly amassed a fortune from the stash of stolen jewellery kept in his garage. Of course, if he had succeeded in appropriating the money allegedly bequeathed him by Mrs Grundy, he could well have afforded to up sticks and move overseas. However, Shipman was too dyed-in-the-wool for that sort of malarkey, so my feelings are that he tried to effectively 'stuff Kathleen's estate into his back pocket' because this arrogant and self-centred man believed that he actually could pull the fraud off.

This leaves us with the other suggested motive put up by Whittle and Ritchie: *that he wanted to get caught because his life was out of control.* While this is an interesting theory, it is a consideration I don't buy into at all, although perhaps it may more appropriately have been said that he (subconsciously) wanted to get caught.

Where I think Whittle and Ritchie may have misinterpreted this suggested motive again concerns Shipman's rash attempt to forge Mrs Grundy's will. This was a deed of momentous stupidity, richly embroidered with such clumsiness, yet exhibited by a clever, devious man; indeed at first glance it gives the impression that Fred had completely lost the plot. That in forging the will he was consciously, or subconsciously, 'offering himself up' to police as a serial killer because he wanted the murders to stop – all of which totally contradicts the idea that he wanted the money so that, aged fifty-five, he could flee abroad.

For decades the hackneyed scenario of a serial killer subconsciously wanting to be caught has been bandied about by the psychiatric profession. One has been led to believe that because the killings (the 'events') become closer together as a serial murderer gains confidence with his *modus operandi*, at once getting even more addicted to killing, there arrives his final confrontation with real world morality, which suggests a conscience. Psychopaths, and to a lesser degree aggressive narcissists, *do not* have a conscience. Conscience simply does not enter into their psychopathological vocabulary.

Dr Shipman was one such aggressive narcissist and here it is worth consulting Professor Bob Hare's Psychopathy Checklist, which includes the following traits, all of which are applicable to Shipman – indeed, to most psychopaths as well:

1. Glibness/superficial charm.
2. Grandiose sense of self-worth.
3. Pathological lying.
4. Cunning/manipulative.
5. Lack of remorse or guilt.
6. Callous/lack of empathy.
7. Failure to accept responsibility for his own actions.

Psychopaths and narcissists never admit they are in the wrong, even when faced with contradictory, completely overwhelming evidence against them – unless it suits a purpose in their manipulative scheme of things. Indeed, in all of my years of working with psychopaths, never once have I heard a word of contrition from any of them, and I have got right inside their heads in doing so. Consciously or subconsciously, none of these deviants wanted to get arrested, with one exception being Wayne Adam Ford.

> 'Hey, Juan. I have a nut ball... is a real one-off... He's got a woman's breast in his jacket pocket, for Christ's sake.'
> – Humboldt Sheriff desk sergeant in a phone call to lead investigator Det. Juan Freeman on 3 November 1998.

CASE STUDY – PSYCHOPATH: HAROLD SHIPMAN

'The Killer with a Conscience', Ford was convicted of mutilating and killing four women – one of whose remains are still unidentified – between 1997 and 1998. Wracked with guilt, he turned himself in to the police during the evening of Tuesday, 3 November 1998. He went to the Humboldt County Sheriff's Department, 826 Fourth Street, Eureka, California, where he introduced himself to the desk sergeant. He brought out a plastic Ziploc bag containing the severed breast from victim Patricia Tamez and then he 'coughed' to all of his shocking crimes and later sentenced to death.

Individuals, like Shipman – who tick-box Professor Hare's entire Psychopathy Checklist – are too self-centred, grandiose and callous to do such a thing. Blessed with a 'God Complex', they consider themselves far, far superior to mere mortals. It is almost as if it is written in their DNA. These killers get caught because they are addicted to killing. They keep on committing antisocial acts as if they are immune to the dictates of law and order – as if they are living in a society where human decency no longer exists. These people kill for fun; they kill for personal gain. They kill, as did Dr Shipman, because they *can* and they *will continue doing so* until they are caught. Meanwhile they become addicted to snuffing out human life by any means at their disposal. Eventually they overstep the mark and the police close in.

Aside from Wayne Adam Ford, of the psychopaths I have ever interviewed thought of themselves as being untouchable and this is how I evaluate the psychopathology running through the wires of Shipman's mind. The very conscious or subconscious thought – or any other self-imagined thought in between – of 'handing oneself in' can never exist, but now, before I close on Harold Shipman, I'd like you to look at '215'.

'215': 'Two hundred and fifteen'. It's a number that rolls off the tongue; easily assimilated as an abbreviation for pounds sterling to be paid for an electricity bill, a cheap laptop even. But what is '215' in terms of the human life destroyed by Dr Shipman?

To begin with, let's consider the epitaphs lovingly engraved on many of his victims' headstones, aside from the scores of cremations this 'doctor' ordered to disguise his crimes. What follows is not just an easily digestible 215 decedents, so it is chilling to think of your own mother, father, beloved grandmother or grandfather being among them. It makes for a shocking, indeed terrifying, indictment of the failure of the NHS and shows that Dr Shipman's aggressive narcissism and homicidal psychopathology could run amok, undetected in our midst. He was in contact with dozens of doctors, psychiatrists, psychologists, nurses and medical practice staff, so if these professionals could not spot a homicidal psychopath working among them, what chances have you and I got?

God help us all!

CASE STUDY: SAVAGE
Melanie 'Mel' Lyn McGuire
– 'The Ice Queen'

During my career I have interviewed a number of female killers but none so cold-blooded and calculating as MelanieMcGuire. Dubbed 'The Ice Queen' or 'The Scarlet Woman', the once pretty-as-a-picture thirty-three-year-old slipped her husband a Mickey Finn of chloral hydrate, a powerful but uncommon sedative. She shot him, cut his body into parts and then placed the remains in three suitcases before dumping them off a bridge into the swirling waters of the Chesapeake Bay. This well-educated nurse, a petite mother-of-two, came from an upscale lifestyle, but beauty is only skin-deep. She fed thirty-four-year-old William T. McGuire – a computer programmer at the New Jersey Institute of Technology, Newark – to the fishes.

Melanie held an unshakeable belief characterised by consistently inflated feelings of personal ability or infallibility and a capacity for savagery from which the outcome was shocking.

TALKING WITH PSYCHOPATHS AND SAVAGES

This was a woman I had to make contact with, yet I was on shaky ground. The *femme fatale*'s notorious crime had made headlines across the US. Courted by countless true-crime writers from the other side of 'The Pond', all of them promised a book and then there were other people with good, perhaps misguided intentions, offering to take up her pleas of innocence and campaign on her behalf.

I had no intention of writing a book about Melanie McGuire (a chapter in a book, perhaps, which I did in *Dead Men Talking*, 2009), therefore getting her to make contact with me, being based in England, was to be an uphill struggle so I tried to put myself inside this woman's head: I needed the right bait.

I am a fisherman of sorts; mostly for sea bass when the October/November gales hit the south coast of the UK and the slipper limpet (seasonally favourite fare for bass) are swept towards shore. One can use all sorts of bait when slinging one's hook, but in November, slipper limpets are good-to-go. And it is how one presents the bait that is so important, as any angler will know. Why exert oneself casting two hundred yards when, at my special place, one merely flips the line into a swirling eddy just yards from the beach? Within a couple of hours my friend Andy and me can reel in three-, four- and five-pounders without breaking sweat.

I have adopted this 'fishing' technique countless times to catch the attention of psychopaths. It was successful pulling in Peter Sutcliffe and Paul Beecham with our mutual interest in painting and it proved to work equally well on the vain and savage Melanie McGuire but with a twist. I had just one cast using the right bait to hook then reel her in, while others, like in any fishing competition lined up either side of me – their lines stretched tight.

CASE STUDY – SAVAGE: MELANIE 'MEL' LYN McGUIRE

Among McGuire's flaws is vanity, a love of mirrors and a need of praise from others. To my advantage, as I saw another crack in this woman's psyche being her innate, perhaps ill-founded belief that the British criminal justice system was far more open and honest than the one she self-allegedly didn't enjoy back home in the 'Garden State', New Jersey. While on remand, she hinted as much to a friend who visited with her. Moreover, Mel considered herself born and bred 'class' with a capital 'C'. She and her husband had just closed the sale on a $500,000 house in Ashbury, Warren County, NJ, to move on and up the social ladder, while she was having an affair with her boss, Dr Bradley Miller.

Now, Melanie had determined that husband Bill was no longer fit for purpose. In her mind, his use-by date had expired. Later, her attitude of 'How dare anyone in this hick place accuse me of murder' was indeed Mel's dogmatic mantra to anyone lending an ear. 'Bill mentally and physically abused me,' was part of her phoney narrative. She then claimed it was an alleged 'Mafia kill' because he owed money to the Mob – a defence she would put up at her trial.

To get inside Melanie McGuire's head meant that I had to identify with her mindset; to understand the latent savagery that had brought her to a natural life sentence at the Edna Mahan Correctional Facility for Women, Hunterdon County, Clinton, New Jersey. Without doubt she had killed William. However, precisely where she had shot him, before she dismembered the blood-soaked corpse in their home, not even the most experienced scenes-of-crime officers using state-of-the art scientific techniques can figure out to this day for there wasn't a drop of blood to be found.

Using a little lateral thinking, I put pen to paper. I deliberately used high-quality, inlaid Conqueror cream-coloured paper with a matching envelope, sealed with my family's wax crest, as you do. After completing my homework, I knew she'd appreciate the up-scale brand of Chanel 'Égoïste' perfume which I sprayed onto the letter. I also enclosed a photo of myself.

Think about Professor Annabel Leigh's letter to me referenced at the outset of this book (see also pages 1–3). The scent of Chanel was a subliminal trick, of course it was. Letters are letters... just paper. With scores of correspondence from wannabe suitors and writers entering Mel's cell every month my correspondence, bearing an Air Mail sticker and a British postage stamp, had to stand out. For a woman who had lived 'the lifestyle' and sought only the best clothes and perfumes, for her Chanel was upmarket scent – a memory, another sensory 'push-this-button' – that would signally make my letter stand out among the others. And I knew this was a scent she would return to time and again when, like all US male or female correctional facilities, at the Edna Mahan CF for Women, the reek of cheap disinfectant, greasy food and the unmistakable smell of human sweat permeated every brick.

Melanie took the bait, hook, line and sinker.

With that humble admission out of the way, what I can say is that 'Melanie and Christopher' entered into a lengthy period of correspondence while she put everyone else on hold. And you, the reader, will not be surprised to learn that *never once* did she mention her two children, whom she claimed throughout her trial to adore. They might as well have never existed. Nor did she display one iota of remorse for her crime, even less for her kids, who had lost their mother and father. And she showed a darn sight less concern for her former lover, whom she had tried to implicate in murder-most-foul and, hard as it is to swallow, all of these people were now superfluous to her present custodial needs.

CASE STUDY – SAVAGE: MELANIE 'MEL' LYN McGUIRE

'This is a defendant who puts on a face and shows the people before her whatever it is she wants to show. Even I don't know who the real Melanie McGuire is.'
— Asst State's Attorney Patricia Prezioso, during McGuire's June/July 2007 trial

Straight off the bat, in my second letter to Melanie I asked: 'Why did you respond to me when you have so many guys interested in you and in the sad predicament you find yourself in? Gosh, you, with your lustrous dark hair, could be a real *femme fatale* as the national media portrays you?'

Mel's answer was almost predictable, saying: 'Lots of guys write me, but *femme fatale*, REALLY?'

My bait was working perfectly, massaging her ego. I was now almost inside this killer's head and Melanie was taking to my flattery like a duck takes to water. More importantly, that single statement of hers says everything about her vanity. This was a woman who had been convicted of murdering her husband, whom she argued was a hard-drinking, womanising, gambling, wife-beating man, who had threatened to spirit her doting children away from her – when honourable witness testimony supplied by the prosecution proved otherwise.

There is an old saying: 'One shouldn't judge a book by its cover'. Although still petite, Melanie used to be a pretty, pixie-faced, magazine-cover-glossy, classy act and even her harshest critics might agree she wasn't unattractive either. That was until prison time had washed away the 'gloss' to replace it with a common mugshot – the lank hair, her pasty face now betraying the realisation that she would not see a bottle of champagne again.

Melanie has a personality that manifested itself throughout her correspondence. Her letters were positively enigmatically seductive, as evidenced when I asked her about her favourite food.

> My favorite food? Asian (be it Japanese, Chinese, French). No, you just can't get decent foie gras in prison. Seafood (hey, I'm from the shore). I fail to cite Italian because that is my ordinary food... is that Chanel I detect on your writing paper?
>
> — Melanie Lyn McGuire, to the author in
> correspondence in 2010

When asked about her preferred colour, she answered:

> If I had to choose one, it would be the grey/blue/green of my younger son's eyes... like yours, but I'll spare you the list of hair-care products that enrich my lustrous hair you mentioned. You've suffered quite enough. Oh, I was joking about the color.

Touching upon her present incarceration and how this was affecting her, Melanie replied using skills any psychotherapist might have been proud of – or call it a rant, if you wish:

> Christopher, I won't sit here and cry in prison, but I am steeped in an environment where I am incessantly bombarded with people who seem to have relinquished all responsibility for their lives and blame any deficits in themselves on the upbringing, or lack of it. The women, including the officers, are obese, unkempt and foul-mouthed. How can I be expected to live amongst people like this?

CASE STUDY – SAVAGE: MELANIE 'MEL' LYN McGUIRE

Now, in full swing, Melanie added:

> I don't mean to intimate that one's earliest experiences (or the perception of them) don't impact our psychological development – but if I have issues related to my rearing, they are just that – my issues. As adults, we bear the charge of choosing how we allow these things to impact or dictate our own choices.

On her marriage to Bill, whom she drugged, shot and chopped up – the loyal breadwinner whom she constantly cheated on:

> Did I have a bad marriage? Yes. Was my husband abusive, be it emotionally, and/or physically? Yes. But am I responsible for staying and for bending to his will on issues that I should have remained firm on? So, while I think things like a 'battered woman's syndrome' do, indeed, exist and are appropriate affirmative defenses in some cases, I do place some degree of accountability on the 'victim' [Bill McGuire], albeit limited. In my criminal case, I never waged an affirmative defense – my defense was always that of actual innocence. My husband's abuse does not absolve me of my poor choices, but it lends a somewhat mitigating context for the situation and the perfect storm of circumstantial evidence that has put me here [prison]. I was unfaithful.

After battering me with what amounted to drivel, Melanie McGuire seemed anxious to lighten my load in much the same way as she had seductively teased me about what hair products she had once used. This was, again, her dry humour:

I'm not certain if I'm being clever, or this is going to read like a flight of ideas from Plath [Sylvia Plath, the American novelist and poet], or something. Somewhere, several hundred miles away, I sense my appellate attorney developing an unsightly facial tic, so I'll stop for now.

With Melanie ducking and diving any questions from me about the actual murder and how her crime had impacted upon her two children, I changed tack to ask how proud she must be of her academic achievements. A simple 'yes' would have been sufficient, however 'Manipulative Mel' responded in grandiose fashion – oh so very typical of her once bright feathers, admired even when they have since turned dull and grey.

Chris, my dearest Chris, my achievements are anything but interesting. But I'll run through them if you like. When I was in second grade, someone thought it would be helpful to test my IQ. As a result, I was placed into what was called a 'Gifted & Talented' programme (how politically incorrect). I was in this school programme throughout grammar/middle/high school, where I excelled even in a fairly competitive school system. I was a member of both the Spanish Honor Society (I like the word, honor) and the National Honor Society, and a drama club. I was selected as an Edward J. Bloustein Distinguished Scholar [intended to recognise the highest-achieving graduating high school students from New Jersey and to reward them with awards that are granted regardless of need]. Then I went to Rutgers University, and got a 1.0 GPA my first semester to the acute distress of my parents. I discovered unchecked freedom – and parties.

I think I pulled a 3.0 or better each semester after that: Statistics major, Psyche minor, Religion mini, but my initial fall from academic grace doomed me to mediocrity. I decided in my senior year that I wanted to pursue nursing, but I didn't have the credentials to switch majors at this point, so I completed my first BA at my parents' insistence.

So, Melanie McGuire has her feet placed firmly on Mother Earth and this highly intelligent and self-effacing woman certainly likes her literature, too. Her favourite authors are Stephen King, Janet Evanovich ('selected works' she says) and also P.G. Wodehouse, Martin Amis, Haruki Murakami, Hugh Laurie and Matt Beaumont, whom she described as 'hilarious'. In her beautifully penned correspondence she claimed she intended to read *Duma Key* by Stephen King, *The War against Cliché: Essays and Reviews 1971–2000* by Martin Amis and *The Gnostic Faustus* by Ramona Fraden. 'That's quite a queue I know,' she admitted, and it would be a long wait because the prison library did not hold copies of these books, nor was ever likely to, a correctional officer told me.

Melanie finished off this letter, adding: 'Alas, time for group therapy, so I'll close for now (and before, somewhere in DC [District Court], my appellate attorney has a grand mal seizure). Let the healing begin (yes, that's sarcasm you smell). This should all be duplicative anyway, as I've channeled to your mailman all I wanted to say (the poor bastard).'

'All of this evidence together leaves you [the jury] no doubt that she participated in this murder. While drinking wine to celebrate his new home, Bill had no idea that the drink was laced with chloral hydrate, and his wife wanted to grow old with her lover, and not him. The next day, the kids out of the way and at the day care center, she shot the still-sleeping man, a pillow muffling the noise. The dead man is cut up in the bathroom, stuffed into bags and suitcases. She drives to the Chesapeake Bridge and tossed the suitcases in the air and into the water.'

> – DA Patti Prezioso to the jury at trial.

'The prosecution's case is circumstantial at best. There is no direct evidence that my client killed her husband and no smoking gun.'

> – Joseph Tacopina, McGuire's attorney at summing at trial.

'The depravity of this murder simply shocks the conscience of this Court. One who callously destroys a family to accomplish her own selfish ends must face the most severe consequences that the Law can provide.'

> – Superior Court Judge Frederick de Vesa, Tuesday, 23 April 2007, sentencing Melanie McGuire to thirty years for first-degree murder. Concurrently ten years for desecrating human remains. Five years for one count of perjury and one count of possession of an unlawful weapon.

Having corresponded with Mel for a year, it was now time for me to get down to the nitty-gritty, to firmly hook her in the mouth by asking a few questions – ones that I already knew the answers to:

1. Can you account for the fact that it was proven that

you purchased the suitcases [used to dump the body parts into the Chesapeake Bay]?

2. A search of your computer by forensic experts revealed that you browsed the Internet for advice on how to commit murder and there was your Google search for chloral hydrate just prior to the murder. There was also an Internet search, made by you, for a nearby Walgreens pharmacy. Please tell me about this?

3. Did you ever own a gun?

Melanie McGuire had purchased the matching set of suitcases from Kenneth Cole Luggage. The black, plastic bags used to wrap up Bill's body parts were identical, in every single respect, to those later found in her home containing the dead man's clothing. Forensic scientist Tom Lesniak concluded they had all been manufactured on the same production line and on the same extrusion run.

Melanie's Google search for a local Walgreens pharmacy was significant. Hooking this up led police to a prescription in the name of an RMA patient – RMA as in the clinic where she worked and where her lover, Dr Bradley Miller, was the boss. There was something else about that prescription too: it featured the signature of Dr Miller. This star witness was asked if he had written and signed the prescription. 'No,' Dr Miller answered. Asked if he recognised the handwriting, he affirmed that it was indeed Melanie McGuire's.

Mel had purchased a .38-calibre handgun from a small gun shop in eastern Pennsylvania just two days before her husband's murder. She had told some friends that it was Bill who wanted the gun, but she later told another man called James Finn that she wanted it for her own protection. Melanie's response to my nitty-gritty questions was, perhaps, anticipated:

Oh, my dearest, dear Christopher. (No Chanel this time around and I missed it). Have you lost interest in me? Why was I drawn to you? We share so much in common and in another life we could have enjoyed so much (fun) together. Your mailman will like this. Yes, I'll answer all of your questions when we meet and I look into your eyes. (Not flirting. Smile). All too complicated for me to put together when the people around me are so crude and gross. Please understand?

Then, in a heartbeat, Mel's mood changed, adding:

Have you been throwing me bones? I didn't fucking kill anyone. I told the judge that I didn't do it. I didn't do any fucking thing. Yes, Christopher, I'd love to meet you. Just give me some advance notice, please. Chris, think about my lovely hair. I want to look my best (no decent hair salon in here) though. My senses tell me that you are going to cheat on me. I'm intrigued.

I was working on a TV documentary series in New York, NY – the 'Garden State' being just across the river. In the past I had visited several NJ prisons and had interviewed several incarcerated male offenders with mixed results. Therefore, with equally mixed feelings, I telephoned the Edna Mahan Correctional Facility for Women to make an appointment to meet Mrs McGuire. 'She's expecting my visit,' I told the duty officer. The reply was, 'Sir, if you could call back tomorrow, I am sure that our inmate will confirm this and you'll be welcome. Thank you for calling, sir. Have a nice day.'

And I made that call bright and early the following morning:

CASE STUDY – SAVAGE: MELANIE 'MEL' LYN McGUIRE

CBD: Melanie McGuire, I spoke to you yesterday about an appointment... a visit to meet with her?

OFFICER: Ah, yes, sir. Inmate McGuire says that it would be inconvenient for her to see you at such short notice.

CBD: Inconvenient... why?

OFFICER: Sir, we are not allowed to discuss inmate McGuire's personal regime management in this facility. Perhaps if you could reschedule an appointment...

CBD: No, I can't.

OFFICER: Sir, thank you for calling the Edna Mahan Correctional Facility. The New Jersey Department of Corrections prides itself on offering visitors and inmates a comfortable, safe environment for the purposes of visitation. Full details are available on our website. Please enjoy New Jersey. Have a nice day!

In other words, the officer and Melanie were telling me to 'F-OFF'!

Criminal history affirms there are thousands of individuals who callously plan the perfect murder. However, they mostly fail, to their cost, to plan the perfect getaway, for like Dr Shipman and Oscar Pistorius and Kenneth Bianchi, the devil is in the small print.

Melanie was too careful, too highly educated, too arrogant and complex for her own good, yet too plum-dumb stupid at the same time. She was lacking in common sense. Her first big mistake was leaving a trail of links that formed a chain of evidence so strong even a possibly sympathetic jury of her peers could not ignore the significance. Her second mistake was her infallible self-belief in a world where elephants fly, lead balls bounce and fairies reign supreme. She is charming, cocky, self-centred, ultra-manipulative, antisocial, histrionic and a pathological liar with delusions of grandeur beyond her station in life, through and through to her very core.

Michael Bruce Ross – Psychopathic Master of Manipulation

'I admitted most of my murders to Detective Mike Malchik within hours of being arrested. I told everyone that I was sane. I volunteered for execution and that really screwed up the entire Connecticut judicial system cos everyone argued that anyone who volunteers to be sat down in that chair must be mad, an' they don't fry mad people in Connecticut.'

– Michael Bruce Ross, Death Row interview with the author, Somers Prison, CT, Monday, 26 September 1994

Although I had been corresponding with serial killers for many years, Michael Ross was the first homicidal psychopath I'd ever met in the flesh, and this was long before he trusted me enough to allow myself and a British film crew to catch this killer on-camera as one of my 12-part documentary series *The Serial Killers*.

TALKING WITH PSYCHOPATHS AND SAVAGES

I have fully documented Ross in *Dead Men Talking: The World's Worst Killers in Their Own Words*, first published in hardback by John Blake, 2009, but the book you are reading now is not so much about his life and crimes, it is about how this highly intelligent, former Ivy League Cornell University student (admittedly from an abusive childhood) came to get a kick out of committing sado-sexual murders. These offences included the killing of two schoolgirls – one of whom he sodomised after death – and how this man went on to run rings around the psychiatric profession, bringing one eminent expert to the point of mental collapse.

Taking Michael at face value, I found him quite the most charming, polite, oft-times giggly type of guy – one who could easily hold his own in any mixed company. With an IQ of 150, intelligent he most certainly was. However, while ticking him off against Professor Hare's Checklist, I could find only one item: (No. 16 – Failure to accept responsibility for his own actions) absent, for Ross had done quite the opposite. In so doing, effectively he carried out a masterstroke of manipulation, a *tour de force* deception. He brought a trial judge and later a string of appellate court judges to a position where the State's death penalty statute was held to be unconstitutional. Thanks to Mr Ross, Connecticut would later consider abolishing execution, most certainly execution using 'Ole Sparky'. The electric chair was a gruesome relic – I know because I once sat in it (see also page 122)!

Apart from the morality of executing a man in the liberal 'Nutmeg State' there was also a financial cost to consider. 'Ole Sparky' had not been used since Joseph 'Mad Dog' Taborsky had 'ridden the lightning' on Tuesday, 17 May 1960. Since then the chair had fallen into disrepair. So here it was, now unemployed, within a very short walk from Michael's Death

Row cell. There were no cables; had they even existed there was not an electrician nor 'electrocutioner' in the entire State who had a clue how to wire things up. Then there were the leather restraints, the redecorating of the witness viewing area and the Death House Suite to sort out. Finally, the 'Electrocution Protocol Manual' had been lost along with the moral will of the local electricity company to hook up the juice to kill someone.

Now the State of Connecticut found itself in an awful fix. The state prosecutor was demanding that Ross be put to death – he was a serial killer everyone thought was mad because he had volunteered to die, therefore he should not be executed in *any event*. Added to which it would cost at least $30,000 in old money for today one might treble that figure to make 'Ole Sparky' useable again. Hedging their bets, Connecticut opted for the more 'humane' lethal injection method instead. It would cost close to $1 million to refurbish the machinery of death. At least another $5 million went on legal fees, not including the psychiatrists' bills to try and get Michael off the hook nor the medical profession's bizarre attempts to cure his incurable psychopathy using chemical castration, in one of the most sickening medical experiments carried out on a condemned man in US history.

> 'I've always felt that I had to be in control of myself and, even to this day, I feel the need to be in control. What scares me the most isn't prison, or the death penalty. I'm not afraid of dying, I just don't wanna be around when it happens. What I fear most is insanity. I'm scared of losing touch with reality. Sometimes I feel I'm slipping away and I'm losing control. If you are in control you can handle anything, but if you lose it, you are nothing.
> – Michael Ross, at interview with the author –
> 26 November 1994.

Having admitted most of his crimes to Detective Mike Malchik just two hours after his arrest – indeed, he would have coughed up everything within the hour had a cleaner not burst into the interview room to start mopping the floor – Ross was also adamant that he was sane. He made it clear that he had no intention of trying to duck responsibility, or ending up in an asylum for the rest of his life. Nevertheless, what he wanted, and what he would get, were two different things. To his credit, he wanted a quick hearing. The State, however, demanded he enter a 'Not Guilty' plea. It was not for Mr Ross to determine his own state of mind for this was a matter for psychiatric evaluation.

Enter the shrinks.

It is a rare thing for defence and prosecution psychiatric experts to agree on both a diagnosis and any mitigating ramifications, but the Ross case *was* unusual and, in this instance, there *was* consensus that he was suffering from sexual sadism: a mental disease that resulted in a compulsion in Ross to 'perpetrate violent sexual activity in a repetitive way'. Unknown to the judge and members of the trial jury, the forensic psychiatrists from both sides had agreed that the crimes committed by Ross were 'a direct result of the uncontrollable sexual aggressive impulses to which he was prey'. However, the State, led by the tenacious Robert 'Bulldog' Satti – now aware of the damage that could be caused by their own psychiatrist effectively giving evidence against them by concurring with the defence psychiatrist – refused to allow their psychiatrist, Dr Miller, to take the stand.

This uncomfortable state of affairs, combined with prosecutor Satti's almost pathological desire to fry Michael Ross, kept the entire court proceedings in the dark as to a 'possible mitigating factor' – one that could have removed the threat of the death penalty from the accused man.

CASE STUDY – PSYCHOPATH: MICHAEL BRUCE ROSS

Satti's suggestion to the jury was that Ross had been examined by a State psychiatrist who had found him *not* to be suffering from a mitigating psychopathology – something which was patently untrue, even a bald-faced lie, bordering on an attempt to pervert the course of justice. Amazingly, the defence failed to ask why the State's psychiatrist was not being made available for cross-examination. Also, the jury had been led to believe that there was a difference of opinion between the opposing teams when there was not. This resulted in rulings that improperly excluded evidence, disingenuous summations and instructions that allowed the jury to draw inferences that were insupportable.

In June 1987, after four weeks of testimony, the jury took just 87 minutes to convict Ross of capital felony murder. On Monday, 6 July, 20 days before his twenty-eighth birthday, he was sentenced to death. Under Connecticut law, he would have been spared if the court had found one single redeeming factor, or quality, that the jury believed to indicate remorse or mitigation. They could not; for Ross, it seemed, did not have a conscience and couldn't give a damn.

But what had happened to the State's expert? Of course, unknown to the jury, Dr Miller had concurred with the defence expert's assessment and in his report to the State's Attorney a year prior to the trial, had concluded: 'Were a specific diagnosis to be attached to Mr Ross's condition at the time of his offences, it would be DSM-111, 302.84, Sexual Sadism.' To this Dr Miller added a rider: 'Notwithstanding this diagnosis Mr Ross could still conform his behavior to the requirements of the law.' In other words, Dr Miller was *actually supporting* the State's argument that Ross *was not* insane. Whether Robert Satti fully grasped this is uncertain, but one thing is for sure, he chose not to present his star witness, Dr Miller, in court.

Some time later, Dr Miller explained to me that he had suffered sleepless nights, having been influenced by the media reports of the case and the awfulness of the crimes. This, he claimed, had coloured and tainted his otherwise professional opinion. His conscience now weighed heavily on him for his diagnosis could help a man into the electric chair, something the doctor said he could not live with. If the State had its way, they might as well 'be using me to push the switch', he said.

To rectify this error of judgement, and to clear his conscience, just two days before the trial, Dr Miller did something unprecedented: he wrote to the trial judge explaining his reason for having to withdraw from the case. In any event, Ross was found to be sane, therefore guilty, and was sentenced to death.

In due course, this distasteful issue was brought before the State of Connecticut's Supreme Court and the prosecution, led by Robert Satti, came in for a roasting.

> The State was able to seize upon inflammatory connotations of the sexual sadism diagnosis to turn a legally mitigating factor into an aggravating factor and the judgment of the trial court is reversed.
> – later Connecticut Supreme Court ruling

Rightly concluding that Ross's trial had been rigged, the matter of completely reversing the sentence of the trial court became another matter entirely, so the Supreme Court ordered a fresh evaluation by independent psychiatrists who would determine, then report back, to a lower Court on Michael's state of mind. However, whether a now-furious Ross would agree to be examined again was his decision and his alone. For the time being he would remain on Death Row, so he vowed to run rings round Connecticut jurisprudence to the end of his days. As mentioned earlier, Michael told me that what he feared most was a loss of mental control. He had played God with both women's and children's lives; some lived, some died. He had become addicted to terrible acts of sexually motivated homicide and now his powers of control had been removed and, as we have noted before, psychopaths hate losing control.

In her book *Pictures of Childhood*, psychoanalyst Dr Alice Miller refers to the German writer of novels Franz Kafka, who once noted in his diary that a writer must cling to his desk 'by his teeth in order to avoid madness that would overtake him if he stopped writing.' Dr Miller adds: 'I suppose the same can be said of any creative activity that somehow permits us to come to grips with the demons of our past, to give form to the chaos within us and thereby master our anxiety.'

How correct Dr Miller and Franz Kafka are.

Then, am I being obscene by suggesting, indeed, if I say, that most sexually motivated psychopaths regard their crimes as a 'creative activity'? Repugnant as it may seem (the FBI will confirm this), serial killers develop their murderous craft over time. These murderers learn from their mistakes. They learn from experience how to improve their modus operandi. For instance, finding which restraints are best suited to the task, or the continued development of a 'murder kit', if needs want. Moreover, they learn how their deadly craft affords them better pleasure – an addicted pleasure – through stalking, entrapping, sometimes torturing and the eventual kill time and then repeating this process again and again.

Undeniably, after he was incarcerated Michael Ross clung 'by his teeth' in order to avoid the madness that he believed would overtake him. He said this so many times himself without prompting. But, paraphrasing Dr Miller, was he *truly* trying to get to grips with the demons of his past, to give form to the chaos within him, thereby mastering his own anxieties? Ross would soon attempt to have us believe that he was trying to understand himself, but as a psychopath was he truly trying to regain his lost sense of control? I got to know Michael extremely well and we know that apart from being highly intelligent, he was a cunning games player too. Therefore I suggest that by playing the 'I need to understand myself' card, which was bound to guarantee great media and medical interest, he was also striving to wrestle back his sense of loss of control.

Robert Theodore 'Ted' Bundy was a manipulating psychopath, as were the countless killers before him and those yet to come. In my opinion, however, they could never come close to Michael Ross for he is a benchmark, being the master of homicidal, psychopathic manipulation. Nevertheless, I would use his manipulation for my own ends and to try and gain admission for two cold-case homicides and in so doing I would have to think like him and get right inside his head.

Recalling Professor Hare's Checklist (No. 16 – 'Lack of remorse of guilt'), I later asked Michael if he had any feelings of remorse for his crimes. Under normal circumstances one might reasonably expect some sign of contrition – a little soul-searching, shame, even a bit of conscience-stricken sorrow, topped up with a large helping of 'I'll never forgive myself. I wish everything could be undone'. But there was not much chance of that and Ross didn't disappoint, telling me: 'Nope! I don't feel anything for them. I really wish I did. I don't feel anything. I feel really bad for the families. I mean, I feel lots of times, like I can see Mrs Shelley, the mother of one of them girls I killed, on the witness stand. And, ah, I can't remember her name, but I can think of another one on the stand describing her daughter – she went to the morgue and saw her at the morgue. But the girls themselves I feel nothing for, and I never have.'

Having seen all of the crime scene and grim autopsy photographs I considered numbers 2 – 'Grandiose sense of worth', 7 – 'Shallow affect' and 8 – 'Callous/lack of sympathy' – so I asked if he had any detailed memories of the murders.

Ross chuckled and said: 'Yes, and no! I used to fantasise over the crimes every day and every night. When I was out free, I sometimes went back to the bodies and masturbated over the remains. In prison I would masturbate to the point of, um, actually having raw spots on myself from the masturbation. I would bleed. It's weird. I get a lot of pleasure from it. It is a really pleasurable experience. But, when it's all over, just like right after I had killed someone and it's all over with, it's a very short-term thing. I guess it is like getting high. You know I've never used drugs, but you can get high, then you come down and crash. That's almost how it is. It's not an easy thing to live with.'

Most psychopaths and narcissists are control freaks and with two TV cameras rolling, a pretty female assistant paying attention to the matt she applied to his face and teasing his hair into place, Ross was now centre stage. He felt himself important – in fact, so important that a British crew had travelled thousands of miles just to hear his words to be screened into millions of homes worldwide. With his IQ of 150, he was finally among his peers: intelligent TV people who had clout and power, people who could go where they wanted, travel when they wanted and do whatever they liked (which is not quite true as any producer will agree). Ross was in control, with his over-inflated ego bursting at the seams. Finally, he felt that he was being internationally regarded as a serial killer bigwig. This was his chance to belittle the psychiatric profession, the cops who had at long last tracked him down; his opportunity to lash out at the criminal justice system and the Connecticut Department of Corrections, whom, in his opinion, were fools.

You will remember my previously mentioned 'fishing' method of getting people to talk to me (see also page 96). Unbeknownst to Ross I was using it now: the master-manipulating psychopath was almost hooked. He was also unaware that I had bigger fish to fry, therefore an inevitable question was to ask him what had been going through his mind while he was raping and killing. I would like to be able to tell you that he turned cold as a wintry day, but the man sitting unshackled just a couple of feet in front of me didn't budge in his chair. He didn't blink and unlike many other serial killers I have interviewed at close quarters, he didn't break into a sweat, nor did the colour of his face change when confronted with such a blunt question.

Ross paused for a long moment; not to consider what I had asked, but because a tannoy screamed out 'YARD TIME... TIME IN THE YARD!' I recalled Mike Malchik of the Connecticut State Police telling me that Ross's confessions to him had been interrupted when a cleaner burst into the room, mop and bucket in hand. That it had taken Mike twenty or so minutes to get back on track. The clock was ticking... so too was Michael's mind. I could almost see it ticking; hear it ticking... Tick, tick, tick... However, I knew that he was trapped because the clock was also ticking – our valuable two hours together was running out. Then he spoke:

> I felt nothin'! That's what's so weird about this thing. Everybody seems to think, you know, the State's theory that I'm a rapist and I kill them so they can't identify me. Look, most of the time it's broad daylight. Chris, I

mean I'm not a stupid person. As sure as hell if I was going to do something like that, as sure as hell wouldn't do it that way. There was nothing going through my mind until they were already dead.

And then it was like stepping through a doorway. And, uh, I remember the very first feeling I had was my heart beating. I mean, really pounding. The second feeling I had was that my hands hurt where I always strangled them with my hands. And the third feeling was, I guess, fear, and the kind of reality set in that there was this dead body in front of me.

And, again, I don't want to mislead you because I knew what was going on, but it was like a different level. I mean, it was like watching it [on TV]. And, after it was all over, you know, it kind of sets in, and that's when I would get frightened and stuff. I would hide the bodies and cover them up, or something.

I abused them, I used them and I murdered them. What else do you need?

And as those last words passed his lips, I snagged my line tight.

Crystal Run (NY) Police and Connecticut State Police had the murders of Paula Perrera and Dzung Ngoc Tu still outstanding and Ross had cockily refused to be interviewed by law enforcement once he'd arrived on 'The Green Mile' (the execution suite of rooms – in Somers Prison it was then a mucky brown). Now on the floor beside me were documents supplied to me by the Crystal Run PD – material never made public before and information only the police and the killer would have known about. Furthermore, I knew that the families of the two victims needed closure.

'You are not really such a big-hitter, are you, Michael?' I asked, leaning closer.

'Uh?'

'Just six murder victims... that's all.'

'What?'

So I listed them: Wendy Baribeault, Tammy Lee Williams, Robin Dawn Stavinsky, Debra Smith Taylor, Leslie Shelley and April Brunais. 'Mike, that makes six in my book. Okay, think about Carignan and Henry Lucas, whom you know I've interviewed. They did around 40 victims apiece.'

There can be many slips between cup and lip but Ross took the bait.

'No, no, no!' he blurted out. 'No, no! I killed that Vietnamese girl, Dzung-something, and that schoolkid, Paula Perrera.'

'I don't think that's true, Mike,' I replied. 'I know the police have never spoken to you about those murders.'

At this Ross started to look a bit hot under the collar. 'Chris, I have *never* lied to you. We are friends. Yes, the police didn't interview me about those girls 'cos my attorney wouldn't let them. There are appeals going through for the other cases. Now I'm upset 'cos you don't trust me.'

'What did you do with the body, Michael?' I asked.

'What body?'

'Paula's.'

'Dumped it by a low stone wall,' he told me. And then without further prompting he added, 'There was a willow tree there. I remember that.'

'Where'd you pick her up, Mike?'

On this he seemed unsure. 'I can't recall. But it was in New York State where I killed her. Someplace called Crystal Run, I think... Yeah, Crystal Run.'

I called for a break in filming with the excuse that he might feel more comfortable after taking a visit to the bathroom and enjoying a cup of coffee. Michael liked that and the correctional lieutenant gracefully extended our time by a further 30 minutes because I imagine he sensed what was coming.

Now it was my turn to be put on the spot. I was thinking 'entrapment'. Here I was, with a folder full of police documents, which Ross didn't know I had. Because of ongoing appeals, acting on his attorney's strict orders he had declined to be interviewed by cops about Paula and Dzung Ngoc Tu. Perhaps even more worrying was that I had not long previously filmed an interview with prosecutor Robert Satti (now deceased) at his office in New Haven, Connecticut. Still smarting from his scrap with the Supreme Court, this no-nonsense legal veteran of the 'Whip 'em, flog 'em and hang 'em' brigade was still determined to see Ross in the chair – if needs be he'd pull the switch himself. And 'Bulldog Satti' had asked me if I could sweat anything more out of Michael to firm things up for him.

Yes, there was '*serious* entrapment' written all over my approach to Ross. By using lateral thinking and my psychological manipulation against him I was effectively acting by proxy for the police in attempting to extract a confession, at once in collusion with a state prosecutor while doing so. If an irate circuit judge had got wind of this the least charge against me would be attempting to pervert the course of justice for pissing all over the Supreme Court's parade. Then I might be the one sitting in the electric chair, not Mr Ross!

So, I turned to my producer, Frazer Ashford. Thinking along the same lines, under his breath he muttered: 'We're going to get sued here, Chris. The cops are going to demand copies of the film tapes. We'll have to hand them over. For Christ's sake, forget the confession. Let's wrap this up and get out of here, fast.'

The one thing you don't do when filming a documentary is to rock the boat with the 'Money Man', aka the producer. Previously I had upset Frazer while interviewing two female serial killers – Cathy May Wood and Gwendolyn Graham – after which he had threatened to send me home on the first available flight. Indeed, he was still angry with me from the time when I sat down in Connecticut's 'Ole Sparky'. 'There's only one problem with this chair,' he told an officer. 'It isn't switched on!'

'Whose interview is this?' I told Frazer. 'The bastard has killed those two girls! You've seen the photos. Don't worry, I'll sort it out, so let's get on with it.'

However, now I was thinking 'Miranda Warning' – as in the advisability or not of reading Ross his legal rights before he said another word. Michael was now back, sitting in his chair.

'Mike,' I said. 'If I showed you a map of Crystal Run, and of course you don't have to say another word, but could you indicate on the map where you think you might have killed Paula?'

With that I took from the folder a map of the area around Crystal Run and gave it to him.

For a minute Ross looked at the map before indicating a location where there was a rest stop called 'Crystal Dip'. 'There,' he said. 'It was quite marshy. I pulled over and killed her here.'

I then asked why he had been in that area. Ross explained that he was on his way back to Connecticut after an argument with his former girlfriend, Connie. He said that he had spotted Paula hitching a ride along Route 211 and had offered her a lift home. The date and approximate time were near on perfect.

'What was Paula wearing?' I asked.

'Gosh, I can't remember that, Chris.'

'Can you recall what she looked like?'

CASE STUDY – PSYCHOPATH: MICHAEL BRUCE ROSS

'I have already told you, I can't remember the faces of any of my victims.'

In the police folder was a press cutting with a photo of Paula Perrera. I considered showing it to him to ask if he recognised the face. For a second I fingered the article and then thought better of it for obvious reasons.

'Well, that's about it now, Mike. I think we are all done now.'

Ross was now under more pressure. At this point, I was in control for he imagined that I was about to close him down. His ego, however, demanded even more attention, for I had not reacted to his repulsive confession in any way. Once again he had failed to shock me with the awfulness of yet another murder.

To understand a psychopathic killer one almost has to think like one. Now, I was reeling him in.

'What about the Vietnamese girl?' he asked. 'They think that I killed her. That ain't strictly true.'

Mindful again of entrapment, I came back with, 'You mean Dzung Ngoc Tu? She *does* have a name, you know. Sweet, hard-working student at Cornell... You must remember her. You helped her a couple of times with her classes.'

Ross then gave me a rapidly potted account of how he had convinced the twenty-five-year-old student to let him escort her back to her dorm. It was dark. He had explained to her that as several rapes had recently taken place on the campus (ones that he himself had actually carried out), she would be safe with him. Ross told me that he had raped and strangled Dzung Ngoc Tu in a wooded area before throwing her body off a bridge into the swirling waters of Beebe Lake.

'Technically, I didn't kill her,' he protested. 'She drowned.'

This cold-hearted statement confirmed the autopsy report carried out on Dzung Ngoc Tu: she *had* been alive when she hit the water. It stated: 'Cause of death: attempted strangulation. Death by drowning'.

Reflecting on my discussion with 'Bulldog Satti', with less than 15 minutes before we had to cease filming, after which Ross would be returned to his Death Row cell, I asked him, in passing, about fourteen-year-olds Leslie Shelley and April Brunais – two homicides for which he had already been found guilty. As far as I was concerned he would have nothing more to add – why would he need to add anything?

He had admitted killing the two girls and had given police a verifiable account into the bargain. Then again, one must never underestimate a psychopath and this monster simply had to have the last say. What follows is taken verbatim from Michael's last words to me. Shocking, disgusting and evil in extremis, it will make your blood boil as it did with 'Bulldog Satti' when he later heard Ross's words to me for the first time.

The trial record shows that it was Easter Sunday, 1984. Leslie and April, inseparable friends and neighbours in Griswold, Connecticut, had decided to walk into Jewett City. Their parents had disapproved but the girls went on regardless and that decision would cost them their lives. Now darkness had fallen. Leslie and April were getting scared. They phoned their respective parents, pleading for a lift home. Both girls were ordered to walk back as punishment. At 10.30 p.m. when neither girl had returned, their concerned parents called the police, reporting them as runaways despite the fact that April and Leslie had not long called home and had begged to be picked up by them.

Nevertheless, Ross's admission of guilt in this double homicide went more or less as follows. Although he could not recall the exact time he had stopped his car and offered the kids a lift back to their homes, he told me that April was the more assertive of the two. She had climbed into the front passenger seat, while the petite and fragile Leslie sat behind.

Both girls were understandably startled when Ross, now overwhelmed with thoughts of rape and murder, drove right past the end of their street. Despite their protests he wouldn't stop. April then pulled out a pocketknife, with which she planned to threaten their abductor. Ross easily disarmed her. Driving east out on Highway 138, he headed for Voluntown and the nearby Beach Pond separating Rhode Island from Connecticut.

Parking up at a still undetermined location, Ross tore off April's jeans, cutting them into strips with the pocketknife. These he used to bind his victims' hands and feet. He shut Leslie into the trunk of his car, and then dragged April a few yards and forced her to her knees. There can be no doubt that Leslie overheard her spirited friend arguing with Ross. As Ross had previously admitted, brave April fought for her life as he raped, then strangled her.

When asked by police to recall the murder of Leslie Shelley, Ross had clammed up. He had nothing more to say. Indeed he had remained silent on the matter until my last minutes with him on camera at the Osborn Correctional Institution on 26 September 1994. What he told me was intermingled with crocodile tears and occasionally hysterical laughter. Indeed what he told me was something not even Robert Satti had ever experienced in all of his years as one of the toughest prosecutors in the United States.

Leslie had made a great impact on him, Ross said, his voice flat, devoid of any emotion once again.

'I took her from the trunk. She had wispy blonde hair. She was calm as I talked to her in the car. I told her I didn't want to kill her, and she cried when I told her that her friend was already dead.' He paused then looked into my eyes, perhaps seeking disgust but there was nothing he could see. 'Yes, I suppose she started shaking,' he added, 'and she appeared resigned to her fate when I rolled her over. This is what bothers me. I can't remember how I strangled her. With the others, it was like someone else did it, and I watched from afar through a fog of unreality. This was real but somehow unreal. It was fantasy but not really fantasy. Her death? Leslie? It wasn't someone else and for the first time it was me. I watched myself do those things and I couldn't stop it. It was like an invisible barrier was between us. I didn't want to kill her.'

During those final moments of the interview, Ross showed the first signs of stress, maybe a hint of remorse. He stopped talking, lowered his head and sucked in a lungful of stale prison air. Behind me there was movement. One of the guards, a father of two young daughters, had quietly been ordered to leave the room. When Ross resumed his sickening account of the murder of Leslie Shelley, there were tears in his eyes.

'Chris, I couldn't do anything but watch as I murdered her, and you want to know something outrageous? Well, I cried afterwards. You know something else? Well, ah, I don't know but nobody knows this.'

There was still no reaction from me, a reaction he so desperately needed. But I was precisely mirroring his coldness, his sickening callousness and his lack of empathy.

'And, so, what?' I asked him.

There was a long pause.

'Well, I wanted to have sex with her straight after I raped and killed April, but I couldn't get it up. So, I had to sit back with Leslie for an hour, just talkin' and stuff. Then, because she started crying again, saying that she would be in trouble for being late home, I had to kill her. But, ah, I raped her, after death, to release the tension. You see, nobody has been told this before.'

Then he smiled sheepishly before adding, 'You know, they call me a serial killer, right? Well, I've only killed eight women. Big deal! There are a lot more guys you have met and they've killed dozens more than me. So, you're right, an' in that context I'm a nice guy. I'm such a nice guy really.'

With that, he burst into an uncontrollable fit of laughter before telling me that he had dumped the bodies of April and Leslie at another location near Beach Pond, occasionally visiting the site to masturbate over their remains. 'I'd just sit there, just to look at their decomposing bodies. Like my childhood fantasies, they were there for me and they gave me pleasure when I needed it,' he recalled.

Ross took police to the bodies of April and Leslie shortly after his arrest on Tuesday, 28 June 1984, although the precise location of the murder scene was never established. This was put down to an 'oversight' by the Connecticut State Police, and later proved in court to be a deliberate attempt by them to avoid a jurisdictional dispute with Rhode Island law enforcement, who then had to foot the bill for the murder inquiries into the two young girls. This proved yet another complication in the legacy of Ross's killing career, one from which he enjoyed much satisfaction at the expense of the police.

When Robert Satti learned of Ross's confession to me concerning the post-mortem rape of Leslie Shelley, he flipped. This was yet another very serious charge he could bring against his target.

'I am going fry that sumbitch murdering fucker if it's the last thing I do before I die,' he raged.

Sadly, 'Bulldog' never got his wish. He passed away before the chair was thrown onto the scrapheap, long before Ross was strapped to the lethal injection gurney at 2am on Friday, 13 May 2005. As he had volunteered for execution he had the topsy-turvy option of saving his own life by changing his mind right up until the moment the needle went into his arm – he didn't!

IN SEARCH OF THE GRAIL

Of course I'm not talking about the mystically religious artefact. Maybe the Holy Grail is a heavily bejewelled goblet, or perhaps it's a simple cup carved from cypress wood used by Jesus at The Last Supper, or else it's Christ's blood. Others believe it not to be a physical thing but something less tangible yet even more intriguing – a doctrine, being a creed or body of teachings presented for Christian acceptance or belief.

No!

I'm referring to the 'Holy Grail of Psychopathy', one that psychiatrists and medical people have been struggling to fully understand and find a cure for since the French psychiatrist Philippe Pinel suggested way back in the nineteenth century that there was a madness that involved mania or depression, or psychosis. Our present thinking is that psychopathy is untreatable. Therefore, if a person could find this particular Grail, he would become rich beyond the dreams of avarice. And there is no want of trying, for try the experts did when Michael Ross came onto the scene.

As soon as the psychiatric profession in the US got wind that the psychopath Michael Ross suffered from sexual sadism with his overpowering, uncontrollable urges – which technically mitigated his actions – lights went on and burned throughout long nights in medical clinics and facilities across the country. Doctors everywhere pored over editions of the *The Diagnostic and Statistical Manual of Mental Disorders* (DSM), trying to find a link between sexual sadism and psychopathy, for scores of psychiatrists started to believe that if they could control, or even eradicate Ross's uncontrollable sexual desires, then a cure for his psychopathy was just around the corner.

On my first visit to Ross's Death Row cell, he was on top form and eager to point out two huge piles of letters. 'Look, Chris,' he said. 'That lot is from doctors and psychiatrists, and the other pile is from women who want to marry me. Letters, letters everywhere, with almost no place to sleep!' Indicating towards the adjoining cell, he laughed: 'See in there? Well, they tell me that I am the only condemned man in the US with two cells. It's where I keep all of my legal and medical books. It really pisses the officers, I can tell ya.'

Much has been written about Ross's alleged determination to discover what, exactly, was wrong with his head; he had this overwhelming compulsion to masturbate day and night, and stalk young women and brutally kill them. Indeed, he has published his own concerns about his state of mind, which can be found on the Internet. Moreover, it would be fair to say that this highly-educated man comes across as very plausible if not for the fact that he was a sexual psychopath through and through. Did Michael, for one moment, hold any feelings of remorse for his crimes? No! He certainly was not concerned about his state of mind when he was killing young women and two schoolgirls, so why, while on Death Row, did he belatedly embark on this so-called quest for self-discovery? To try and understand his reasoning, forget we are examining a 'normal person' and enter the mind of a fully emerged psychopath – it's not a good place to be.

To the end of his days Michael Ross was a game player. His aggressive narcissism demanded that he detest those who did not admire him. He believed himself to be more important than he actually was, and now with a pitiless chain of days, weeks and years ahead of him with nothing better to do, he surrounded himself with law and medical books, to include a copy of *The Diagnostic and Statistical Manual of Mental Disorders*, and he then started claiming to be an 'expert' on many things.

His best wheeze was to run the Department of Corrections ragged with his application for surgical castration while knowing this would be denied. Michael had time on his hands, so after going through the law books and other material, he wrote letter after letter to members of the medical profession and the prison warden. Eventually, after spending a small fortune arguing the toss, an agreement was reached: Michael could submit himself to what he called 'The Chemical Cosh' – chemical castration – so he put himself forward for a series of tests.

Many experts, including several from The Johns Hopkins University School of Medicine, Baltimore, Maryland, seemed to believe that this treatment could separate the beast from a possibly decent Michael Ross and, for an extended period, he was prescribed massive doses of the female contraceptive Depo-Provera to reduce his enormous sex drive. At the same time as he was taking this drug, he was being prescribed Prozac, a powerful anti-depressant, and this cocktail certainly reduced his abnormal desires, along with any chances of him falling pregnant!

However, there soon emerged problems, the first being legal in nature. Upjohn, the British manufacturer of Depo-Provera, had issued no licence for their contraceptive to be used in this manner. The second snag was a physical one. Unfortunately, excessive use of Depo-Provera ballooned his weight by several stone and, as a result, Ross suffered pathological changes in liver function and hormone levels. Now that he was terribly ill, quite understandably his depression reappeared. He was back to being a walking time bomb, making it perfectly clear that if ever he found himself alone with a female officer he'd kill her. This attempt at curing psychopathy by castration had failed dismally.

When I asked Michael why he had volunteered for execution, he explained, probably tongue-in-cheek, that he didn't want to put his victims' families through more court cases again. As a retired judge explained, 'Ross will probably outlive everyone else involved with this case. If he really wants to be executed that bad, then he should kill himself.'

The serial sex killer Keith Hunter Jesperson was not slow in coming from another angle, and perhaps he has a point when he explains: 'If you volunteer to die, chances are the prosecutor will not give you what you want. Serial killers I know of asked to be killed at their trials. Reverse psychology. The juries opted for life – wanting the guilty men to suffer. It's a good defense to play.'

Thank you, Keith, for that.

> 'He [Ross] was real humble. He wouldn't look you in the eyes when you talked with him. He was very educated and a talented twenty-year-old kid. He didn't appear to be the kind of guy who would go out to towns and do this kind of stuff. He more or less kept his mouth shut, and he was subdued and spiritless.'
> – Sergeant Lewis, La Salle PD to a journalist after his final arrest for the La Salle offence committed Monday, 28 September 1981.

We can read all the psychopath checklists ever published but if we can learn anything from Ross's psychopathology and his life, crimes and manipulations, it has to be that his rape and murder victims didn't realise that he was a stone-cold killer until it was too late. His parents, his tutors at Cornell, fellow students, employers, landlords and landladies and his several girlfriends might have realised that he was narcissistic, but never in their wildest dreams did they regard him as a sexual psychopath.

> 'If I had been walking along a dark alleyway at night and heard footsteps behind me, I would have been relieved to have turned around and seen Michael. Bespectacled and bookish, he looks just like the All-American Boy, someone living next door to you. That's how normal he looks.'
> – Karen B. Clarke, New York investigative journalist on Connecticut's most notorious serial killer, the now-executed Michael B. Ross

Cocky Ross, with his glibness and superficial charm, grandiose sense of self-worth, need for stimulation, pathological lying, cunning and manipulative nature, lack of remorse or guilt and shallow effect ticks many of Professor Hare's Checklist. Added to which are: callous/lack of empathy, parasitic lifestyle, poor behaviour controls, promiscuous sexual behaviour, early behaviour problems, lack of realistic long-term goals, impulsivity, irresponsibility, many short-term relationships, juvenile delinquency and criminal versatility.

Actually, when super-sleuth Mike Malchik first knocked on Ross's front door, on 28 June 1984, he actually felt that the personable young man who opened it could not have been a serial murderer. As the officer was leaving to rejoin his colleague Detective Frank Griffen in their car, Ross called him back to invite the cop in for coffee. He then asked Malchik a question: Ross asked if such a killer would be declared insane and thereby escape the electric chair if convicted? It was such a pointed question that it prompted Malchik to return to Ross's sitting room.

Although Ross's blue Toyota roughly matched the vehicle that had been seen tearing away from the area close to where Wendy Baribeault was murdered, after a few more minutes of general conversation Malchik got up to leave for the second time. He was only a few yards away before a gut instinct prompted him to turn around and ask Ross a question of his own, which was: 'What were your movements on Friday, 15 June, the day Miss Baribeault went missing?'

Amazingly, thought Malchik, Ross immediately reeled off his movements for that day almost to the minute, with the exception of the hour encompassing 4.30pm. This was the time when witnesses had seen Wendy walking along the side of the road, followed by a man answering Ross's description. Malchik thought it remarkable that anyone could recall his or her exact whereabouts, along with solid timings, two weeks after an event, so he reckoned that 15 June must have been a special day for Ross. He then asked him what he had been doing on the two days either side of this crucial date. Ross couldn't remember a thing and the detective was stunned for the implication was now obvious.

Michael was taken into custody.

Acknowledging this author's work in gaining confessions for the murders of Dzung Ngoc Tu and Paula Perrera, the full transcripts of Ross's interview with NYSP detectives, along with crime scene photographs, are now with DCI Martin Brunning of the Bedfordshire, Cambridgeshire and Hertfordshire Major Crime Unit. DCI Brunning was the lead investigator in the murders committed by serial killer Joanne Christine Dennehy in 2013. The definitive book on Dennehy called *Love of Blood*

TALKING WITH PSYCHOPATHS AND SAVAGES

written by this author is published by John Blake (London) 2015. A full account of Ross's awful murders is included in my book *Talking with Serial Killers* first published HB by John Blake (London) 2003.

CASE STUDY: SAVAGE
Kenneth Alessio Bianchi – Conman Supremo

Another futile attempt to 'cure' a wholly manipulative sado-sexual murderer of his 'illness' was attempted in Bellingham, Washington State, circa March 1979, when leading psychiatrists appearing for Kenneth Bianchi's defence and the prosecution were convinced that Ken suffered a Multiple Personality Disorder. I have touched on Bianchi earlier in formatting this book.

Charged with the murders of Washington State University co-eds Karen Mandic, age twenty-two, and Diane Wilder, twenty-seven, a lot more charges emanating from Los Angeles would later follow: Kenneth Bianchi, aka 'the Hillside Strangler', was figuring out a plea bargain deal so that the threat of the gallows no longer hung over his head. In the event, his attorney, Dean Brett, advised his client to plead 'Not Guilty by Reason of Insanity' (NGRI). Although not having anything like the high IQ of 150 enjoyed by Michael Ross (see previous chapter), Bianchi was street-smart.

Had Ken been abused as a child this just might have unhinged his mind. Furthermore, saying that he failed to remember killing the two co-eds could result in a much lesser custodial sentence. If the defence succeeded there would be a specific period before parole or, better still, his time could be served in a psychiatric institution, where the silver-tongued killer could work his ticket to freedom as so many killers do – the previously mentioned Paul Beecham, for example (see also pages 13, 48–53, 155).

Allegedly Bianchi displayed a multiple-personality disorder (MPD). MPD seems to be caused by severe psychological traumas in childhood, such as sexual abuse or extreme cruelty – of which Bianchi suffered none – and these experiences can be so painful that the victim literally blots them from his mind. In later life a violent shock can reactivate the trauma, causing the 'everyday' personality to blank out, hence his so-called 'amnesia' over the co-ed murders.

Although the medical profession had been aware of the enigma of the MPD since the early nineteenth century, the general public learned of the 'illness' largely through the 1957 movie *The Three Faces of Eve*, which was based on the book of the same name written by, of all people, two psychiatrists. Shortly after Kenneth's arrest we find him sitting on his bunk, reading the very same book. Furthermore, he had even watched the film on a TV positioned on the wall outside his bars.

The most remarkable case of MPD in recent years was that of Billy Milligan. In 1977 he was arrested in Columbus, Ohio, for rape. Billy later declared to a social worker that he was not Billy but 'David', and subsequent examination by psychiatrists made it clear that Billy, aka David, was a genuine MPD case.

Sexually abused in childhood by his stepfather, Billy had become another personality to escape the misery. Eventually, he split into no less than twenty-three separate personalities, including a lesbian, a suave Englishman who also spoke Arabic, an electronics expert and a Serbo-Croat, although it has never been established how he learned the language. Nevertheless, all these personalities were so distinctive that only a remarkable actor could have simulated them. It was later discovered that apparently the 'lesbian personality' committed the rape – presumably while the other twenty-two personalities watched from the sidelines, one of whom becoming so disgusted that he turned Billy in to the police.

The Milligan case was much publicised in the late 1970s. In 1977 a 'Dr Kenneth Bianchi' was setting up his own bogus psychiatric counselling service. Using genuine diplomas by sleight of hand garnered from students who applied for a post with him, he conned Dr Weingarten into allowing him to rent an office at his practice.

Bianchi would later write this to me: 'People in California are big on window dressing. Joining the *Psychology Today* book club, I took in books [one of which concerned Billy Milligan] to decorate my shelves. I was introduced to Dr Weingarten, and I asked him if I could rent part of his office at night. I sounded literate, and he accepted me on the reference of a mutual friend. There was no extraordinary effort to fool the doctor, and if he had asked me just some basic questions about psychology he would have seen right through me.'

The killer went to say: 'Placing ads in the *Los Angeles Times*, I received credentials from other psychologists and students [notably a 'Steve Walker'] applying for a job with me. A diploma service provided more (phony) decorations for my walls and shelves. Also, I had several basic psychology books from back east. I knew I was doing wrong, but I took every precaution to not harm any one [*sic*].'

Among the books from 'back east' was general psychology reading for his studies at the Rochester Monroe Community College. He failed to complete many of the classes, which included Psychology, in which he drew 'incomplete'.

To add further authenticity to his crooked scheme, our 'Dr Bianchi' forged letters from well-known institutions, who thanked him for his 'generosity' and for the 'small cash donations' and his 'valuable time in giving such enlightening lectures'. And, at the same time, he was telling his common-law wife, Kellie Boyd, and his own mother, that he had earned his Psychology degree way back in Rochester, and that he was helping Dr Weingarten with his overload of patients. But then, like all of Bianchi's schemes, it fell apart.

During a visit to California to see her son, Frances Bianchi could not fail to notice the many fraudulent diplomas he had displayed in his home as well as in his office. Not impressed, she berated Ken, threatening to expose him as a cheat. However, her warning went unheeded, like water off a duck's back. He continued to pour money into advertising until his limited funds dried up. Indeed, even patients dried up because, most fortunately for them, particularly so for potential patients who also happened to be pretty young women, no one failed to materialise.

It is also known from Bianchi's Bellingham custody records that he had watched the 1976 miniseries *Sybil*, which concerned another multiple-personality disorder. His attorney duly arranged the first of many hypnosis sessions.

Forensic psychiatrist Professor Dr Donald T. Lunde recommended that Ken should accept a course of hypnosis under the expert supervision of a Dr John Watkins. Dr Lunde, MA, MD is a Clinical Associate Professor of Psychiatry and Behavioral Science and Lecturer at Stanford University. He is

CASE STUDY – SAVAGE: KENNETH ALESSIO BIANCHI

also the author two excellent books, *The Die Song: A Journey into the Mind of a Mass Murderer* and *Murder and Madness*, as well as co-author with Herant A Katchadourian of *Fundamentals of Human Sexuality*. Dr Lunde is also a member of the American Academy of Psychiatry and the Law, and eminently qualified to assess accurately Kenneth Bianchi's state of mind. If anyone could pronounce on a genuine case of an MPD, then it had to be Dr Watkins, whom Professor Lunde recommended.

The idea that Bianchi may have been sexually abused as a child came from research carried out by John Johnson, a highly experienced social investigator, and his team. However, Johnson didn't interview Kenneth's adoptive mother, Frances, although he did unearth a report dating back to 1960 when the nine-year-old child was seen briefly at the Strong Memorial Hospital Clinic in Rochester, NY. Ken's appointment was prompted by a complaint from The New York Society for the Prevention of Cruelty to Children. In a nutshell, this issue was based on school and adoption agency evidence, suggesting the lad was not being properly cared for and, of course, at face value there was every reason to believe this was the case. The report published below followed Ken's visit:

> Kenneth is a very anxious lad who has many phobias and counter-phobias. He uses repression and reaction formation. He is very dependent on his mother. She has dominated him, and indulged him in terms of her own needs. He is anxious, protective, and this clinging control has made him ambivalent. But he represses his hostile aggression, and is increasingly dependent upon her.

When I asked serial killer Keith Hunter Jesperson to respond to this in 2014 he didn't mince words, saying: 'So, what! She is his mother by all rights. An only child, considering the circumstances surrounding his father, what else could she do but be protective and indulge her boy? Days full of each other alone in the house.'

Jesperson has a point. Kenneth's adoptive father, Nicolas Bianchi, was an inveterate gambler who spent the better part of his wages at the bookies. Loan sharks were constantly hammering on the front door, threatening Frances, chasing Nicolas for his gambling debts, the result being the family had to move home several times, with Ken changing schools almost as often as he changed his socks. It got so bad that in 1953, the Bianchis were forced to flee their home on Saratoga Avenue in Rochester, New York, and move to Glide Street, where the loan sharks soon tracked them down. So they upped sticks again for Los Angeles, where they stayed with Frances's sister, Jennifer Buono – whose son, Angelo, would later become Ken's accomplice in 'serial murder most foul'. However, the defence of NGRI was solely based on John Johnson's report.

Professor Lunde was not informed about Kenneth's phoney psychiatric counselling service back in Los Angeles and could not have known that Bianchi was soon to be arrested for at least twelve murders committed in LA between 1997 and 1978, or that as a teenager he had been sexually abusing girls as young as nine years old. Dr Lunde had no knowledge that Bianchi was – and still is – the prime suspect for the three 'Alphabet Murders' committed in Rochester between 1971 and 1973. That he and his half-cousin Angelo Buono previously ran a call-out prostitution service in LA or that he had raped, tortured and strangled to death Sonja Johnson, aged fourteen, and Dolores 'Dolly' Cepeda, twelve, on Sunday, 13 November 1977, after which he and Buono dumped their naked bodies on a garbage tip at Landa and Stadium Way. The Professor recommended that Dr Watkins should hypnotise Kenneth in an effort to hunt down a multiple personality.

On Wednesday, 23 March 1979, Dr Watkins, a specialist in multiple personalities and hypnosis from the University of Montana, arrived at the jailhouse in Bellingham to perform the first of many sessions with Ken. Watkins also had no knowledge or information of all the above facts concerning his previous life, nor indeed that Ken had watched *Sybil* and *The Three Faces of Eve* from his cell, and that he had recently read the book *The Three Faces of Eve*, and the book concerning Billy Milligan back in LA, just two years previously.

It appeared to Dr Watkins that within minutes Ken was in a trance. He began speaking in a strange, low voice, introducing himself as 'Steve Walker'. This 'Steve' came across as a highly unpleasant character with a sneering laugh. He told those present that he hated Ken. 'Ken doesn't know how to handle women,' he snarled. 'You gotta treat 'em rough. Boy, did I fix that turkey! I got him in so much trouble, he'll never get out.'

The amiable Dr Watkins was in no doubt that what he was witnessing was indeed a multiple personality speaking from within the head of Bianchi.

With little prompting, and although unaware that he was about to be visited by LA homicide detectives investigating the Hillside Stranglings, 'Steve' turned to the Los Angeles murders, describing how Ken had walked in on Angelo Buono while he was murdering a girl. At this point 'Steve' admitted he had taken over Ken's personality and had turned Ken into Angelo's willing accomplice for all of the Hillside Stranglings.

Dr Watkins leaned across the table and softly asked, 'Are you Ken?'

'DO I LOOK LIKE KEN? Killing a broad doesn't make any difference to me. Killing ANY FUCKIN' BODY doesn't make any difference to me. Angelo is my kind of man. There should be more people like Angelo in the world. I HATE KEN,' snapped 'Steve' (aka Bianchi) in response.

To Dr Watkins it seemed perfectly clear that Kenneth Bianchi was made up of two opposing personalities: the loving father, kind friend and hard worker who made up Ken (none of which was actually true) and the vicious rapist, sadist-cum-serial murderer who was 'Steve Walker'. Watkins firmly believed now that Ken had subconsciously invented 'Steve' as a repository for all his hateful feelings towards his adoptive mother, Frances. And, in this way, he could remain a loving devoted son, the affectionate guy almost everyone 'allegedly' knew and 'allegedly' liked, because Bianchi had previously told anyone lending an ear that he was a perfect gentleman. 'Steve', however, and apparently unknown to Ken, periodically emerged to wreak horrific vengeance on young women.

Word soon leaked out that Bianchi was 'coughing' to the LA murders and that he had implicated his accomplice, Angelo Buono, who was still carrying on with his car upholstery business in Glendale, LA, so homicide cops flew to Washington State. Previously Bianchi's name had cropped up several times during the Hillside Murders inquiry and the Bellingham PD had now alerted them that he was in custody. As a couple of LA cops sat quietly close to Bianchi's cell, they wondered, in anticipation, what might happen next. In his jail diary, on Wednesday, 18 April 1979, Bianchi penned an entry for everyone to read:

If this person [Steve Walker] is more real than just my dream, and if this is the same person haunting me, which according to Dr Watkins is more than likely, this person could have been responsible for the uncontrollable violence in my life, the instigator of the lies I've done. The blank spots, amnesia, I can't account for, and the deaths of the girls, all the ones in California, and the two here. But if he is in me, then killed them using me – why can't I remember for sure? I want to know if this is so – what if?

When BPD Detective Terry Wight heard this, all he had to say was 'Bollocks!' Meanwhile slick-suited Detective James Ritter and a colleague from Rampart Division, LA, were getting impatient. They wanted Bianchi extradited back to California ASAP, but frustratingly, they had to sit around and twiddle their thumbs as tension mounted between the cops, while Bianchi was observed by the psychiatrists.

'Hey, Terry,' quipped Ritter. 'You arrested the wrong guy! You should have cuffed Stevie, and let poor Ken go home.'

Wight came back with: 'Know what, they ought to be hypnotising this Steve to see if he corroborates Bianchi's bullshit. That'll fuck things up. If you two fellas are so smart, when you put the cuffs on Buono an' ask him if knows anyone called "Steve Walker".'

For his part, to be absolutely sure of his diagnosis of multiple personalities, Dr Watkins also administered the Rorschach inkblot test to check out both Ken and 'Steve', the results of which supported his overall hypothesis. Both tests differed and were consistent with two personalities – so he reported back to attorney Dean Brett, saying, 'It is one of the clearest cases of Dissociative Reaction and Multiple Personality I have diagnosed over forty years.'

But Dr Watkins was not setting out to determine Bianchi's state of mind for that was Professor Lunde's job. Watkins was there merely to find out whether or not Bianchi was a real MPD case.

Somewhat condescendingly, Bianchi would later write to me, saying: 'Dr Watkins is a kind, soft-spoken, honest behavioral expert who was caught up in the excitement of the moment.' Indeed when all of the hypnosis sessions stopped 'Steve' never appeared again! But the damage had been done. A leak to *Time Magazine* caused a headline: 'BIANCHI – A MULTIPLE PERSONALITY'. This so outraged Judge Kurtze that he ordered the appointment of a panel of experts to evaluate Bianchi. He summoned Dr Watkins and Professor Lunde to act for the defence with Doctors Ralph Allison and Charles Moffett representing the Court, while Doctors Martin Orne and Saul Faerstein acted for the prosecution, inter alia 'The State'. This was an honourable move by the judge, or, as one police officer remarked, 'An effort to sort out the bullshit from the bullshit.'

But Dr Watkins had an ally in the Court's camp in Ralph Allison, who is also the author with Ted Schwarz of a famous book called *Minds in Many Pieces: Revealing the Spiritual Side of Multiple Personality Disorder*. His credentials were impeccable and, under apparent hypnosis, Ken, through 'Steve', claimed, 'I fuckin' killed those broads... those fuckin' cunts. That blonde-haired cunt, and the brunette cunt,' which implied a disgusting reference to Karen Mandic and Diane Wilder.

'Here, in Bellingham?' asked Allison.

'That's right.'

'Why?'

'Cause I hate fuckin' cunts.'

Now aware of the list of Bianchi's alleged victims back in LA, after that short exchange, Dr Allison pressed his subject about the murder of his first kill – that of Yolander Washington on 18

October 1977. At this 'Steve' piped up with the fact that she was a hooker – 'Angelo picked her up an' I was waiting in the street. He drove round to where I was. I got in the car. We got on the freeway. I fucked her and killed her. We dumped the body off and that was it. Nothin' to it.'

At last here was something akin to music to the ears of LA Homicide. Now they had probable cause to have Angelo Buono arrested forthwith.

After a breather while Ken/Steve collected his thoughts, Dr Allison regressed Ken back to his childhood. Zeroing in on Kenneth when he was nine years old, Allison found an environment filled with pain and suffering, which he thought had spawned Ken's 'Steve' alter ego.

Under hypnosis, Ken claimed to have met 'Steve' while he was hiding under his bed. 'Mommie was hitting me so bad, I met Stevie,' he whined in a childlike voice.

Despite the fact that Ken had previously told Dr Watkins that he'd first met 'Stevie' when he was five years old while playing with a train set, Dr Allison probed a little deeper. 'How did you *first* meet him?' he asked quietly.

'I closed my eyes. I was crying so hard,' Bianchi whimpered. 'All of a sudden he was there. He said "Hi" to me. He told him [*sic*] I was his friend. I told him "If Mommie finds you here I'll be in a lot of trouble." I felt really good that I had a friend to talk to.'

Professor Lunde began his report – dated Monday, 23 July 1979 – by explaining how he had formed his evaluation and upon what sources he was intending to base his diagnosis of Bianchi. By his own testimony, this boiled down to a four-month study, including three short sessions with Ken, which took place on 11, 12 and 13 July 1979. Lunde had read some 3,000 pages of police documents, witness statements, medical and psychiatric reports and school records. The Professor also gained access to the information compiled by attorney Dean Brett, social investigator John Johnson and, somewhat remarkably, the District Attorney's Office. He reviewed the audiotape and videotape interviews conducted by Dr Watkins and read transcripts of examinations performed by his colleagues. Donald Lunde also interviewed Bianchi's common-law wife, Kellie Boyd (a State witness), along with 'dozens of other people who knew' Bianchi. Frances Bianchi had refused to speak to him.

After four months' toil Professor Lunde started his report. Using social investigator John Johnson's findings he claimed that Ken had been fostered for the first eleven months of his life, when in fact it had only been *three* months. Lunde also reported that Nicolas Bianchi was 'overshadowed and overpowered' by his wife. It is ill will that speaks ill of the dead, but Nick Bianchi was one of life's losers. Hardworking without doubt, he was nevertheless also addicted to gambling. As soon as the whistle blew at the end of his shift at the factory, he was off to the bookies or ducking and diving from his long list of creditors. In reality, he made Frances's life a misery.

Relying on John Johnson's information, Lunde gave the wrong dates for Kenneth's schooling. He concluded that Ken's bedwetting (enuresis) problems were psychosomatic. Finally, Professor Lunde suggested that Bianchi's mental condition was of a 'Dissociative Reaction, with extreme stress bordering on psychosis'. In his report, the Professor wrote:

> This condition (Dissociative Reaction) has been present since at least the age of nine years, and is manifested by periods during which the defendant acts without awareness of his actions, and for which he subsequently

has amnesia. During some of these periods, the incredible amount of unconscious (repressed) hostility towards women present in this man surfaces. The best demonstration of what I have described is seen in some of the videotapes, which were made while Bianchi was under hypnosis, and emerged as a quite different personality calling himself 'Steve Walker'.

Professor Lunde did say that it was debatable whether Bianchi represented a true case of multiple personality. Watkins, the doctor he had brought in, had reported back with: 'It is one of the clearest cases of Dissociative Reaction and Multiple Personality I have diagnosed over forty years.' Lunde felt that Bianchi could have been faking his symptoms. He concluded that 'Bianchi is not psychologically sophisticated enough, nor is he intelligent enough to have constructed such an elaborate history which gives him the mental defense if he were subsequently charged with a crime.'

The Professor wrote next: 'Furthermore, one would have to assume that Bianchi began plotting his strategy for these crimes and his defense at about age nine since this is when the first documented symptoms of his mental disturbance occurred.'

Dr Watkins had reported that it was at around the age of five – and Watkins had based aged five on social investigator John Johnson interviewing Ken in the first instance. In ending his report to defence attorney Dean Brett, Professor Lunde stated that Bianchi was mentally competent to stand trial in Bellingham, while agreeing with Dr Watkins that Ken was *indeed suffering from a Dissociative Reaction*.

It [Dissociative Reaction] has affected him in such a manner that he would have been unable to perceive the nature and quality of his acts with which he has been charged. It is my opinion that the defendant did not have a moral sense of right and wrong, but was aware that what he was doing was against the law, and for this reason, precautions were taken to avoid incriminating evidence.

So, Professor Lunde believed that Bianchi was only taken over by 'Steve' when he needed to rape and murder, and at no other time, which would be first-class mitigation for a defendant who could face the death penalty.

Enter Dr Charles Moffett, who represented the Court.

Having studied the case file, and having interviewed Bianchi for some eight hours, Dr Moffett concluded that Bianchi was 'psychotic and probably schizophrenic'.

Three eminent psychiatrists having found that Bianchi was suffering from multiple personality disorder, the fourth leaned towards a different diagnosis altogether, Dr Moffett, like Lunde and Watkins, firmly believed that Ken had been hypnotised but found that 'Steve' was the result of an 'ego, or an identity split' rather than the 'different personality' which his colleagues agreed upon. Moffett added, 'Is this so different from a patient hearing the voice of Satan and struggle against alien control?'

Dr Moffett diagnosed Bianchi was suffering from 'delusional grandiosity' and added, 'Ken lives on the brink of regressed and infantile terror. He literally wakens in his cell at night, hiding under his bed in nameless terror.'

Ken *did* wake from his sleep, and he *did* hide under his cell bunk. Several times it was noted in the custody log that Bianchi was crying, simpering and begging 'Stevie' to leave him alone.

Dr Moffett eventually concluded in his summary to Judge Kurtze: 'He [Bianchi] intellectually knows right from wrong. The combination of his grandiose alter ego, and his dissociation, and his lack of awareness of the violent aspects of his own being, would not permit him to effectively control and govern his actions.'

But, then the shit hit the proverbial fan.

When Doctor Orne from the Department of Psychiatry at the Pennsylvania Medical School arrived in Bellingham, almost immediately he fired a single salvo in what can only be described as a flash of pure brilliance. Aware of the benefits to Bianchi of a diagnosis of a multiple personality disorder, Dr Orne decided to analyse not so much Ken's personality, but the *assumption* of multiple personality itself. And this is why I suggest that Judge Kurtze (quite the most fair and impartial of legal referees) had decided to seek a perfectly sound independent opinion from him. Dr Orne's unique move was a lateral test to determine whether Bianchi had really been hypnotised at all, for Orne figured that, if this man was not a multiple personality disorder then the hypnosis had not been effective. In Dr Orne, Bianchi was about to meet a sceptic who had serious doubts about the concept of multiple personality disorder.

Before attempting to hypnotise Bianchi, Dr Orne mentioned in passing, and deliberately *almost* out of Bianchi's hearing, that it was extremely rare in the cases of MPD for there to be just two personalities. Bianchi overheard the doctor and shortly after he entered a trance, out came 'Billy', who amounted to personality number three.

Minutes later, Dr Orne asked 'Billy' – not 'Steve/Stevie' – to sit back and talk to his lawyer, who wasn't even present in the room, but on this occasion Bianchi overplayed his part. Of course 'Billy' had no lawyer at all, but this did not stop Ken from leaning across the table and shaking the non-existent, obviously invisible lawyer's hand. Then Dr Orne arranged for Dean Brett to walk into the room. 'Billy' immediately shifted his attention to the newly arrived visible attorney, asking, 'How can I see him in two places?' This behaviour caused Dr Orne to conclude that Bianchi had not in fact been hypnotised and following a few other tests that he was not suffering from MPD, too.

When I later asked Bianchi how he had suddenly come up with this 'Billy', he said this: 'I sensed that Doctor Orne was sharp. He threw a wild ball in my direction and I got a surprise from it so I came up with the first name that crossed my mind. I guess that it was because Orne had mentioned it [Billy Milligan] just before trying to hypnotise me. When Dean walked in, I knew I was fucked.'

Like so many serial murderers, Bianchi is a pathological liar from the top of his head to his little toes. To suit himself he will deny guilt in any way he can and when the cards are stacked against him, lie repeatedly at the drop of a hat to suit the circumstances.

Up until a few years back Bianchi was still involved in appeals against his convictions for the murders of Karen Mandic and Diane Wilder, quite forgetting that he gave police details of the murders that only they and the killer could know. He also concocted a risible scenario whereby a former staff member at the Whatcom Security Agency (where he worked under the self-styled rank of 'Captain') conspired with Karen Mandic's two boyfriends not only to kill the two co-eds but also to shift the blame onto him. As soon as I learned, our Ken was up to this 'game', which would have cost Washington State a small fortune to defend. Somewhat mysteriously, copies of all his correspondence to me found their way onto the DA's desk. The Appeal Court subsequently threw his case out.

But what of Professor Lunde, and Doctors Watkins, Allison and Moffett? I entered into a brief correspondence with

Donald Lunde, who agreed that my considerations concerning Bianchi's psychopathology were correct.

Dr Ralph Allison is of the view that Ken is 'Someone with an "Internalized Imaginary Companion (IIC)".' Allison prevails in his view that: '"Steve" was made by Ken's personality as a way of getting back at his mother when she was "yelling at him at home during his youth"... it was then that Ken imagined "Steve" into being, and he became Ken's hit man in expressing his hatred of women like his mother.'

When investigative author Christine Hart pressed Dr Allison on what an IIC was, he replied as follows:

> An IIC is what is called a "Thoughtform" in para-psychological literature, or an imaginary playmate or companion in pediatric psychology. However, the pediatric doctors assumed that all imaginary companions exist outside the bodies of the children who created them. That is false, as the child can place it anywhere he wants it to be, outside sitting in a chair, inside a doll, or inside his body taking over his body to do its deeds. It is designed by the child to take care of the child's emotional needs, whether that be to combat loneliness or to avenge some insult to the child by a hostile adult. It is made voluntarily by the child with a vivid imagination and can, therefore, be destroyed by that same child as an adult.

Dr Allison went on to explain to Christine Hart:

> IIC is a term I invented to describe these "other selves" which were not alter-personalities. Initially, I called them IMPs, for Internal Malignant Personalities, which

seemed to be a good acronym, as an IMP is a playful spirit. But I realized that only some were malignant, and others were benign, so I changed the label to something that was morally neutral, Internalized Imaginary Companion, or IIC.

Hart then asked Dr Allison to explain who Dr Martin Orne was, and why Orne was diagnostically against him. After a preamble, Allison replied:

He was well known to the State prosecutor to be a sceptic of MPD, so he was hired to disprove the diagnosis of MPD initially offered by Dr Watkins. We were aware that Dr Orne was not likely to diagnose anyone with MPD, so we were not surprised when he maintained that Ken was just a liar. In Buono's preliminary hearing, Dr Orne also stated that Ken had never been hypnotised by any of us, something I greatly dispute. I was caught in the middle of a "battle of the experts", with Dr Orne on one side saying that Ken was only a liar, and Dr Watkins saying that Ken was a bona fide multiple. I knew he wasn't a multiple, but I didn't know then just what he was.

Source: *In for the Kill: A True Story of Hunting Evil* by Christine J. Hart, 2012

Ken would love it if I would give him a little self-promotion on his behalf. He has/had a website in which he modestly describes himself as a 'God-fearing man'.

Hi, my name is Kenneth Bianchi. I have been wrongly incarcerated for many years. My desire is to develop friendship beyond this edifice of political smoke and mirrors is, in part, because I need to dispel the myth that I am void of humanity and, in part, because most of my family and friends are either deceased or have faded away.

Wrestling clumsily with his vocabulary and losing the battle, he continued:

My basic interests are Law, philosophy and spirituality. My desire is to meet people who are obviously cogitative on which they can develop a mutually inspiring relationship through some engaging mental intercourse. I welcome women of all races. I weigh 210 lbs. Solid as a rock 'smile', healthy, compassionate, sincere, loving, honest and good-looking.

In order to try and raise money for my day-to-day items and additional art materials, I would be prepared to sell a small number of my prints of any of my featured drawings. Thank you for your attention and I look forward to hearing from you. Signed Revd. Bianchi.

In an attempt to convince me just how artistically talented he is Ken sent me a cardboard tube containing half a dozen of his pencil drawings, all signed by him. This artwork came with a note: 'Chris, I send these to you as a sign of our friendship. Please keep them to show your children. If you don't want them, you can sell them on the Internet, where they make a lot of money. If you do, I would be grateful for a small donation. Kenneth.' Several of the pictures were quite excellent: detailed with a nod to talent. Others were pretty poor!

'The Hillside Strangler' made no mention of his homicidal CV anywhere on his web page. Maybe this can be put down to a slight oversight on his behalf, for we do have to remember that he is a very busy man, with his legal studies and immersed in his deep interest in philosophy and spirituality.

Kenneth Bianchi later went on to plead guilty to seven of the LA Hillside Stranglings and gave evidence against his accomplice, Angelo Buono. He is now serving a life sentence at the Washington State Penitentiary at Walla Walla. If the reader feels inclined to write to Bianchi, one can find his full details and address by looking up the Department of Corrections website – only please say that you have been recommended by me. He'll like that, I don't think! But don't bother with Angelo – he died from a heart condition at the Calipatria State Prison on Saturday, 21 September 2002. He was sixty-four. As for 'Stevie' and 'Billy'... well, their current status is unknown – at least to me.

CASE STUDY: PSYCHOPATH
The Shawcross Confession

The Law isn't justice. It's a very imperfect mechanism.
If you press exactly the right button and are also lucky,
justice may also turn up in the answer.
— Raymond Chandler, *The Long Goodbye*, 1953

The US criminal justice system was perhaps fortunate that soon after his arrest in Bellingham, savage sexual killer Kenneth Bianchi pleaded guilty to the murders of co-eds Diane Wilder and Karen Mandic, so there was no need for him to stand trial nor to have his fate determined by a jury.

It must appear bizarre to the reader to learn that Michael Bruce Ross managed to run rings around psychiatrists and manipulated Connecticut's criminal justice system for several decades. It was frankly shocking that homicidal schizophrenic mass murderer Paul Beecham was released from Broadmoor Hospital having served a mere sixteen years in custody, only for him to kill again after it was determined that he 'no longer posed a risk to society' by Dr Pat McGrath, one of the UK's leading psychiatrists.

Let's move on to the case of Arthur 'Art' John Shawcross. Dubbed by the media as the 'Monster of the Rivers', Shawcross was convicted of the second-degree murders of ten-year-old Jack Blake on Sunday, 7 May 1972 and eight-year-old Karen Hill on Wednesday, 2 September of the same year. Although he pleaded 'Not Guilty' on Tuesday, 17 October 1972, a disgusted Judge Wiltse sentenced him to the maximum term of 25 years for the murder of Karen Hill. The murder of Jack Blake was more or less put on the back burner and Shawcross only gave the details of this crime to me when I interviewed him in 1994.

Shawcross served just over fourteen years in prison, where he experienced a rough time from other inmates, whose brotherly admiration for each other's offences did not extend to the rape and murder of children. The beatings and abuse started on his admission to Attica, and this treatment followed him through the penal system until he arrived at the notoriously tough Green Haven Correctional Facility at Stormville, New York State. (Incidentally, it was at the Green Haven CF that I later interviewed Ronald 'Butch' DeFeo Jr of *The Amityville Horror* movie fame.)

Set in rugged hill country between the Hudson River and the Connecticut border, some 40 miles north of New York City, this penitentiary houses many of the State's most evil criminals, where, at the time of writing, at least 33 per cent of the inmates are rapists and savage killers. However, for Shawcross even Green Haven was still not the safest place to be.

After being given exclusive access to Shawcross's medical files, I learned that prison psychiatrists had diagnosed him as 'a dangerous schizophrenic paedophile, suffering from an intermittent explosive personality' and it was noted that 'he heard voices when he was depressed or engaged in fantasy as a source of satisfaction', leading one doctor to add: 'he also has an oral-erotic fixation for the need of material protection.

The same prison record shows that Shawcross was placed in the A-1 protective segregation unit for his own good (Kenneth Bianchi lives on such a unit today). Art's custody file shows that he was a troublesome inmate in the unit of 41 men. For the greater part of his sentence, he continually faked illness or psychiatric problems to gain attention. However, like so many psychopathic personalities, Shawcross was nobody's fool.

He started to behave himself and became a model prisoner, earning his high-school equivalency certificate, and qualified in carpentry. Many years later he would write the still unpublished *A Cannibal's Cookbook*, the manuscript of which I have the only copy. Nevertheless, now well into his sentence Arthur was found to be exhibiting all the welcome behavioural traits of a 'reformed' man. He figured it was better to accept responsibility for the murder of Karen Hill and also started attending the religious services, where he found 'Our Lord', and obtained a counsellor's job in the prison's mental health unit.

There you have it in one. The prison psychiatrist has a convicted child killer and cold-blooded psychopath counselling other inmates, who were probably all as crazy as one another. Nevertheless, and this will come as no surprise either, while there, Arthur educated himself in the language of psychiatry and psychology and, in so doing, he eventually gained the support of a three-man State Parole Panel, who granted his freedom.

Shawcross walked out of the gates of Green Haven on Tuesday, 28 April 1987. Although he had been receiving excellent evaluations from one group of psychiatrists, their high opinion of his transformation from homicidal maniac to one fit for release back into the community was not shared by several of their colleagues. A report from senior parole officer Dr Robert T. Kent noted: 'At the risk of sounding dramatic, this man could be possibly the most dangerous individual to have been released to this community in years.' Green Haven prison psychiatrist Dr Y. A. Haveiwala concurred, adding, 'Mr Shawcross is a grave parole risk. He has an antisocial personality disorder [sociopath/psychopathic] and schizoid personality disorder with psychosexual tendencies.'

This monster was released 10 years before his full 25-year tariff had been served. He went on to kill at least nine other women between March 1988 and December 1989, before being arrested and sent to prison for life.

Although I interviewed doctors Kent and Haveiwala during the research for a TV documentary, *The Monster of the Rivers*, and for my book, *Talking with Serial Killers: The Most Evil People in the World Tell Their Own Stories,* I also popped in to see Edwin Elwin, then director of the State Division of Paroles. He told me: 'Mr Shawcross did a comfortable adjust to parole. We simply hate it when one of our people goes bad. Goodbye!'

The trial judge for the later Rochester homicides was His Honor Donald J. Wisner, who is one of the nicest and most self-effacing men one could meet. In a meeting with him during a court recess – during which he was trying a murder case where a man had pushed his girlfriend under a moving train – he told me upon reflection: 'the prosecution should have pressed a first-degree murder charge against Shawcross for the two earlier murders [Jack Blake and Karen Hill] when they had the opportunity. Indeed, the prosecution could have gone even further and pressed for an aggravated charge, which would have ensured that he would never have been released again.' Judge Wisner added: 'He most certainly would have received a life sentence, had that been the case, instead there was some mitigating evidence given by a psychiatrist so they opted for a lesser charge and, in doing so, the prosecution behaved like Monday morning quarterbacks [rank amateurs].'

Bearing in mind that Shawcross actually ate the penis and the heart of Jack Blake – and what he did to Karen Hill is almost indescribable – I think that any right-minded person would have to agree with Judge Wisner. The State prosecutor for the later string of Rochester homicides felt exactly the same way in supporting Judge Wisner's sentiments to the hilt. Charles 'Chuck' Siragusa – later to become a Justice of the Supreme Court – told me that he was 'disgusted' that Shawcross was released from prison after 14½ years only to kill again and again.

'My position dictates that I keep all of my personal thoughts and emotions about Mr Shawcross to myself. Please understand this, Christopher,' he said. 'I think that the State of New York has much to answer for here. It was an institutionalized mess.'

During my time in Rochester, New York, I was granted a grace-and-favour interview with Arthur's then girlfriend. Clara Neal transpired to be an extremely large woman. Aged fifty-eight in 1994, she already had ten children of her own plus seventeen grandchildren. She had known 'Art' for several years before his conviction for the Rochester murders and her love for him knew no bounds. He used to borrow her cars – either a small, metallic-blue Dodge Omni saloon, or a grey Chevrolet – using them for day outings, or to go fishing, she told me. These were vehicles also used by Shawcross to transport his victims to his killing ground alongside the banks of the slow-moving Genesee River.

'Ya know, Chris,' she said. 'I love Arthur and he has told me that you might be the Best Man at our wedding. I have spoken to a psychiatrist and he's told me that if Art were to be released from jail, he would prescribe drugs to make him better.'

'Clara, but he returned to many of the rotting bodies to masturbate over them... to discuss his life with them...' I suggested.

'I don't believe a word of this,' she said confidently. 'He has always been a perfect gentleman to me. I really love him. He is just such a wonderfully gentle man.'

All of the above proves, at least to me, that we *are* living in a world where elephants fly, lead balls bounce and fairies reign supreme.

As a tailpiece, and gross and unprofessional as it appears, yes, it *is* true that Arthur Shawcross had asked me to be his Best Man at his upcoming marriage to the buxom Clara. It *is* true that I had, tongue-in-cheek, agreed – and for a very good reason.

I needed to manipulate this heinous man into giving me a full confession to the murder of Jack Blake.

Prior to interviewing Shawcross at the Sullivan Correctional Facility, NY, I had visited Mary Blake, Jack's mother, in her home on the outskirts of Watertown. She was terminally ill with cancer, yet knowing I was coming with a film crew, she obviously had made a great effort to tidy the place up. She'd been to the hairdressers too. For a small family, living on the breadline, she had gone to some trouble to buy and serve a pot of tea – because she knew that the Brits like tea – and there was homemade apple pie, sandwiches and biscuits for my crew and me.

There were photographs of Jack everywhere, and there were tears in Mary's eyes as she said that because Shawcross had never admitted killing her son, she reasoned the dismembered, decomposing remains found by police at Kelsey Creek surely belonged to someone else. 'Ya know, Christopher,' she told me, 'not a day goes by when I don't look out of my window expecting to see Jack walk up the street and come home. I believe in God. I am a good woman.'

Jack was just ten years old when he bunked school to go fishing with Shawcross in 1972. Had he suddenly come home when I visited with Mary, he would at that time have been thirty-two.

At this point Mary broke down. 'I'm so sorry,' she sobbed. 'We cannot accept that Jack is dead. It is impossible. Can you please ask Mr Shawcross to tell us the truth?'

How tragic, and how sad is that, I thought. So I vowed to myself that I would get that confession if it was the last thing I would do, period, and I would use my friendship with Clara, and the promise of being Arthur Shawcross's Best Man at the wedding to do just that.

Prior to my interviews with Shawcross, correctional officers had warned me that he was still considered to be a highly dangerous and formidable killing machine. 'He can revert to type within milliseconds if you upset him,' they told me. 'Now, before you and your team sign this waiver and not hold the Department of Corrections responsible if he attacks you, we can proceed.' Then the officer gave us another word of advice: 'My officers will not be in the room during your interviews. We have to wait outside. Should his features whiten, then tighten up, or should he break into a sweat, then get out of his way as fast as you can. He is strong enough to rip your head right off. If he loses it, it will take us at least fifteen seconds to get to him. By then it will be too late.'

At this juncture the reader might wish to acquaint himself with Mr Shawcross by watching one of the recorded TV interviews with Arthur that followed mine, for I was the first to talk to him on camera. You can locate these programmes on the Internet, or you could obtain a copy of my interview by ordering it online. The TV series is called *The Serial Killers*. (And no, I don't receive any royalties from the sales.)

Okay, having watched 'Art', you may think that he looks harmless enough but in the flesh he weighed in at around twenty stone and is about five-foot eleven inches tall. With a potato-shaped head, topped with thin, silvery hair, a bulbous nose and small, black, ever-watery porcine eyes set close together, he is quite an intimidating sight when one is sitting just six feet away from this unshackled piece of disgusting humanity. Massive arms hang from immensely strong, sloping shoulders, his chest merging into a pot belly which sags in folds over his belt. From the waist down, the shape of Shawcross is reversed: from the rolls of fat circumnavigating his middle, he has short, stumpy legs terminating in very small feet. All in all, I got the impression that he was top-heavy and could topple over, like two inverted cones – or like some cartoon character – at any minute, but guards had also informed me that Mr Shawcross can manage a good turn of speed when the situation demanded. Possibly these 'short bursts of speed' had been needed to react to his experiences way back at Green Haven when large, black Gangstas chased him round the exercise yard with the intention of running a shiv into his fat ass for raping and killing a little girl.

But it was Arthur's hands that fascinated me. They constantly fidgeted, as if he was suffering some kind of nervous condition. During one interview I had been locked alone in a small cubicle with 'Art' while he was engrossed in eating his lunch. As he greedily stuffed the food in his mouth his eyes were furtive, darting around as if someone was about to snatch the meal away.

After he wiped the grease and food particles away from

his face, I asked him why he had eaten some of the intimate body parts – including a vagina – from several of his victims. Shawcross smiled and said, 'Yes, sir, I have. The human meat... well, ah, it tastes like pork. I eat meat, uncooked meat, and it's like that. I eat hamburgers raw. I eat steak raw, an' I eat pork raw. I don't know why I ate parts of people, but I just did.'

For a long moment he fell silent. Podgy fingers fiddled nervously with a Styrofoam cup. His eyes scanned the room as if searching for an invisible fly, then he added, 'Yeah, an' I ate another one [vagina] with the bone. I just remembered that.'

'God,' I thought. 'How can someone *just* remember that?'

From the outset, Shawcross had made it perfectly clear that he would not, under any circumstances, discuss the murder of Jack Blake. Arthur was by no means an intelligent man, but he possessed a certain animal cunning and could smell a rat a mile away, so I knew that broaching the subject would not be an easy task.

It was to be my last interview with the 'Monster of the Rivers' and I had on my mind Mary's desperate plea to get the truth about the murder of her son. To warm things up a bit, I made reference to the 14 and a half years he'd previously spent at Green Haven. I put it to him that for me to document his life thoroughly, as indeed he wished, just rubbing those years out as if they had never existed was simply not good enough. What follows is taken verbatim from my TV interview, which was edited somewhat for public consumption so as not to upset anyone of a delicate disposition:

AS: So, whaddaya wanna know about it?
CBD: Fourteen years' prison time, Art. How do we deal with this?

AS: We don't. You ain't taking me there, so don't fuckin try.
DON'T FUCKIN' GO THERE!
CBD: Okay, so I take out an eraser and out goes 14
years, right?
AS: Yes, sir.
CBD: What about Jack Blake?

By asking this question, I knew that I was treading on thin ice because if the prison population at Sullivan CF heard in the past Shawcross had raped and murdered two small children then his problems with other inmates, who would try and kill him at the drop of a hat, could resurface.

Within a blink of an eye, Shawcross's expression changed. His skin tightened like bat's skin, taut as fabric over a biplane's wing, and a curious paleness washed over his face. Beads of perspiration formed across his brow to run in glistening rivulets, staining the collar of his prison-issue shirt. Just a moment before, a smug smile had masked his simmering fury, now that mask of apparent sanity slipped for the first time and the fire of homicidal insanity flared in his eyes as he struggled to get his head around the fix in which he now found himself and to overcome the murderous emotions boiling within. The interview room went quiet, deadly quiet – quiet as an old grave with the sides falling in. Then, in anger, he suddenly reached out and grabbed my arm in a vice-like grip.

'You don't know who ya dealing with, fuck face,' he snarled. 'You don't know WHO I am, or WHAT I am.'

Since this interview took place, I have often been asked: 'Did Arthur scare you when he flipped?' My answer is always a categorical 'Nope!' because Shawcross was only capable of raping and killing children and sometimes ordinary women or prostitutes down on their luck. Just like Bianchi when he went berserk at me, all alpha-male bravado comes to naught when they are faced down, for they are bullies and cowards at heart.

'You don't need to do this, Arthur,' I responded. 'Okay, you have a problem with Jack, and now you have a problem with me. Hey, and you'll have an even bigger FUCKIN' problem with Clara! You mess up this interview and Clara's gonna climb the fuckin' wall, pal. We all had dinner with her last evening. She's a good person, Art. She's waiting for us outside right now.'

At the very mention of Clara's name it was as if something had flicked a switch inside his head. Shawcross's expression reverted to normal and he released his grip to let his hand fall away. Now he looked very confused. Shaking his head negatively from side to side, he started to mumble a form of apology.

As he shifted back into his chair, I moved forward. Now, I could see right into the abyss that was this man's psychopathic mind. Tick, tick, tick... 'Clara, Clara, Clara. Best Man at my wedding. My friend who had come so far to talk and understand me.' Tick, tick, tick... 'TV interview.' Tick, tick... 'Clara's waiting outside.' Tick, tick...

Then came my *coup de grâce*. I got up close to his ear and did what he had just done to me, moments beforehand: a physical touch, a comforting grip even, to his wrist. I was now in his space and inside his head, so I whispered: 'Arthur, Clara loves *you so much*. Don't let her down.'

'Okay,' he said, his voice shaking. Then he screwed his eyes up – they were watery. His facial expression looked as if his mind was chewing on wood. A pause, a glance around the room, then: 'Yeah, I killed him. Okay, I told him [Jack] to go home, and he wouldn't. An' then I got kinda mad at him. Yeah, I killed him, an' I buried his body under the dirt, and went fishin'. It was his fault he died. It ain't got nothin' to do with me... I'm sorry.'

    CBD: And the clothes, Arthur. What about Jack's clothes?

    AS: He took 'em off, an' I told him to just fold 'em up and stuff.

    CBD: Why?

    AS: Dunno. Maybe to keep him shut up, ya know. Let him think that he's gonna put 'em on again. Stuff like that. I dunno. Just went back to him and did stuff to him the next day.

    CBD: What did you do with the body, Art?

    AS: I ain't going there.

    CBD: Why?

Again I reminded him that if I walked out of the interview, Clara would be furious with him because she was expecting him to be totally honest with me. Then, letting him off the hook for a moment, I asked Arthur about Karen Hill:

    CBD: What about little Karen Hill? Why did you murder her?'

    AS: Same reason, ya know. She kinda wanted it, ya know. Sex, an' stuff like that. Then, I get started, an' she starts cryin' and wants her mom, so I suffocated her. Not with my hands. Covered her mouth with dirt and stuff.

    CBD: But you did have sex with her... Vaginally and anally, Arthur.

    AS: Yeah, but that was after she was dead. Then I went home.

After a few more questions regarding his murders in general, I told him, 'Arthur, there is a lady out there, Mrs Blake. I have visited with her. Decent woman and she has asked me to ask you just to give her closure about Jack 'cos she still thinks he's going to come home. Imagine if this was *your* Clara asking Mary Blake's question? I have seen all of the photos of you with Clara and all of her kids. Great loving family photos, Art. It is a great album of memories that she cherishes. So, can you please look into the camera and talk to Mary Blake? She is a mother just like Clara.'

For a few seconds I saw something of a decent human being in this 'Monster of the Rivers'. Now, my trap was about to snap shut. I reached over to him again because physical contact – even to those who are devoid of compassion, lack of empathy, a coldness that most of us can never understand – sometimes allows one to communicate with a hidden goodness that rarely surfaces. And, according to the somewhat naive Clara Neal, this goodness was, in her mind, always there in Shawcross.

'Look into that camera,' I asked him. 'Please talk to Mrs Blake, now.'

By God, did Shawcross struggle to get the words out. Then he cracked.

'Mrs Blake, I am sorry,' he murmured. 'Christopher has asked me if I killed your son. Yes, I did. It was not my fault but I killed your son. He won't be coming home. I'm sorry.'

> 'Chris, we gotta tell you that Mr Shawcross is now down in the hole [punishment segregation]. After he got back to the dorm, he was bragging about you becoming the Best Man at his wedding. Then they all saw you being interviewed straight after by that Rochester TV station. He is really pissed with you.'
> – Media relations officer in a phone call to the author, who told the media that Shawcross was a 'murdering scumbag' just minutes after leaving the Sullivan CF

As tailpieces to this chapter I'd like to confirm that after my last interview with the 'Monster of the Rivers' I never spoke to him again. When we parted company, we did not shake hands, nor did we say our goodbyes. Shawcross simply left the interview room and was cuffed by guards and escorted away; he didn't even look back at me. His job in the prison was repairing locks and radios.

I never spoke to Clara Neal again: I had conned Shawcross into believing she was waiting for me outside the prison after the last interview had wrapped when she wasn't. My film crew and I did return to see Mary Blake, however. Out of respect we left our cameras outside. What followed was one of the most truly heartbreaking moments of my life. As we parted company, she said: 'Thank you so much for coming back and telling us what Mr Shawcross has said but I know that I will be with Jack again soon. He's not really dead and I'll always watch out for him coming home some day.'

As a result of this author's interviews with Arthur Shawcross and Clara Neal, and working with the complete cooperation of Captain Lynde M. Johnston, Captain of Detectives Rochester PD, the previously cold case murder of Kimberley Logan, a slightly retarded thirty-year-old black mute who was killed on Friday, 15 November 1989, was cleared up.

On 10 November 2008, inmate # 91–B–083 Arthur Shawcross died of natural causes at the Sullivan Correctional Facility, Fallsburg, New York State.

CASE STUDY: SAVAGE
John David Guise Cannan – A Very British Monster

> The authors, using skills any psychotherapist would be proud of, encouraged Cannan to give a very full account of himself and his actions... here we can see the mind of a murderer probably more starkly than he can ever see it himself.
>
> – David Canter, Professor of Applied Psychology –
> Foreword to *Ladykiller* by Christopher Berry-Dee and Robin Odell, first published in hardback by John Blake, London, 1992

As psychotherapist Dr Alice Miller says: 'the grandiose person is never really free. First, because he is so excessively dependent on admiration from others; and second, because his self-respect is dependent on qualities, functions and achievements that can suddenly fail with far-reaching consequences.'

John David Guise Cannan was a robber and a serial rapist and if not an established serial killer he certainly murdered Shirley Banks, in Bristol, on 8 October 1987. Police believe that he also killed Suzy Lamplugh in London on 28 July 1986 although he was never tried for this.

We must also consider the murder of Sandra Court, in Bournemouth, on 3 May 1986. In letters to me, Cannan categorically denied being in Bournemouth on the date in question. However, I discovered a screwed-up 'Pay & Display' parking ticket amongst his property being held at a Bristol police station. The time, date and location proved, without any doubt, that Cannan was lying. When all of this was brought to the attention of a senior detective, he laughed me and my colleague Tony Brown out of the door. The 'Cold Case' of Sandra Court is still regarded as an 'Open Inquiry', so I hope that taking all of the material previously published in my book *Ladykiller: Inside the Mind of John Cannan* – of which some is published abridged in the book you are now reading – gives the police an incentive to reconsider the case.

But *Talking with Psychopaths and Savages* is not so much concerned with John Cannan's crimes or *his modus operandi* (MO), this book is all about what made this evil man's mind tick for he is a combination of vanity of latent savagery.

We can plot his history from being a well-educated youngster through to his developing spiralling vanity and his ever-uncontrolled plunge into becoming a murderous, sexually deviant savage. Indeed, one can almost plot each point as he turned, or shifted course, throughout his violent career.

Put simply, the question is, are these killer types born evil, or are they born with healthy minds that 'become evil' over time? It is the Nature versus Nurture topic of discussion, these days more generally called the 'Nature and Nurture debate', one that has been for decades at the forefront of criminologists' minds and especially the minds of psychologists. My friends at the FBI, and many of the forensic psychologists of my acquaintance, have been struggling with this question for ages when trying to determine with some degree of accuracy when these 'points' are reached in any specific offender's history in whom they have an interest.

Local law enforcement does not really care too much about such things as Nature versus Nurture: the body of a murder victim is found and their sole responsibility is to bring the offender before the courts. Job done, they move onto the next corpse found on their patch. But for those who have a professional interest in what makes these killers tick it is tantamount to trying to get fingerprints from running water. To do so you must try to understand how their deviant minds work and how they graduate from being, say, a 'Peeping Tom' to a stalker, to committing what may be termed a 'minor sexual assault' to go on to become a rapist and serial rapist, before finally graduating to homicide then serial murder and at what points along the way an offender's buttons are pressed to escalate the nature of his crimes. So now we have John Cannan, and to understand and plot his waypoints, I had to get right inside his head – as you the reader will also, all too soon.

Mr Cannan first came to my attention in October 1987 when it was reported in the local press that a crash-helmeted man had entered the Ginger boutique in Leamington Spa at around 3.55 p.m. on Thursday, 29 October. After closing the door of 20a Regent Street, he browsed through a clothes rail before producing an orange-handled serrated knife, which he used to threaten the owner, Carmel Cleary, and her assistant, Jane Child. The man's intention was robbery and rape. Later, Cannan's name would be tentatively linked to one of the most mysterious and heavily publicised unsolved murder cases in British criminal history – that of missing estate agent Suzy Lamplugh.

TALKING WITH PSYCHOPATHS AND SAVAGES

The incident in Leamington Spa intrigued me. Looking at the press photographs of John Cannan – and while some women might consider his dark looks, blue eyes, slim physique and those eyebrows that meet in the middle as attractive – I sensed something sinister. Vanity and savagery writ right across the smug face of Cannan for his pretentious hairstyle, thin lips and cruel mouth did nothing to make me think otherwise.

> 'Before we go further, you do realise that I am a direct descendant of the Holy Order of the Knight's Templar. I am named "Guise" after the Duc de Guise. My family's motto is "*A chacun son tour*" [My turn will come].'
>
> – John Cannan to the author in correspondence
> now with MetPol's SOII.

Following Cannan's conviction for the murder of Shirley Banks (whom we will come to later), he became headline news throughout the UK. 'In droves, true-crime writers are begging their publishers for a book commission,' he alleged after I initially wrote to him. So, like Kenneth Bianchi, femme *fatale* Melanie Lyn McGuire and Michael Ross, here was a story that had to be told, for the mystery of Suzy Lamplugh was, and as we go to press still is, in the forefront of our minds.

Allegedly coming from such an historical bloodline as the Knights Templar, John Cannan would have expected nothing less than to be recognised, appreciated and lauded as such, for why did he mention this to me in the first place? So, using my cream Conqueror stationery, with its matching envelope sealed with red wax, I told him that I was related to Dr John Dee, Court Astrologer to Queen Elizabeth I. And that Sir Joshua 'Uncle Josh' Reynolds, PRA, was an ancestor, too and this is completely true. I explained to him that I had already anticipated that he would join up with a writer more qualified than me. Then, as a footnote, I added that the national newspapers had painted him in a bad light (Cannan was not permitted to read any articles mentioning him so he was in the dark, so to speak) and one should not believe everything that was printed in the press.

'My concern,' I explained to him, 'is that you will *not* get a fair crack of the whip.' My punchline came as: 'Please find enclosed copies of the covers of several of my previous books [pictures paint a thousand words] and a commissioning note [drawn up on a wing and a prayer] from my publisher, so I'll get on with my book. It is a shame that you feel that you cannot assist me with the true facts. I wish you well.'

Game, set and match! If you could have been a fly on Cannan's cell wall, you would have watched manipulative John suddenly realise that his self-esteem, glibness and superficial charm and all of the edifices making up his evil mind, along with the need to control others, were being eroded by the minute. Now the facts – as they seemed to him – concerning his over-inflated ego and its promising demise were in the hands of someone else. I had not only pricked his ego, I was about to pop it, and this is something that the vain fear more than anything else – we might call this 'Mind Control'. For John Cannan the only way out was to mediate with me, regain what he was losing, placate me, communicate with me, and he did so with scores of letters. However, the more he put his Biro onto prison-issue paper, the more this horrible man exposed evidence of the evil which makes up the mindset of a savage sado-sadistic killer.

John's claim that he was a descendent of the Knights Templar was certainly news to me, as indeed it was to the several historians I contacted who *do* know their stuff. Moreover, this claim resonated with one previously made by serial killer

Arthur John Shawcross (see pages 19–20, 155–68), who told me that he was a distant cousin of Sir Hartley Shawcross, former Attorney General of Great Britain and Chief British Prosecutor at the Nuremberg trials (which Arthur was not).

I would correspond with Mr Cannan and, using the psychological fishing skills I have mentioned earlier with Melanie 'Mel' Lyn McGuire (see also page 99), I threw in some bait – the sort of 'classy bait' I had used with Melanie – but this time with a male-orientated twist.

My dealings with Cannan together with my study of the case papers left me in no doubt that here was a super-inflated ego flying high like a balloon on a thin string – when burst, the results can be unpredictable. Apparently stable on the surface, these egos become unstable and fall down when the ground collapses beneath their foundations, like buildings constructed on shifting sands – as in 'One puff and I'll blow your house down!'

I stress that I cannot give the reader any professional credentials to support this, but it did cross my mind that if I could try and use several of the innate characteristics so depended on by him in order to do what he has to do to support his ego and then remove them brick-by-brick, in so doing his very façade would crumble as we communicated over time. With that ever-so-vital ego under threat, everything that makes up his vain personality would fight back. However, no longer is that ego 'controlling' (as it subconsciously believes it is) for it is actually being manipulated and controlled, unbeknownst to its host.

In his mind John Cannan could never, ever have realised where I was coming from, for to truly understand such a personality one has to get right inside the head – and this is not a groundbreaking line of thought, not one jot of it! Let's think 'consumerism' and 'reverse psychology'.

CASE STUDY – SAVAGE: JOHN DAVID GUISE CANNAN

When one signs up for a 'loyalty card', the issuing company begins to know what you purchase, when you buy their products, where you live, your demographic status, whether you are single, married and with children, what ages they are, their birthdays, your birthday, and you are thereafter sent discount vouchers and offers.

For example, you buy a branded bottle of tomato ketchup from a well-known store. A week later, you get an email from the producer offering a FREE booklet showing all of the Italian recipes, their sauces and products you might be interested in. Click 'accept' and the next thing you receive is a four-page questionnaire asking if you are 'satisfied with the product and would you recommend it to a friend'. Complete this form to receive a 10 per cent discount voucher and once again you are bombarded with nuisance phone calls, perhaps telling you that because of the car accident (the one you have *not* had), you are entitled to compensation, or, because you are a regular buyer of dog food, would you give a donation to the 'Mutt's Dog Home'? I think you know exactly what I mean!

If you haven't read the very small print – most especially if you prefer buying online – soon you'll be inundated with offers from other firms you've never heard of, trying to sell you something you never considered buying in your wildest dreams. However, what we all fail to realise is that what these companies are truly up to is getting right inside the consumer's head, often manipulating them into the bargain. It's a subtle, oft-times sinister marketing tool, aka 'Mind Control'. And I'd put money on it that if, for example, one subscribes to an Internet dating website (something I do not), one's personal details will be flashed across to scores more dating websites, including suppliers of sex industry hardware and software.

This is 'Marketing Psychology'. It is all about getting inside a customer's head, finding out what they like, or *may* like, then selling them something they had not considered previously. And this is more or less what I do when communicating with the criminals who interest me. I spend time learning about my target, getting to know what s/he likes, or *would* like to have. It's about interpersonal relationships, non-threatening issues where I encourage them to talk about themselves and their lives. All overblown egos take to this form of attention, this ego massaging. They hugely enjoy having their feathers preened, being admired, feted and recognised, for it supports their fundamental nature.

Next, close your eyes, for you are now keen to fully understand John Cannan. Let's imagine that you have him standing on a plinth in front of you right now. If you study photos of him, you'll know what he looks like. There he is, stationary, akin to a mute Madame Tussauds' wax figure. Please walk around him. The dark hair is well groomed. Examine his face, his mouth, the way his eyebrows meet over the bridge of his nose and his slim, athletic build. What is he wearing? A spotlessly white shirt, cufflinks, wide 'Kipper-style tie', a smart, well-cut dark suit and highly-polished shoes. He is dressed immaculately.

Now, push the button on the control panel next to this Mr Cannan and hear a recording of him talking. His voice is soft, almost upper-class – perhaps affectedly so, you may think. He talks in a measured manner. Confident, he is seemingly a worldly person who could almost certainly hold his own in any company. He tells you that international travel and philosophy are his main interests and as might be expected of a man whose genealogical history dates back to the Knights Templar, he likes the finer things in life, among them champagne, fast cars and sunny climes.

'But none of this is materialistically important to me,' he

adds with conviction. 'I am seeking a decent woman of good faith with whom I can share my theological interests. If she is divorced with children, I would make the perfect husband and dad.' (This is precisely what he alluded to when interviewed on camera during his application for a dating site.)

So far so good, for there is nothing to worry about in what you see in John, is there? But 'Buyer Beware', because what he portrays is a mask, when everything behind it can be demonstrably monstrous. He is like a fake Rolex watch – all shiny and false – then, when you rewind it, the spring breaks, and savagery is unleashed.

Actually (and this can be great fun), you can try this off-the-wall exercise with anyone you do, or don't, like, or indeed, have some reservations about. It could be a potential adult partner, or the guy you bring home to meet your parents for the first time. 'Look, Dad, he's brought me some flowers,' says the enamoured daughter. 'He's got a smart car parked outside, he's an executive.' Dad, however, might have noted that the sleeves on the guy's suit are too long with no cuff visible, his shirt collar is frayed, his shoes are not leather and he hasn't even cleaned the welts. His offspring's potential suitor's hair is lank and cheaply cut. Actually, more pertinent to this subject, is that Dad is subconsciously already starting to look inside the young man's head because Pop knows all that glitters is not gold. Do you catch my drift?

With the killers I have an interest in, I also walk around them and examine their façades. I go through their life's history without them knowing it before even meeting with them, which is often in the flesh, in prison. Then, and only then, do I compare fact with the inevitable fiction (or might I say bullshit?) coming from their lips.

Overly vain characters and those of their ilk do love to be flattered; well-educated psychopaths even more so. The more you stroke their feathers and asks their advice on issues that they consider themselves to be 'experts' in, the more they respond and the more *they* talk and therefore the more *you* learn. However, what they do not realise – because their nature will not allow it – is that I can ladle out bullshit to them like the Chinese ladle out rice.

Here's an example. John Cannan considered himself the expert on high-end cars, so I sought his 'expert advice' on whether I should go for a 5.3-litre V12 XJS or an Aston Martin V8. I suggested that 'Fire Engine Red' was my choice for the Jag, perhaps with cream Connolly hide interior and the additional extra footplates in polished aluminium. John's reply covered six sides of prison-issue notepaper, among other technical drivel such as 'Red is far too flashy, the birds don't go for red. Opt for what I strongly recommend, silver,' before adding, 'an Aston has always been my favourite driving machine. At one time I owned a green DB6. It echoed understatement and my character. All very low-key.'

Of course, I already knew that John had never sat in an Aston Martin in his life. I was merely 'acknowledging' his vain belief in his own self-importance. It was my 'honey trap'.

'When you were on day release from Wormwood Scrubs prison, when you were visiting car auctions in the West Country, you didn't have an Aston then. How did you get about?' I wanted to know.

'Oh yes, I borrowed the prison hostel's red Ford Sierra,' he volunteered. 'Not quite to my liking, but it was acceptable for me to drive at the time.' The amazing significance of his mention of a red Ford Sierra will shortly become apparent but I digress.

Returning to Leamington Spa, with great presence of mind Carmel Cleary dashed across to the front door of the shop and ran out into the street, screaming, 'Help, help! There's a man in my shop with a knife!' Her desperate screams attracted the immediate attention of Andrew Riley, a builder who had just entered Regent Street from Portland Street. He ran towards her, asking, 'What's up?' 'He's got a knife,' the boutique owner gasped. As they spoke, the attacker ran out of the shop, turned left and ran down Portland Street. 'I decided to chase him,' Riley later recalled and 'almost immediately I was joined by another man [Robert Filer] and the two of us ran down Portland Street after him.'

By now the hue and cry was up. Police, including PC George Sears and PC Robert Calvert, raced to the scene. A police dog handler arrived and with Riley and Filer's assistance, Sears and Calvert soon stopped a man near the Smithfield garage. They took him around the side of the Regal cinema to question him away from the curious gaze of bystanders, who had begun to gather round. After failing to say very much, the man was arrested on suspicion of attempted robbery and conveyed to Leamington Spa Police Station.

On arrival the man was identified as John David Guise Cannan, whose address was Flat 2, Foye House, Bridge Road, Leigh Woods, Bristol. While in the Charge Room, he cockily denied everything, using his affected upper-class accent; he also demanded to speak to a solicitor and asked for a pack of cigarettes. He was placed in a cell.

PC Sears's attention had also been 'drawn to' (as they say in police parlance) a black BMW car parked in Dorner Place. The vehicle, index number A936 FJU, was about fifty yards from the boutique. A Police National Computer (PNC) check of the plate by personal radio revealed that the registered keeper was John Cannan. Further information showed that the owner was Mercantile Credit – a finance house selling the vehicle on a hire purchase agreement to Cannan. It also transpired that John Cannan was a convicted robber and serial rapist, who had already spent a lengthy time behind bars. Now, like his car, he was about to be taken apart by the seams.

Shortly thereafter, the BMW was towed to the police garage. Inspector Robert Kitchen briefly searched the vehicle and found a replica .38 Smith & Wesson revolver in the glovebox. When confronted with the imitation firearm and asked if there was anything else in the car that might be of police interest, Cannan retorted 'No! Nothing contentious.' Asked if he owned a crash helmet, Cannan again demanded to speak to a lawyer. Pressed on whether he had entered a ladies' dress shop at any time that day, he responded with, 'I did not go into a ladies' dress shop as far as I can remember.' Following this, he replied 'No comment' to every other question put to him.

The next morning, DC Fletcher made a further examination of the black BMW and removed a black briefcase from the front passenger seat. When Peter Ablett, a forensic scientist summoned to Leamington, arrived, the two men donned protective anti-contamination suits and began a systematic examination of the car, inside and out.

Most people's cars become an extension of their homes and, in many cases, translate into a subconscious repository for all manner of miscellany. Cannan's car was no exception. Although externally all shiny and black, this was merely a Series 3 1.6-litre first-entry model with skinny wheels and tyres, but the boot was full of clutter and junk. There was clothing, toiletries and personal documents. Items included a blazer, a man's jacket and an overcoat, a pair of trousers, a pair of jeans, two ties, a shirt, a pair of socks, slippers and a pink blanket. There were three coat hangers and, for a rainy day, two umbrellas – one a lady's, the other a gent's.

CASE STUDY – SAVAGE: JOHN DAVID GUISE CANNAN

The documents in the car included a Woolwich Building Society account book with almost zero funds in it, and a Lloyd's Bank chequebook personalised to J.D.G. Cannan. Subsequent inquiries proved that Mr Cannan was extremely overdrawn. Among the bric-a-brac were a bottle of Paco Rabanne aftershave lotion, a can of air freshener, a disposable razor, chewing gum, sundry parking tickets, a number of newspapers, a brochure featuring kitchen units, plus a solitary champagne cork.

Other items of more sinister interest were found, to include a length of rope (discovered in the glovebox) and a clothesline still in its package. A pair of handcuffs was found in the jack well of the boot, along with a British Visitor's Passport in Cannan's name, a driving licence and a vehicle excise licence disc in respect of an Austin vehicle, registration number HWL 507N, which did not belong to Cannan. This car belonged to a missing woman called Shirley Banks, who had left her home to go shopping in Bristol on Thursday, 8 October 1987 and was never seen alive by her husband, Richard, again.

The 'flashy' exterior of the bottom-of the-range entry model BMW, aligned with the cocky façade of the well-spoken Cannan, completely contradicted the junk-filled, untidy interior of his car. It was as if it was all shop-front window display with only rubbish inside. This sort of attention to detail tells forensic psychologists more about a suspected offender – the workings of his mind – than most things. Cannan was a 'disorganised' offender, and this is why he was finally arrested for attempted robbery, culminating in his life term for committing homicide.

And that is why one should never believe a word that a handsome, allegedly highly-decorated US Marine Sergeant serving in Afghanistan spiels out to 'Miss Needing Love and Companionship' on an Internet dating agency website. I would say that the moment alleged 'Congressional Medal Sgt Privy' asks for a penny, drop him, because the odds are high that he is really an obese shoe salesman, living with his trailer-park Mom, and on his uppers, from Turdsville, Shit Creek, Alabama. Trust me! Cannan would later tell me that he went to Leamington Spa solely to commit a robbery, as he only had £6 to his name. He had selected the boutique as being 'a quick haul'. When I asked him about rape also being on his mind as he entered the Ginger boutique, he replied: 'There was absolutely no question of sex, in fact it was the last thing on my mind.'

Pressing him further, I suggested that the police might construe the handcuffs, the lengths of rope and the imitation revolver as being a 'Rape Kit', similar to one he had used previously during a terrible attack on a pregnant Sutton Coldfield shop owner, who was with her toddler son; an offence for which he had previously been convicted, receiving an eight-year prison term on 26 June 1981. Ever the pathological liar, cunning and manipulative, with a callous lack of empathy, and packed full of a grandiose sense of self-worth, John came back with: 'You and me are highly intelligent people. Would you agree? This is why I selected you out of the dozens of authors who wanted my story. But they all wanted the sensational stuff while you wanted to really get to know me. I had a top-end BMW [which he didn't] and you drive a red Jaguar XJS [which, at that time, I did]. As a very experienced car dealer [which he wasn't], I appreciate men with good taste like mine. I can tell from your stationery that you are a perfectionist [which I am not]. I'd put money on it that you like Remy Martin and Moët Chandon rather than cheapo plonk. That would never impress the girls, would it?'

(Actually, authors don't get paid much these days, so I'll drink pretty much anything!)

'But the alleged "Rape Kit", John?' I persisted.

CASE STUDY – SAVAGE: JOHN DAVID GUISE CANNAN

'Well, I would not read too much into this,' he replied. 'I have no idea why the gun was found in my BMW. I suspect a conspiracy by the police and leading members of Freemasonry. I had bought the washing line because my line at home broke. To prove it, it was still in the plastic bag I bought it with the price tag. I will tell you later about the handcuffs. It's a long and complicated story about those and I don't want you to go off-track with silly side issues when we have more important things to concentrate on.'

The proverbial shit hit the fan for John Cannan when, following his arrest in Leamington Spa, police opened his garage door at Foye House and found a recently blue-painted Austin Mini with the licence plate SLP 386 S. The plate was false, for the Mini had belonged to a missing woman called Shirley Anne Banks (*née* Reynolds).

Born in Edinburgh on 4 August 1958, Shirley Banks was married, and lived and worked in Bristol. She had vanished without trace after shopping in the city centre on Thursday, 8 October 1987. The Mini Clubman – its original colour was orange – was registered to her. The correct index number was HWL 507N (the vehicle excise licence for the same car having just been found by police in Cannan's BMW).

At first, the false number plate, SLP 386 S, didn't register with the Avon & Somerset Constabulary, but SLP 386 S certainly did with me for I noted a remarkable coincidence: 'SP' – Suzy Lamplugh – and '86' being the year that the twenty-five-year-old estate agent disappeared.

Much later, I asked John why he had chosen SLP 3 86 S as a false number plate. He replied, 'Oh, that was just arbitrary. The truth is that I'd bought the car from a colleague at the St Phillip's Bristol Car Auction. It was a side deal, cash in hand.

Twenty-five quid. I can't remember the man's name, and I told DCI Saunders this. When I read that Shirley was missing, and that I had innocently bought her car, I became confused. I put it in my garage and repainted it.'

I phoned DCI Bryan Saunders, who was leading the hunt for Shirley Banks, and explained the possible significance of SLP 386 S. For his part, Saunders said that he was into astrology and had even consulted the stars in his desperate efforts to find Shirley. He and I were now singing from the same hymn sheet. I liked this... In fact I liked Bryan very much indeed!

Cannan's letters to me were always meticulously crafted. His handwriting is good and the grammar is spot on. With a limited amount of stationery at his disposal, he had to think before he wrote a word, a sentence or a paragraph. Nothing, however, appeared to be spontaneous, or from the heart, for everything seemed carefully calculated, even contrived.

John rambled on about having wanted to 'qualify for entry at a really great university like Oxford or Cambridge,' adding, 'Academia is where I really wanted to be.' (In fact what he was really doing at this time was sponging off his parents, robbing petrol stations at knifepoint and attacking and raping young women, including a devoted lover.)

He had joined the Merchant Navy but soon left. For a very short time John was a car salesman – of sorts. His father, Cyril, was the general manager at Reeve & Stedeford, whose prestigious showrooms in Birmingham were filled with the 'latest models of the famous marques in British car manufacturing: 'Through them I grew up enchanted with names such as Austin of England, Morris of Oxford and MG at Abingdon,' John boasted. Yet, here in Leamington and Bristol we now found him driving an entry model BMW on hire purchase, struggling to make the payments and with an overdraft at his bank. Undeterred, and imagining that I knew none of this, he grandiosely expanded: 'The life of a car salesman has its advantages, of course. I used to have high-flying times with the fast crowd. Dancing at the Belfry and screaming through the back lanes of Sutton in our Jag, TR7 and company demonstrators. We were factory-trained sales executives and conversant in financial depreciation, projection, motor engineering and responsible for six-figure sales turnovers.'

I interviewed John's mother, Sheila. Of the 'old school', she was neat in her personal appearance: short, fair-haired, in a well-ordered way. She laid on tea and biscuits for my visit. Her late husband, Cyril, was a solid, perhaps overbearing man, she told me. When I asked her to confirm John's employment at Reeve & Stedeford, she said: 'My husband gave little Johnnie a job. Cyril was an exacting man with a quick temper. He had been a flight lieutenant in the Royal Air Force during the Second World War and served as an instructor on aero engines. He was widely respected in the motor trade throughout the Midlands. Johnnie started with Reeve & Stedeford as an odd-job lad. He cleaned and washed the cars. He couldn't even do that properly so my husband despaired and eventually fired him.'

'Was Johnnie conversant with car depreciation and price projections?' I asked her.

'Oh, I think he must be referring to... is it called *Glasses Car Guide*?' she replied. Delicately pressed further, Mrs Cannan added, 'Johnnie always considered himself as "Top Gun". He characterised himself as a "Big Head – big mouth", while his friends and colleagues called him "Billy Liar".'

'Top gun', 'Big Head – big mouth' and 'Billy Liar' was writ large throughout every letter John Cannan sent to me. 'I left my father's firm because all of the other salesmen could not match my devotion to work and my excellent sales turnover,' he explained. 'They were jealous and it made my life unbearable. I could have owned that company within a few years.'

This contradiction between Sheila Cannan's statement and her son's deceptive account of his employment at Reeve & Stedeford gives us a focused look into the workings of this man's mind, for even way back in the early 1970s and while, to give him due credit, he worked hard to further educate himself, he was becoming increasingly vain, detesting those who did not admire him, pretending to be more important than he really was, exaggerating his achievements and claiming to be an expert in all things concerning the motor trade.

In May 1978, John met and married June Vale, a pretty, home-loving girl with light brown hair. She worked at an off-licence near his father's garage. According to Cannan, she was his one and only girlfriend and their engagement lasted for seven years. (This was false, for he cheated on June at every opportunity.) He told me that June had other boyfriends before committing herself to marriage and that he was very popular among men. The truth is that he was a loner with few, if any, pals at all, as Paul Scott, a former salesman at the showrooms, confirmed.

'John Cannan?' Paul told me. 'Did he have a large chip on his shoulder, or what? Because his father was the boss, John thought that he deserved special treatment amongst the sales staff. He treated the workshop mechanics like dirt. His dad had told him that he had to start at the bottom and work his way up like anyone else Cyril employed, so he had to clean the cars, make the coffee and these sorts of things. John hated it. A Mr "Know All, No Nothing", and we didn't like him. Did he use a Jaguar demonstrator? What? No, he was never allowed to drive our demonstrators. He had to use a bus to get to and from work.'

And Scott's testimony stands up. When John married June at

CASE STUDY – SAVAGE: JOHN DAVID GUISE CANNAN

Four Oaks Methodist Church, Birmingham, his younger brother Anthony was Best Man. John had the customary stag night celebration, but those who attended were mainly Anthony's friends, not his. 'My marriage was motor-trade blessed,' John told me, 'with two beautiful dark blue Rolls-Royce Shadows provided by the company.' (Apart from the two 'Rollers', which only existed in John's imagination, it was 'such a blessing' that no one from the motor trade attended his stag night, either.)

Cannan would later blame his parents for rushing him into marriage. With the benefit of hindsight he claimed, 'I never would have married her but everybody was trying to hassle me into it, her side especially.' The couple didn't have a home of their own so they stayed with his parents and then June fell pregnant. 'I really could have done without all that extra trouble,' he later wrote me from prison, adding, 'that ruined all those previous years of happiness and success. From a spiritual point of view things got on top of me at that point and I began to slide downhill.'

We can now add more traits to his character: an obvious self-focus in interpersonal relationships and problems in sustaining satisfying relationships.

By 1980, at the age of twenty-six, John Cannan was practically an alcoholic. He had effectively deserted June and their small daughter by the end of 1979. In February 1980 he met Sharon Major (her name has been changed to protect her identity). Aged thirty-two, Sharon was a vivacious woman with an open, trusting face, framed by longish fair hair, and she was on the verge of a divorce. When John first asked her out, she accepted and he explained that he was divorced (which, at that time, was untrue), and that he worked as a sales manager at a local car showroom (also untrue).

Now kicked out of his job and booted out of his disgusted

parents' home, Cannan began living at Sutton House – a B&B in Chester Road, Erdington. He had stayed there before while cheating on June. 'I used to visit the hotspots of Birmingham,' he bragged. 'Buy 'em a drink, tell 'em I love them, tell 'em they were the best thing since sliced bread, then take them to the Sutton Guest House for a cheap night of easily forgettable passion.'

Can the reader smell misogyny here?

After a sparkling start to their relationship, Sharon soon started to see the flaws in John's character when he moved in with her. After a chance meeting with June in a supermarket, she discovered that he was still married; in fact he even had a daughter, a fact he'd never mentioned before.

As tensions grew, with Cannan out of work and stealing money where he could find it, his vanity threatened" as Sharon started to find fault with him more often. Already intolerant of criticism, he became hypersensitive to any insults, or imagined insults, and flew into uncontrollable rages. Sharon would turn up at work with black eyes and bruises on her arms. Drinking a bottle of Scotch a day, John had the extra pressure of finding cash to pay June's maintenance.

'I now realised that he had an evil streak in him, but I tried very hard to settle John down,' a tearful Sharon told me during our only interview. 'One part of me still wanted to be with him but common sense told me it had to end.'

Matters came to a head with the approach of Christmas Eve 1980. Sharon asked John to move out for a few days because her ex-husband was coming over to visit the children on Christmas Day and Boxing Day. 'He wasn't coming to stay at my house,' she explained to me. 'Just for lunch and to bring gifts for me and the kids.'

John was livid. Utterly humiliated and extremely jealous, he returned to the guest house. Once there he drank himself stupid and his fury grew and grew. After the festive season, he returned to June's house, anticipating a warm welcome. But he was mistaken: she told him that their relationship was over.

What followed has to be one of the most savagely violent and sexually sickening attacks ever carried out on a woman who, by the Grace of God, survived and did so only by a whisker. Amazingly, following his arrest, Cannan was released without charge. It would be over six years before he was questioned again about the assault on Sharon Major, when he was taken to Bristol and held in custody on suspicion of the murder of Shirley Banks.

Exhibiting no signs of remorse in his letters to me, John blamed his assault on Sharon Major; that it had been a sex session that got out of hand. He told me that he loved her children – a boy aged four and a daughter aged six. 'I took very seriously my role as a surrogate dad,' he insisted, claiming that he occasionally bought them toys and took the little boy to his first football game, Aston Villa v. Birmingham City. 'We sat munching hamburgers,' John recollected, 'and he learned how to call the referee a "pillock".' He said the girl was backward for her age and that he and Sharon took her to see a specialist at a children's hospital.

After the break-up with Sharon, whom he called 'the most gorgeous creature' one moment and a 'slag' the next, Cannan says he was distraught. 'I left my wife,' he complained in his letters, 'lived with this lover, supported her and her two kids for twelve months, paid all the bills, gas, electric, rates, mortgage, housekeeping, children's money, entertainments, clothes, food, paid my wife maintenance and for Louise, my daughter, our relationship ends.' He loved Sharon, he said, and with greatly exaggerated emphasis, claimed that he was, 'very, very, very, very, very, very, very upset that we'd broken up and I was also upset that I'd hit her.'

John had mixed feelings about what had happened. He said that he missed Sharon and the children but he also blamed her for triggering his subsequent misfortunes. 'Everything I had loved for years had just gone. Believe me,' he said, 'I didn't want the birds, the booze, the clubs... I wanted the family again.' To his mind the affair with Sharon and its unfortunate outcome was pivotal too in regard to his future behaviour. 'When we broke up, I broke up,' he explained. 'Suddenly, everything was a shambles.'

Drowning in self-pity, he whined on: 'No home, no money, no job, and no hope. Drink, debt and despair was all that remained. I was just losing control. I let myself go and genuinely felt I could no longer cope. Tears, shakes, depression, it was a terrible time. Everything, it seemed, had been such a waste. She was the trigger but not the cause.'

Several days after Sharon dropped him, Cannan, armed with a lock knife, walked into Yenton Service Station just a few hundred yards from his guest house. Here, he terrorised two young girls and stole about £260.00. With funds at his disposal, he changed clothes and went out to buy a bottle of brandy.

For her part, Sharon categorically denied her former lover's assertion that he assisted her financially: 'John was always broke,' she told me during our meeting in a Bristol waterfront cafe. 'He never gave me any money. The household bills were paid by my ex-husband and I made a contribution to the welfare of my family through my own earnings, working in an off-licence.'

As for Cannan's description of the time he spent with the children, Sharon's view was that he had overstated it. He did buy a secondhand bicycle for her daughter at a cost of £10 and repainted it in the kitchen but he certainly did not spend hours teaching her daughter to read, 'patience not being one of his strong points,' she stated, adding, 'You know, Christopher, there is a good side of John trying to get out, but even though he'll never be released from prison, I am still terrified of him, even today.'

Let's go back to an earlier time. At 2.45pm, on Friday, 6 March 1981, John Cannan had walked into a ladies' knitwear shop in Sutton Coldfield and savagely raped a thirty-seven-year-old pregnant woman in front of her son. Cannan was shortly afterwards arrested and sentenced to eight years behind bars.

While at the Verne semi-open prison at Portland, Dorset, he sought advice regarding access to his daughter from a Bristol-based solicitor. An extremely attractive, dark-haired woman, lawyer, Annabel Rose was right up John's street: classy, well-dressed, and there was something about her that convinced him that he could 'pull her' – the term he used in a letter to me. Annabel, however, was married to a barrister whom John later claimed was 'a dull professional man'.

I have written extensively about the relationship that developed between this lawyer and her client in my book *Ladykiller: Inside the Mind of John Cannan*, but for the purposes of *Talking with Psychopaths and Savages*, here we see quite the most extreme example of how manipulative a man like Cannan can be. Annabel Rose, who had all the money, status and privilege that Cannan always aspired to, fell for him hook, line and sinker. Indeed he swept her off her feet.

> 'She found me a romantic rebel, who loved life passionately and one who allowed his impetuosity to triumph over reserve and caution.'
>
> – John Cannan, on Annabel Rose, to the author in correspondence

One might immediately pre-judge Annabel Rose as being somewhat naive in starting out as what would transpire to be 'one of my hottest lovers', as John claims. As a lawyer acting for Cannan with regard to access to his daughter, it is most probable that she didn't know the details of his rape conviction for which he was now serving time and therefore it could best be argued that her heart ruled her head when faced with the sort of charm offensive that he was most capable of. Nevertheless, when John was released from prison in 1986, they were so attached that he relocated to Bristol. Here, they continued their steamy affair until Mr Rose got wind of it and for John Cannan crunch time came about again: Annabel called off the relationship but John didn't take it lightly.

He pestered her, and stalked her and her husband. With £2,000 left to him in his now deceased father's will, and a further gift of £5,000 from a distant relative with the apt name of John Perks, he hired Tom Eyles, a private investigator, who ran Tom Eyles Legal Services of Fishponds, Bristol, to follow his former lover, stake out her home and office, and report back to him almost every day. Armed with the reports, Cannan tried to blackmail Annabel, threatening to spill the beans about their affair to her husband. She, however, had already confided in her spouse and so his threats fell on deaf ears.

I interviewed Tom (now deceased) at his home. Present was his wife, who remembered Cannan very well and she didn't like him at all. A tall, striking blonde, she explained that she always felt uneasy when John was around. 'He gave me the creeps,' she said. 'He was coming onto me and I could read him like a book.'

Just before lunchtime on Monday, 28 July 1986, twenty-five-year-old blonde estate agent Suzy Lamplugh, later described by her friends and colleagues as a 'smashing girl', left her office to meet a client called 'Mr Kipper' outside 37 Shorrolds Road.

This is confirmed by her diary entry, which recorded the essential details of the address with the annotation: '12.45 p.m. o/s' (outside).

At approximately 2.45pm, a close friend, Barbara Whitfield, who was a partner in a flat-finding agency, saw Suzy. Barbara was riding her bicycle along the Fulham Palace Road. 'I waved at her,' she later told police, 'but she didn't see me and there was a man sitting next to Suzy in her car [a white Ford Fiesta, index number B396 GAN]. I was absolutely certain it was her... she looked scared. I had known her for about five months. We would go and look at flats together. She was one of my best contacts.'

Suzy Lamplugh was never seen alive again. Various witnesses passing 37 Shorrolds Road recalled seeing a man whom police believe to be John Cannan talking to a pretty, young, well-dressed young woman. Suzy's car was later found abandoned in Stevenage Road, close to Fulham football ground. The vehicle had been badly parked about a mile from Shorrolds Road. There was every indication that it had been abandoned in haste: the handbrake was off, the driver's door was unlocked, Suzy's straw hat was on the parcel shelf behind the rear seats and her purse nestled in the driver's door pocket.

A local woman called Wendy Jones later told police that she had noted seeing the white Fiesta at around 3pm on Monday, 28 July. She thought it rather odd that it was parked askew. Wendy had gone to the cinema and when she returned home at about 10.30 that evening, the car was surrounded by policemen. The police believe that some time between the sighting of Suzy by colleague Barbara Whitfield at 2.45pm and the witnessing of the abandoned vehicle noted by Wendy Jones just 15 minutes later, Suzy was under the control of John Cannan and had been taken away in another vehicle to be murdered.

In November 2002, the police held a press conference at which officers named Cannan as the man they believe murdered Suzy Lamplugh. No evidence was found linking Cannan to Suzy's murder and he has consistently denied any involvement.

But who was Sandra Court? Was there anything to link John Cannan to her death?

While staying in the prison hostel, John often borrowed the hostel cook's red Ford Sierra to drive down to the West Country – specifically to Bristol, where he met up with Annabel Rose – and to visit a car auction at Poole, Dorset, to hone up on his 'factory-trained' skills in buying and selling old bangers when his discharge from prison finally came through. He explained that over bank holidays he could stay over with friends, one of whom lived on the outskirts of Southampton.

Twenty-seven-year-old Abbey Life Assurance clerk Sandra Court had been reported as a 'missing person' following a night out at Steppes nightclub in Bournemouth's town centre on Friday, 2 May 1986. She was last seen alive at about 2.45am on the Saturday morning, walking barefoot, apparently drunk, in the Bournemouth suburb of Lansdowne. Her naked body was found in a slow-moving stream close to the Avon Causeway, near Hurn, Christchurch, the following day at 7pm.

Neither robbery nor sexual assault appeared to have been a motive for the killing. There were no signs of a struggle and the cause of death – evident by the strangulation marks – was 'slight'. Some of Sandra's belongings were discovered strewn about at scattered locations nearby. A shoe, found by the side of the A31 near Picket Post, had possibly been thrown from a car heading for Southampton.

Ten days later, a letter posted in Southampton was sent to DCI Rose of Dorset CID, who was leading the murder inquiry. Its content suggested the death of Sandra was an accident and that the killer was truly sorry. Examination of this note reveals that the writer, although right-handed, completed it with a left hand in an effort to disguise authorship. The envelope was postmarked Southampton.

Although I also know the New Forest like the back of my hand, it is vital in my work to visit crime scenes and associated locations where possible. This I did in the company of my colleague Tony Brown, who never misses a thing, and we started off at the Poole car auction, then to Lansdowne where Sandra Court had last been seen alive staggering home – now just a few hundred yards away.

Our next task was to inspect the shallow stream where Sandra's corpse was found. It is along a quiet lane, much quieter in the dead of night. The stream runs under the road; there is a small bridge. Kids out riding cycles had spotted the body. The police had been summoned. Using a police map, Tony and I located all of the places where items belonging to Sandra, including her purse and handbag, had been found. Finally we arrived at the very place where her shoe had been discovered – along the eastbound carriageway of the A31, near Picket Post leading to Southampton. Other bits and pieces had also been thrown from a moving car along the same route.

We decided that it was Tony's job to have the note examined by several independent experts. He would then have them compare the handwriting with known samples belonging to John Cannan. Although obviously disguised by the writer using the left hand instead of the right hand, there were over twenty-five similarities. There appeared to be a very strong link between both sets of script, style and spacing. As John Cannan had never been considered a possible suspect in the Court case, Tony and I thought this warranted a fuller investigation by the police.

While this was going on, I wrote to Cannan on general matters, to include asking him if he had ever visited Poole over the Bank Holiday in question. He denied travelling to Poole over any weekend, but then he corrected himself, saying, 'Once in September or October of 1986. I was with Gilly Paige, the former Olympic ice-skater. I am not sure. I forget these things.' In fact he had dated Gilly for a short while. On their last date he had driven her to an isolated spot, put his hands around her throat and started to strangle her. 'This is how Suzy Lamplugh might have been murdered,' he snarled. The beautiful young ice skater later told police that she was so terrified by this sudden change in Cannan's demeanour that she never saw him again.

Now serving life at HMP Wakefield for the murder of Shirley Banks – whose naked body, like that of Sandra Court's, was also discovered in a remote stream – John Cannan had managed to get hold a copy of *Ladykiller*, my book about him. The foreword was written by Professor of Applied Psychology David Canter (at the time he was based at the University of Surrey).

On reading it, John flipped and he wrote to police, saying my book was rubbish. Furthermore, that my quotes from his letters were all made up by me, he argued, adding that some of the letters I had mentioned he had never written at all. This of course piqued the interest of SOII MetPol, who also had a copy of the book. Then, one afternoon, I received a call from the police. It was a detective asking if I still had all of Cannan's letters in my possession. Yes, I told him, I did.

'Sir, we would very much like those letters, if possible,' the officer asked, as polite as can be.

'You most certainly can, on the proviso that you copy them and return those copies back to me,' I replied.

'Thank you, sir,' came the response. 'I'll drive down to Portsmouth and pick them up this afternoon.'

Two weeks later, I was invited up to Buckingham Palace Road Police Station to meet with DCI Jim Dickie and DI Stuart Ault.

To be fair to these police officers, they really didn't have the time to wade through the scores of Cannan's lengthy and wandering correspondence, looking for something that might not even exist that would help pin him down for Suzy's apparent murder. However, to my delight they confirmed that everything I had written in *Ladykiller* seemed to be correct. Cannan had, indeed, given me the material he was now denying knowledge of. 'Billy Liar' was up to his old tricks again!

'There are a lot of references to the Holy Bible in these letters,' pointed out Stuart Ault. 'He likes his Biblical quotes, doesn't he? Christopher, do you think there is any hidden meaning in this?'

I promised that I would take a closer look. In fact, now that the Met were so interested in Cannan's denial of ever writing much of what he clearly had written, this renewed my interest. My thoughts bounced back to Cannan's trip to the Poole car auction and the vehicle he had used over that Bank Holiday.

Poole, Dorset, the Park & Display ticket I had found in his property in a Bristol police station? A bell rang inside my head. John knew that I had once lived in Southampton and as an aside he had explained that he knew the city quite well. He had friends who lived in or on the outskirts of the city. He had bought a camera at University Cameras, Below Bargate. He had a soft spot for the New Forest, especially the hamlet of Buckler's Hard, where he had a drink. 'I know the New Forest like the back of my hand,' he claimed. 'I visited the car auction at Poole twice...'

Previously, I had been allowed to examine the contents of several black bin liners containing the detritus and paperwork collected from John's BMW. DCI Bryan Saunders and his colleague Supt Tim Bryan had produced this material when I visited the Avon & Somerset HQ. Did I, or did I not, find a crumpled-up Pay & Display parking ticket for Poole, Dorset? I went back to Bristol. Yes, the ticket had been issued at Poole and was dated 3 May 1986 – a Bank Holiday.

For years, police had tried to figure out specifically what car Suzy Lamplugh's abductor and killer had used to convey the young woman to his killing ground and body disposal site (still unknown). It could not have been Suzy's white Ford Fiesta, for Wendy Jones first saw it abandoned in Stevenage Road, just an hour after Suzy's appointment with the mysterious 'Mr Kipper'. In his letters to me, Cannan had mentioned that he'd often borrowed the hostel cook's red Ford Sierra. I brought this information to the attention of DCI Dickie and DI Ault, who told me that no link between Suzy Lamplugh and Sandra Court had ever been considered by them before. Likewise, it also transpired that the Dorset Police had made no connection between the murder of Sandra on their patch and the disappearance of Suzy, which came under the Metropolitan Police's jurisdiction.

Although the Pay & Display parking ticket was of great interest to SOII, I had something else that I could offer the Metropolitan Police too. Although DCI Dickie and Stuart Ault gave me no indication that they would be interviewing Cannan about the murder of Suzy Lamplugh, I sensed this was about to happen when the detectives asked me how they might approach him with their line of questioning. Indeed, they had contacted colleagues in Bristol, asking if the transcripts of their interviews with John could be made available. Alas, much time had since passed and the files had been destroyed – there had been no need for them to be kept because the murder of Shirley Banks had resulted in a conviction in May 1989. These files also included details of the interviews carried out by Thames Valley Police regarding the rape of Donna Tucker, at Reading, Berkshire, among other matters.

During the course of my 'relationship' with John Cannan, and acting upon John's instructions, his solicitor, Jim Moriarty of Blackham, Maycock & Hayward, had handed me a full set of folders (about eight in all). This was the only record of John's interrogation by police that now existed. I handed it all over to SOII.

By dint of sheer hard work and diligence, SOII tried to track down the hostel cook, only to learn that he had since passed away. However, excellent detective work linking the man's name to the Vehicle Licensing Office gave officers the year, make and model of a red Ford Sierra, which they hoped they could still find. They discovered it in a London scrapyard and had it towed away. Upon forensic examination they discovered Cannan's and Suzy Lamplugh's DNA. Sadly, forensic scientists did not look for a DNA link between Cannan, the Sierra and Sandra Court.

'We feel very relieved that, in our estimation, the man who killed Suzy cannot kill anybody else.'

– Diana Lamplugh (mother of Suzy),
The Suzy Lamplugh Trust

'Impressive... a detailed and balanced portrait of a murderer.'

– Diana Lamplugh on *Ladykiller* by Christopher Berry-Dee and Robin Odell

There was now physical and circumstantial evidence associating John Cannan with Suzy Lamplugh and much of the physical evidence came to the law's attention following my time working with Cannan for my book, *Ladykiller*. The Metropolitan Police submitted the file to the Crown Prosecution Service (CPS), who concluded that 'DNA belonging to Miss Lamplugh has been found in the car. DNA belonging to Cannan has been found in the same vehicle. But this does not imply that both persons were in that car at the same time.'

The two senior investigating officers called a press conference, which was televised on TV. In an unprecedented event DCI Jim Dickie and DI Stuart Ault of MetPol's elite SOII vented their frustration and anger during the broadcast.

At around the same time Tony Brown and I took John's handwriting samples and a copy of the Southampton postmarked letter, along with a copy of the Pay & Display parking ticket to Bournemouth Central Police Station, where we had an appointment with a detective. Our discussion lasted less than ten minutes. He admitted that no such handwriting comparison had been made by his officers and, with a dismissive wave of his hand, asked us to leave. 'Oh, and you might use the public car park if you come again,' he added as he closed the door.

At the time of writing, the murder of Sandra Court remains unsolved. Occasionally the dust is blown from its cover as part of Cold Case reviews. As far as I am aware, at no time since Sandra's death have Dorset Police contacted SOII Metropolitan Police, who are responsible for the Lamplugh inquiry. If they have done so, they've certainly not had the courtesy to inform me!

Nevertheless, several years later I had lunch with the ex-head of Dorset CID. This former detective officer was somewhat reluctant to be drawn on the Sandra Court case, explaining that while Sandra's homicide had fallen within his jurisdiction, Suzy Lamplugh's disappearance had come under the Met's remit.

'No, we didn't talk to the Met at all... at least not to my knowledge. We didn't get on very well with them, anyhow,' he said.

'You must have known about my meeting with DI Stent,' I countered.

He looked me straight in the eye, saying, 'Nope! As I've just explained, the Lamplugh case was of no concern to me.'

Perhaps what galls me most is that the Dorset Police appear not to have followed up the initiative taken by SO11, whom, upon learning of John Cannan's use of the red Ford Sierra, arrested him at HMP Wakefield and had him brought down to Buckingham Palace Road Police Station for further questioning. Cannan denied everything in his usual 'Fuck you' manner, but here was a golden opportunity for detectives to also ask him to account for his movements during his trip to Poole over the Bank Holiday of 2 and 3 May 1986. John may well have told them to go to Hell, but explaining away the Pay & Display parking ticket would have certainly proved a point of interest, for I had handed this vital item of evidence, along with the handwriting comparisons, to the police on a plate. And did they even consider asking the Met if their own forensic officers could examine the red Sierra for any possible DNA links to Sandra Court?

At 1 pm, on Monday, 6 October 1986, an attempt was made to abduct a young woman in Whiteladies Road, Bristol. Although never charged with this offence, a photofit of the abductor bore a remarkable likeness to John Cannan. Moreover, his bank statement revealed that at 1.31pm that day he withdrew £25 from an ATM at Lloyds Bank in Clifton. This placed him close to the scene of the offence and within 30 minutes of its time of occurrence.

'I'm sorry about this. Do you have any children?'
                    – John Cannan to Donna Tucker following
                                              the 1986 rape

Later that same day (and we know this from another ATM withdrawal), Cannan was in the Berkshire town of Reading. Thirty-year-old Donna Tucker had had a minor tiff with her husband and had driven off to park up and read a book, allowing a cooling off of tempers. It was late and a man approached her car asking for directions, saying, 'Can you tell me the way to Balfour Drive, please?' Almost instantly, Donna was threatened with a knife and then driven in her Vauxhall Cavalier to the Theale Industrial Estate, where she was raped. Afterwards, John drove her to Reading railway station, where he left her and caught the earliest train back to Bristol.

By the Grace of God, Donna survived, for she could easily have ended up dead. Following the rape (which she reported immediately), officers at Reading Police Station asked her to hand over the clothing she had worn when assaulted. The yellow sweater, blue skirt, slip, shoes, bra and panties were sealed in clear plastic crime bags. Her panties – labelled exhibit AJB/6, a pair of M&S white knickers – were later destined to become a crucial item of evidence. Donna had also given detectives several tissues, one of which she had used to wipe her vagina and anus. These too were sealed in a bag labelled AJB/7. At the scene of the attack, police also found several cigarette butts.

When, months later, Donna was shown a line-up of photos, she identified Cannan in a heartbeat. His DNA was extracted from the intimate items with the chances of the unique profile belonging to anyone other than him being several millions to one. When interviewed by the police he consistently denied this offence. Because this DNA evidence was so overwhelming,

CASE STUDY – SAVAGE: JOHN DAVID GUISE CANNAN

I didn't even bother asking him about Donna Tucker – it would have been a waste of my time, and as John would smugly have agreed, a waste of *his* valuable time, too!

For almost a year, we heard not much more from Cannan until he killed Shirley Banks in Bristol on 8/9 October 1987. He was arrested at Leamington Spa 20 days later.

With the word count allocated to me in this book, I have tried to give the reader just a brief insight into John Cannan's MO and his mind, so what do we find?

Ever-mobile Cannan was always out on the hunt, trawling for attractive young women whom he might charm into bed, yet he was also a savage predator and a vain and violent personality. Oddly enough, although at a superficial level being a romantic, John is also a misogynist, who harbours an underlying hatred and dislike of women. In his letters to me, he makes much of his love of women: how he courted them, swept them off their feet with flowers, champagne and fine dining and how they responded to his flattery, handsome looks and good taste.

Remember also his crass remark: 'Buy 'em a drink, tell 'em I love them, tell 'em they were the best thing since sliced bread, then take them for a cheap night of easily forgettable passion.' This was yet another unintentional boast that echoes a comment made to me by Michael Ross (see page 119): 'I used them, abused them, killed them and dumped them like so much trash.'

As we dig a little deeper into Cannan's mind, we would be looking for the turning points that propelled him downwards into an ever-increasing spiral of violence that culminated in savage sado-sexual homicide. While always willing to be corrected, it is my opinion that John's problems began when he was working at his father's garage.

I believe the following steps mark the development of Cannan's behaviour.

STEP 1

The facts show that Cannan was holding down a menial position but thought he deserved something better because he was privately educated and the son of the boss – his father, Cyril – who demanded from John that he start from the bottom and work his way up to a more senior position. However John took this badly and his attitude reflected on the staff, who regarded him as an obnoxious young upstart whom they could not bear to be around. John 'knew best' because he actually believed he was better than anyone else, so here we find his vanity and self-delusion.

To be fair to Cannan, I have no doubt that he really wanted to become an achiever in his overbearing father's eyes. Although he frequently played truant from school, academically he had done rather well and with admirable self-motivation spent hours in public libraries learning about things that interested him. As the reader might agree, others have indulged this kind of random education, which can create specialist knowledge but often at the expense of structured learning. Therefore, I truly believe that he started out in life with good intentions; there was a decent guy in John but his developing vanity and self-delusion demanded even more of him, more than he was capable of resisting.

As I write this, I recall the words of Sharon Major, whose relationship with Cannan almost came to a fatal end. She told me: 'I know what John did to me was wicked *but there is a good side to John, which is desperately trying to get out.*' (Author's italics.)

Lord Lane, former Lord Chief Justice of England (now deceased), assisted me in my book *Ladykiller* and sent me a signed photograph of him in his judicial robes. Lord Lane said:

CASE STUDY – SAVAGE: JOHN DAVID GUISE CANNAN

'The prospect of a young man spending the rest of his life in prison is appalling. It is a pity that there seems to be no humane alternative. *There is good in the worst of us.*' (Author's italics.)

Then we have to consider the words of Michael Bruce Ross to me during an interview: 'Ya know, I was like a spider climbing up a pane of slippery glass. Every time I almost reached the top, I fell down again.'

STEP 2

This came about during Cannan's marriage to June, which he said was forced upon him by both sets of parents because she was pregnant. What did he say? 'I would never have married her, but everyone was trying to hassle me into it, on her side especially.' Later, writing to me from prison in November 1989, he says, 'that [the marriage] ruined all those previous years of happiness and success. I began to slide downhill.'

So, as we enter John's head, you can see him already trying to apportion blame for the mess in which he unfortunately found himself. This was to be a pattern of behaviour he would repeat time and again when struggling to formulate a defence for later crimes he says he did not commit.

When Sharon Major realised that John was not all he claimed to be – for she was now beginning to understand him a little better – she thought it was best for her to leave him, if only for the sake of her children. How did John react? He violently assaulted her.

STEP 3

This was instigated when Cannan entered the ladies knitwear shop in Sutton Coldfield on Friday, 6 March 1981. He was wearing a crash helmet. Because he was flat broke, his initial intention was robbery with the savage rape of the pretty woman also in mind. That she pleaded that she was pregnant meant nothing to John. He was soon arrested and sentenced to a prison term of eight years (he would serve just five). The MO (modus operandi) of wearing a crash helmet when committing an almost identical offence would be later used at the Ginger boutique in Leamington Spa.

STEP 4

Step 4 was triggered when, while in prison, Cannan asked solicitor Annabel Rose to act for him in gaining access to his daughter. Like the women before her, Annabel fell for John's charms and, like many of his other conquests, she failed to see behind the plausible mask of normalcy that hid the emerging sado-sexual savagery. I believe that Annabel knew nothing of John's criminal antecedent history, making her seem as naive as she may appear to others, but Cannan was extremely charming and manipulative too.

The affair with Annabel continued for some time after Cannan was sent to Wormwood Scrubs. Prior to his final release he was allowed to spend the remainder of his sentence at the prison hostel in Du Cane Road. While here, he borrowed the cook's red Ford Sierra, frequently travelling to visit Annabel in Bristol, until her husband finally learned of his wife's infidelity and she finished with Cannan.

STEP 5

This came about when Cannan realised that Annabel's ardour was cooling. Just like Sharon Major, this attractive lady solicitor wanted to let John down lightly. He sensed this when she started making excuses as to why she could not spend as much time with him as he would have wished. I also believe that his pie-in-the-sky, elephants fly, lead balls bounce and fairies reign supreme ambitions of success in the car sales industry were just that, as in 'bullshit'. This way of selling himself as a high-flying executive was a repeat of his spiel to Sharon Major five years previously, and incidentally also to me in correspondence.

Following his disintegrating and hopeless dreams of settling down with classy Annabel, John's ego was being pricked.

STEP 6

In Cannan's criminal chronology this step brings us to 25 July 1986. It was on this day that he was finally released on parole from the Wormwood Scrubs hostel and, technically, was free as a bird. It was a mere three days later that Suzy Lamplugh disappeared forever. John was still using the red Sierra and was moving in with his mother at Sutton Coldfield, yet the evidence shows that his claim that he was at her home on the day when Suzy was abducted was untrue.

Sheila Cannan told me: 'No, John said that he was in London on 25 July. He was driving a red car, but he returned later that evening for his dinner.'

STEP 7 AND 8

These arrived when Cannan caught a train to Reading, where, during the late hours of 6 October 1986, he abducted and raped Donna Tucker. By now, John had moved to Bristol and his affair with Annabel Rose was cooling off. However, he was still on the prowl for female conquests. Following this savage attack, Cannan caught a train back to Temple Meads Railway Station in Bristol. Later, during the early evening of 7 October, he attacked Julia Pauline Holman at Canon's Marsh Car Park.

'He [John] had women falling at his feet.'
> – statement of Cannan's ex-lover
> Gilly Paige to police

Before he took his flat at Foye House, one of Cannan's favourite haunts in Bristol was the Avon Gorge Hotel, where for a short while he stayed. It was here, on Sunday, 14 June 1987, that he met Gilly Paige, an attractive, twenty-four-year-old showgirl. The former Olympic ice-skater was taking time off from the *Holiday on Ice* show. Earlier that day John had met Annabel Rose and after she'd returned home, he left his room and went down to the restaurant for dinner, where he spotted Gilly. She would later provide an invaluable insight into the methods Cannan used to have 'women falling at his feet'.

As Gilly put it later, 'He kept making eye contact with me,' while John told me in a letter, 'The restaurant staff were aware of my signals and the waiters were taking bets on whether or not I would seduce her. It's a well-remembered incident.'

During my research into the life and the crimes committed by John Cannan, I simply had to follow up on this boast, coming away not disappointed after speaking to one of the staff who waited on him at the Avon Gorge Hotel. 'When we saw his photo in the newspapers some of us remembered him,' I was told. 'He stayed with us occasionally and he was right up himself. He was a guest who liked to snap his fingers when he wanted something from me. Very picky about his food and how the table should be laid. He thought he knew a lot about wine and champagne. Some of the female staff thought that he was "oily" and demeaning. Did we place bets on whether or not he would seduce the guest you are talking about? Absolutely NOT!'

Nevertheless, John did order a bottle of champagne and had it sent to Gilly's room, along with a note giving his room number and saying, 'I'd love to see you. Don't disappoint me.'

Gilly explained to me, 'I thought, "What the heck?" and decided to accept his invitation. I had never met anybody so charming. He had this way of making a woman feel very special. He is very good-looking and has amazing eyes.'

For his part, John told me that he liked the Avon Gorge Hotel very much, alleging, 'It was the only hotel in the area that offered a suite with a jacuzzi. It was in the jacuzzi that I first made love to the ice-skater.'

The following day he gave Gilly a lift to Birmingham in a hired Ford Escort. The contradiction between his flashy persona and this basic, low-end hire car might or might not have crossed her mind. Nevertheless, during the journey he touched on some rather 'odd subjects'. Gilly recalled when I spoke to her, 'He talked about the police searching for bodies in woods and rivers. He gave it as his opinion that the best way to get rid of a body was to put it in concrete on a construction site.' Cannan even ventured to suggest that this was probably what had happened to Suzy Lamplugh. He also asked Gilly if she knew the name to describe people who had sex with dead bodies (necrophilia), and talked about bondage and anal intercourse. 'He also volunteered the information that he enjoyed sex with other people looking on,' she added.

Now, the reader is looking right into the mindset of this perverted sex killer. It's not a nice place to be, is it? John pulled the hire car into a service station, where, at one point, he put his hands around Gilly's neck and said: 'You know I'll never hurt you, you're too nice too hurt. Maybe this is the way Suzy died.'

At some point during the trip, Gilly explained that they drove off the motorway into country lanes and she was questioned as to whether anyone knew where she was. Despite being scared, she was sufficiently entranced by John to meet him again, which she did twice in Bristol and once in Poole. Cannan later told me that she rang him one night and he told her: 'Look, stay where you are and I'll come down.' They stayed at a hotel near Poole old docks (very close to the Poole car auctions). When asked by DCI Saunders during a police interview if he had the ice-skater's autograph, he cockily replied, 'I don't need that, I got everything. She was a trophy, just another notch on a bedpost.'

The relationship between Cannan and Gilly Paige came to an abrupt, though amicable end when she returned to the *Holiday on Ice* show. John spoke of this 'interlude' in his usual misogynistic manner, merely saying, 'It was another brief flirtation,' and adding: 'It was ego, I suppose. She was a very, very, very attractive girl.' He also explained his dalliance in terms of not being willing to sit around tapping his fingers, waiting for Annabel Rose to leave her husband.

All this being said, one might have expected that Gilly would have dropped John like a hot brick, but such was his hold over her – just as with Annabel – that six weeks later Gilly wrote to him from France, inviting him to fly out to see her in Grenoble. John prevaricated: all he wanted was fast and cheaply obtained sex. To him the alleged session with Gilly in the Avon Gorge Hotel was a free bonus, costing him nothing more than a bottle of champagne. The very idea of flying to Grenoble to get between the sheets with an already established conquest was the last thing on his mind when there were easy pickings to be found in Bristol. He politely declined the offer, claiming that he was short of money because he was moving into a new flat at Foye House and was planning a pilgrimage to India and the West Indies – the trips, of course, were a complete figment of his overblown ego and grandiose imagination.

'Under that veneer of charm there lies a most evil, violent and horrible side to your character. You should never again be at liberty outside of prison walls.'
— Mr Justice Drake to John Cannan,
Exeter Crown Court, 28 April 1989

After Cannan's conviction at Exeter Crown Court, *The Sun* carried an interview with Gilly Paige, whom the newspaper described as an 'ice show beauty', which, indeed, she was. She talked about her encounter with John and of her nightmares in which she was haunted by his 'hypnotic eyes'. She told a reporter that during her car ride to Birmingham with John, he spoke of his interest in buying property and his insistence on being shown around by a woman. (Further echoes of Suzy Lamplugh here.) In relation to Suzy Lamplugh, he said that the police were looking for someone called 'Mr Kipper' (Cannan was well known for wearing wide, Kipper-type ties). Gilly added that John's opinion was that 'Mr Kipper' had got rid of the body by putting it in concrete. 'It gave me the creeps,' she added.

Having spent more time inside John Cannan's head than might be deemed a healthy way to pass the time of day, I do not think, for one moment, that John had buried anyone under concrete. Perhaps he had been watching too many Mafia movies, or had read up on something concerning the Kray Twins. However, notwithstanding this, in a letter to me he completely denied the remarks attributed to him by Gilly and called her 'a liar and an opportunist'. Venomously, never short of a theory, Cannan later told police that 'she was a bit of a moody girl' and put this down to 'her unhappy upbringing'.

Throughout the summer months of 1987, Cannan kept fairly mobile. In his letters he bragged about pulling a girl in Paignton while staying at the Commodore Hotel, which he put down to a 'dirty weekend'. When pressed for his companion's name, he told detectives to 'mind your own business'.

John enjoyed the company of other conquests, including Liz (surname deleted to protect her identity), a successful businesswoman in the West Midlands, whom he described as a 'gem'. Rising to the occasion, he bragged of many other one-night stands with: 'Girls I picked up at Racks, the wine bar at the Avon Gorge Hotel. You know, occasionally, you talk to somebody, and occasionally, you know, these things happen.' Rationalising his amorous intentions, he added, 'And why not? I wasn't married nor engaged to be, and I was always hot and cold on forming a permanent future with Annabel anyway.'

STEP 9

This occurred on Wednesday, 7 October 1987. The location was Canon's Marsh car park, a short distance from the Watershed in Bristol. Julia Pauline Holman, a recruitment administrator for Arthur Andersen & Co., whose offices were in Broad Quay House, had just finished work. She was drinking with three colleagues in the Colonial Bar (where I later interviewed Sharon Major) and then at 6.50pm she decided to leave, completely unaware that the suited-and-booted John Cannan had zeroed in on her.

It was dark as she walked alongside the harbour for a short distance and through an alleyway to reach Canon's Road. Using a gap in the fence, she entered the open-air parking lot and strolled towards her blue Ford Fiesta. Cannan was now an arm's length away. She placed a key in the car's ignition and then he struck first by wrenching the door open. He produced what appeared to her to be a handgun – probably the same imitation firearm found in the glovebox of his BMW after his arrest in Leamington Spa. 'If you do what I say,' he demanded, 'you won't get hurt.'

With great presence of mind, Julia swung her legs round to the right and kicked out at him, at the same time pushing him off-balance with her hands. She also shouted at him and let out a loud scream. As he straightened up, she slammed the car door shut and drove rapidly away, noticing her assailant walking casually off in the direction of Bristol's city centre.

Julia immediately reported all of this to the police. She gave a description of the man, which fitted with Cannan precisely – even to his eyebrows meeting over the bridge of his nose. When subsequently questioned about this matter, John described Julia Holman's account as a 'highly original little statement'. He did not know where Canon's Marsh car park was. When DI Bryan Saunders pointed out its location on a map of Bristol, Cannan, in one of his characteristic attempts to pre-empt the police, asked, 'And are you going to say, "Where were you at seven o'clock on that day?"'

'Well, I am ultimately,' replied Saunders.

'I'm having everything thrown at me, aren't I?' was John's rejoinder.

STEP 10

The above step arrived on Thursday, 8 October 1987, when Shirley Anne Banks (born Edinburgh, Monday, 4 August 1958) went shopping at a Debenhams store in Broadmead,

Bristol. She drove to the store car park in her orange Austin Mini, registration number HWL 507N, and was last seen at around 7pm by a close friend called Jeanne Duvivier. Shirley was browsing through the Topshop outlet where, for £24.00, she bought a full-length navy-and-white dress, which she had held up to herself, asking, 'What do you think of it?' Jeanne was complimentary as they parted company, with Shirley saying, 'See you tomorrow.'

She did not see her then.

A till roll recording transaction number '1053', and the item code, all time-stamped '19:26', were later produced to police by seventeen-year-old Nicola Wiltshire – who worked part-time at Debenhams – and it became a crucial piece of evidence after John Cannan was arrested for Shirley's murder.

Shirley's decomposing naked corpse was found on Easter Sunday, 3 April 1988, by Basil Hooper and his wife Jill, who were taking their niece and two teenage children for a walk along a forest trail in the Quantock Hills in Somerset. Walking through a 2,000-acre conifer plantation known as Great Wood, they saw what appeared to be a human body lying in a slow-moving stream (ironically, already known locally as 'Dead Woman's Ditch'). They stopped a Land Rover driven by a man called Kevin Morley and police were called to the scene.

Following a post-mortem examination carried out by Professor Bernard Knight (who also carried out examinations on the remains unearthed during the Fred and Rose West inquiries), it was determined through dental records that the body was of the now 'presumed missing' Shirley Banks. Indeed, a button found close by was positively identified as having coming from the Topshop dress she had bought at Debenhams.

CASE STUDY – SAVAGE: JOHN DAVID GUISE CANNAN

STEP 11

This final step was John Cannan's arrest for attempted robbery at Leamington Spa on 29 October 1987 – just a few weeks after he murdered Shirley Banks.

Shirley was a slim, vivacious blonde, who almost certainly turned many heads. She was also known to have frequented Racks Wine Bar at the Avon Gorge Hotel – a favourite watering hole used by John Cannan. In his letters to me – correspondence I passed onto the Metropolitan Police – he states quite categorically that he had known Shirley for some time. He explained that she had become unwittingly involved in dodgy dealings concerning crooked solicitors in a massive fraud connected with mortgages and conveyancing, and that she feared for her life. It is true that such a major conveyancing fraud had been taking place, following which several men were convicted and sent to prison for a term.

John also alleged that he had known Suzy Lamplugh, who confided in him regarding the same matter, and, to be fair to him, what he claimed to know about this 'mortgage fraud' – which stretched from Bristol to London – bears more than a resemblance to the truth. I can also confirm that what Cannan told me during his lengthy correspondence could *not* have been gleaned from any media reports at that time. I will merely say that he obtained this information through 'pillow talk'. But who would believe this 'Billy Liar' anyway?

However, John Cannan repeatedly told police that he had not bumped into Shirley during the evening she disappeared from her shopping trip to Debenhams and that she had never been in his flat at Foye House, while her thumbprint later discovered by Scenes-of-Crime technicians on a document found on his coffee table proved this claim to be a lie.

I like to think of this as being Shirley 'telling' police: 'Look, I've been here.'

There was no forensic evidence linking Shirley's actual murder to John's flat at Foye House. Two elderly witnesses did see a man apparently hitting a woman in nearby woods the next day, but that evidence is a little obscure. How John conveyed Shirley to 'Dead Woman's Ditch' in the Quantock Hills also remains a matter for conjecture.

John Cannan was found guilty on all of the following 16 charges. He remains in prison today.

THE CHARGES JOHN CANNAN WAS FOUND GUILTY OF

'For that you on 30th December 1980 at Sutton Coldfield in the City of Birmingham had sexual intercourse with Sharon Major [name changed] without her consent.'
CONTRARY to Section 1 (1) of the Sexual Offences Act, 1956

'On 30th December 1980 at Sutton Coldfield in the City of Birmingham did attempt to commit buggery with Sharon Major, a woman.'
CONTRARY to Section 1 (1) of the Criminal Attempts Act, 1981

'For that you on 30th December 1980 at Sutton Coldfield in the City of Birmingham did make an indecent assault on a woman called Sharon Major.'
CONTRARY to Section 14 (1) of the Sexual Offences Act, 1956

'For that you on 30th December 1980 at Sutton Coldfield in the City of Birmingham did unlawfully and maliciously cause grievous bodily harm upon Sharon Major.'

CASE STUDY – SAVAGE: JOHN DAVID GUISE CANNAN

CONTRARY to Section 20 of the Offences Against the Persons Act, 1861

'On 6th October 1986 at Reading in the County of Berkshire did rape Donna Tucker.'
CONTRARY to Section 1 (1) of the Sexual Offences Act, 1956

'On 6th October 1986 at Reading in the County of Berkshire did commit buggery with Donna Tucker, a woman.'
CONTRARY to Section 12 (1) of the Sexual Offences Act, 1956

'On 6th October 1986 at Reading in the County of Berkshire did indecently assault Donna Tucker, a woman.'
CONTRARY to Section 14 (1) of the Sexual Offences Act, 1956

'On 6th October 1986 at Reading in the County of Berkshire did take away Donna Tucker against her will and by force with the intention she would have unlawful sexual intercourse with you.'
CONTRARY to Section 17 (1) of the Sexual Offences Act, 1956

'For that you on 7th October at Canon's Road car park in the City of Bristol did attempt to forcibly abduct and to carry away Julia Pauline Holman against the will of the said Julia Pauline Holman.'
CONTRARY to Section 1 of the Criminal Attempts Act, 1981 and Common Law

'On the 7th October 1987 in the City of Bristol did attempt to take away Julia Pauline Holman against her will and by force with the intention that she would have unlawful sexual intercourse with you.'
CONTRARY to Section 1 (1) of the Criminal Attempts Act, 1981

'For that you between 7th October and 31st October 1987 in the City of Bristol did steal a motor vehicle, namely a Mini Clubman saloon, registration number HWL 507N, to the value of £175, the property of Shirley Anne Banks.'
CONTRARY to Sections 1 and 7 of the Theft Act, 1968

'For that you on 8th October 1987 in the City of Bristol or elsewhere did forcibly abduct and carry away Shirley Anne Banks against the will of the said Shirley Anne Banks.'
CONTRARY to Common Law

'On 8th October 1987 in the City of Bristol did take away Shirley Anne Banks against her will and by force with the intention that she should have unlawful sexual intercourse with you.'
CONTRARY to Section 17 (1) of the Sexual Offences Act, 1956

'For that you between 7th and 30th October 1987 in the City of Bristol or elsewhere did murder Shirley Anne Banks.'
CONTRARY to Common Law

'On 29th October 1987 at Leamington Spa in the County of Warwickshire did assault Carmel Clearly with intent to rob.'
CONTRARY to Section 8 of the Theft Act 1968

'On 29th October at Leamington Spa in the County of Warwickshire did detain Carmel Cleary against her will and by force with the intention that she should have unlawful sexual intercourse with you.'
CONTRARY to Section 17 (1) of the Sexual Offences Act, 1956

Upon casual glance, Cannan seems a contradiction. At face value he appears to be a romanticist; his track record for charming countless women into bed is without fault. As Gilly Paige confirmed: 'John had women falling at his feet.'

During my journey into his life and crimes I met numerous, very attractive women, who testified that Cannan was the most romantic man they had ever encountered. Slim of build, he was tall, some may say handsome; he dazzled the girls with his smart line of chat. He was clean-cut, well spoken, personable, well turned out and, when he spotted a pretty girl who took his fancy, a surprise bunch of roses and a fine dinner (with champagne when he could afford it) followed in short order. Thereafter, many of his conquests (one-night stands or not) initially viewed him through rose-coloured spectacles, their very own Adonis-in-waiting. Their knight in shining armour had finally arrived on the scene. There was nothing colourless, drab, or redolent of stuffy crusty banality about John David Guise Cannan. He was witty, fun to tease, waggish, whimsical and droll. One look into his azure blue eyes simply swept the girls away.

However, as most of these women soon found out, John was like a flashy, storefront window – all gloss with the products advertised being presented in a 'buy me now' light, but the shelves inside the place were full of tat: bargain-basement goods that fell apart as soon as one got them home.

I also interviewed several other women whom John attempted to seduce, to include private investigator Tom Eyles's wife, who said that Cannan gave her the creeps. He struck her as 'smarmy', 'overconfident' and a 'letch'. I sensed that while Mrs Eyles supported her husband's work, she thought there was something dirty about a client who wanted surveillance carried out on Annabel Rose, who seemed to be a thoroughly decent solicitor and who was married to a barrister at that!

Louise (surname removed to protect her identity) recalled

Cannan coming into her furniture shop and ordering a coffee table and two armchairs for his flat at Foye House. He paid for them and wanted these items to be delivered, at once asking Louise if she could call round because he wanted her design expertise for other decorations and the like. However, Louise smelt a rat, unsettled by the way he had been 'looking her up and down'. The smell grew even stronger when she turned up at his flat, where a chilled bottle of champagne was waiting for her, along with an expensive box of gift-wrapped Swiss chocolates.

Despite the fact that Louise wore a wedding ring, Cannan was undeterred. Almost immediately he asked her about the state of her marriage. Was she happy, he wanted to know. 'I can put a lot of business your way,' he went on, quickly adding, 'How about I treat you to dinner at the Avon Gorge Hotel to discuss working together?'

Louise told me that John had boasted that he had his own, permanently reserved table at the hotel. 'He talked about the important motor trade clients he entertained there,' she recalled, adding, 'He said that he always picked up the bill and that they often used the jacuzzi, where they cemented any deals.'

'Christopher,' Louise continued, 'I threw the flowers and chocolates away as soon as I left Foye House and I told my husband about John's proposition. My husband was very concerned. He told me never to speak to John again. John pestered me for several days, and when I didn't respond he threatened to have the furniture sent back to us as being totally unsuitable. His calls were spiteful, very hurtful. It seemed that his mood had changed on a sixpence.'

I asked Louise if Cannan had ever returned the furniture. She told me, 'No! My husband intervened. He is a former rugby player. He told Cannan that if there was a problem then he should take it up with him. I was not privy to that telephone call, but Mr Cannan never troubled me again.'

As to John's contradiction in terms – even his motive for savagely committing rape and homicide – perhaps one might wish to add moral bigotry and misogyny to his characteristics.

When one reads about the above offences for which this 'love of mirrors man' was charged and sentenced to life in prison (with the possibility of parole), it does not take a psychiatrist to inform us that hideous Cannan consciously, or subconsciously, hated women with a passion: he used women, abused women. To him they were utterly disposable, only there to satisfy his perversions before being dumped, like so much trash.

What more can I say?

CASE STUDY: PSYCHOPATH
Kenneth Allen McDuff –
'Big Mac'

'I have been digging up the dirt roads around Waco for years. Every night I go out looking for my daughter [Regenia DeAnne Moore]. Please ask McDuff where she is so's I can give her a decent burial, just like Mrs McDuff would want for her son?'

– Barbara Carpenter, mother of Regenia to
the author during a tearful 1995 TV filmed
interview in Waco, Texas

Following my interviews with Kenneth Allen McDuff, Death Row, Ellis Unit, TX, McDuff was cajoled by me into revealing where he had disposed of seventeen-year-old Regenia 'Tina' DeAnne Moore, plus several other bodies. I cannot claim sole credit for the remarkable results for these were as a result of the sum total of efforts by dedicated law enforcement: US Marshals Service, Texas Rangers, Waco and Austin PD, the DA's office, with me being the man in the middle who gained exclusive access to the psychopathic mind of Kenneth McDuff.

I was merely the 'facilitator' if you will. Bizarrely enough, it was Kenneth's own mother, the 'Pistol Packin' Momma' Addie McDuff, whom I visited at her isolated Belton ranch. She had bought in Earl Grey tea especially for my visit and it was this now frail old lady who led her son up the garden path to the final recovery of bodies that were almost long forgotten.

> 'Christopher. I love Kenneth dearly. I have already lost two of my children and I am on my own now. Some say Kenneth was born on the wrong side of the tracks. He was always a pain to police. I tried my best for him. We didn't take kindly to folk meddling with us McDuffs. No, I cannot take the money [$500.00], but I will sign a letter to say that I have if it helps you. Kenneth need know nothing else.'
>
> – Addie McDuff to the author, Belton, Texas

During the dark hours of Tuesday, 15 October 1991, at a bridge traversing Tehuacana Creek alongside Highway 6, northeast of Waco, Texas, Kenneth McDuff had pulled off the road onto a very steep embankment down to the edge of a creek, where he drove under the bridge. Passing motorists could not have seen his car. The road here is a freeway – vehicles rushing overhead easily made enough noise to drown out any screams that part-time hooker, seventeen-year-old Regenia DeAnne Moore might have made.

A forensic team recovered Regenia's body from a sinkhole on Wednesday, 29 September 1998. She had been hog-tied by her pantyhose in such a way as to allow her to hobble to the spot where she was killed. After being missing for seven years, Regenia was finally going home to her mother.

CASE STUDY – PSYCHOPATH: KENNETH ALLEN MCDUFF

'I have serious health problems. They don't give vital medication to us, so if you want me to give up a body you give my Mom $500 so's I can get treatment. Get her to sign for it so's I can prove she has the money. Now fuck off!'

– Kenneth McDuff to the author and a film crew –
Death Row, Ellis Unit, TX, 1995

Frequently I'm asked who was the worst serial killer I have interviewed over the decades but they are all evil, believe me. However, McDuff stands out as being among the top five by miles. In the flesh he was tall, dour, icy-eyed, rangy, muscular and brutish. Certainly not a man to meet at any time of the day, he was callous, a dope-head, a heavy drinker, a man who boasted and bragged about his sexual prowess to any of the halfwits who looked up to him, either as a result of gross stupidity or fear.

Kenneth Allen McDuff was born on Sunday, 3 March 1946, at 201 Linden Street in the small, central Texas hamlet of Rosebud, Falls County. He was one of four children born to Addie L. McDuff and John Allen 'JA' McDuff. A hardworking, tough, no-nonsense man, JA did farm, masonry and concrete work. Way back then Addie was a hefty, domineering woman who ran a rundown Laundromat. She ruled the family roost with an iron fist and was known as 'The Pistol Packin' Momma' on account of her violent temper coupled with the habit of carrying a sidearm in her handbag, with which she would threaten anyone who crossed her, or her children.

'From the age of five there was murder in Kenneth's eyes. It was quite disturbing, I can tell you that.'

– Martha Royal, McDuff's fifth-grade teacher,
to the author in 1995.

With his IQ of 96, as a junior high schoolkid Kenneth was something of a loner. The town's residents called him the 'Bad Boy of Rosebud'. Even as a teenager he was feared and he beat up any youth who upset him. He was a sadistic bully who thought nothing of roaming the neighbourhood with a .22-calibre rifle, shooting any animal, bird or road sign that fell within his sights, so before I set my own sights on McDuff in an effort to give Regenia Moore's mother much-needed closure, I needed to visit Rosebud to find out where it all began.

This small town – that calls itself a 'city' – has a saying: 'All is Rosy in Rosebud', suggesting a picturesque, out-of-the-way area untroubled by violence. The place dates back to the 1836 War of Independence. Cotton-pickin' slavery was rife and between 1866 and 1890, the Chisholm Trail and Kansas railroads passed close by. During the Wild West days, Rosebud had no less than 11 saloons, all filled with drunken cowboys. Saturday-night shootouts were commonplace and even today the original calaboose remains intact, as does 'open-range law', meaning cows have the right of way.

After visiting with Martha Royal, I met the eighty-five-year-old mayor and Chief-of-Police Wanda Fischer for tea on the stoop of her spacious, clapboard house, just off Main Street. 'I apologise if my maid is black,' she said, adding, 'but she is clean, ya'll know.'

Also present was the aged Judge Ellen Roberts and the daughter (whose name now escapes me) of the publisher of the local newspaper. Ellen explained that she had also been a teacher at Rosebud High; that Kenneth had been incorrigible and she had gone out of her way to try and tame the boy and his elder brother, Lonnie, and that she had tried to help their mother Addie McDuff in every way she could. But these efforts were all to no avail. 'Something in the boys' value system taught them that what they did could not be wrong, because *they* did it,' the judge told me. 'What they said was the truth, because *they* said it; and whatever *they* believed was right, because *they* believed it.'

Wanda Fischer went a lot further, with: 'Like Lonnie, Kenneth existed in an extraordinary self-centred world. He had his own things, but what anyone else had could be stolen. When he spoke, others existed only to listen, and believe, tragically. When he grew to be nearly six-foot-four weighing over 250 pounds, loudmouth Kenneth would see other people as things to be used up. As a result, he took pleasure in performing before an audience. This, of course, led to his downfall.'

> 'McDuff didn't just kill his victims, he savaged them in unspeakable ways. He raped them with a sadism that made veteran police officers cringe. This killer blew off his victims' faces at point-blank range. He slashed and stabbed with knives, and bludgeoned with clubs. He crushed one victim's neck with a broomstick.'
>
> – Sheriff Larry Pamplin to the author at interview in June 1997.

Falls County Sheriff Larry Pamplin told me that McDuff had always been in trouble. In his teens, he had been involved in robberies with his brother, Lonnie, and, more than once, Larry said that he had tried to shoot their police car tyres out, but they always got clean away. And Kenneth McDuff hated Pamplin with a passion. Armed with this knowledge, I had another tool to be later used to get inside McDuff's head.

Although incomplete, Texas Department of Correction Records obtained by me show that what did matter was a string of robberies that eighteen-year-old Kenneth and other boys began committing in the spring of 1964. In March, he and an accomplice burgled Lotts Store in Falls County after cutting a bolt from the front door. They stole about $500 and cheques from the safe. In April, in Milam County, he did the same thing in three stores, taking assorted shotgun ammunition and two bars of ice cream. With yet another accomplice, he ripped off a coin-changer, taking about $20. Later, that same month, he broke into a machine shop in Bell County and stole a saw and tools. That very same night, he broke into a 7-Eleven store, but he could not open the safe and just took a handful of .22-calibre bullets. Kenneth and Lonnie tried to enter a boathouse near Temple, but they could not get in, so they had to leave empty-handed. Moving north to the little town of Troy, they broke into three more business premises.

On Friday, 17 April 1964, the cops finally rounded up Kenneth and his cronies. On 29 January the following year, he was sentenced to a total of 52 years in prison (four years each for thirteen offences) but each of the four-year sentences ran concurrently, meaning that for all practical purposes, he was merely sentenced to four years behind bars. On Wednesday, 10 March 1965, inmate #182279 McDuff was delivered to the Ferguson Unit of the Texas Department of Criminal Justice.

Somewhat remarkably, after serving just nine months and two weeks behind bars, on Wednesday, 29 December 1965, Kenneth Allen McDuff was paroled for the first time. Exactly twenty-six years later, he committed one of his most heinous crimes – at least as far as we know. Nevertheless, McDuff's accomplice in the murder of two schoolboys and a girl was Roy Dale Green. So, it was this man I needed to interview next if I were to try to understand what made McDuff's psychopathic mind tick.

Sheriff Larry Pamplin has since fallen from grace: sacked and then prosecuted for misappropriating his jail's inmate food allowance. With several hundred prisoners in his custody, this amounted to a not inconsiderable amount, and he deposited $23,574 into his back pocket. However, while still holding office, Larry drove me and my TV producer Frazer Ashford in his beat-up car to visit with Roy Dale Green and this was a ride one could never forget. His car, appeared to lack suspension as it screamed along the dusty dirt roads with shotgun ammunition rolling around the foot wells and the sheriff flicking up a finger of acknowledgement to every driver that passed us en route.

Mr Green was not too pleased to see his local sheriff standing at the front door of his lice-infested home. For a few seconds he blustered before Larry barged his way in. 'Ya'll just shut the FUCK UP!' Pamplin ordered. 'Ya sit the FUCK down and hear what this Englishman has to say. He has got questions for you so fuckin' sit down, dick weed. You are gonna tell him how you and McDuff killed those kids.'

What follows is a short summary of the Saturday, 6 August 1996 killing of three teenagers: Robert Brand (eighteen), his cousin, Marcus 'Mark' Dunnam (sixteen) and Robert's girlfriend, vivacious sixteen-year-old Edna Louise Sullivan, all of them pupils from Everman High School.

'The kids were on their knees, begging him [McDuff] not to shoot them. I saw the fire come out of the gun on the first shot. He shot six times into the boys now in the trunk of the car. He shot one twice in the head, and he shot the other boy four times in the head. A bullet went through the boy's arm as he tried to stop the fire. He raped the girl then he told her to get out of the car. He made her sit down on the gravel road, and he took about a three-foot piece of broomstick from his car and forced her head back until it was on the ground. He started choking her with the piece of broomstick. He mashed down hard, and she started waving her arms and kicking her legs. Then he snapped her neck with a cracking noise. We threw the body over a fence. He choked her some more. We put her in some kind of bushes there.'

– Extracted from Roy Dale Green's statement given to Detective Grady Hight, on Monday, 8 August 1966, and confirmed to this author during a 1997 interview

To try and give the reader some perspective, Edna Louise Sullivan was a popular girl who was about to begin her junior year at the end of August 1966. She liked basketball and played on Everman's team, but participated in little else because she had to work extra hard to keep up with some of her grades. At five-foot-two and weighing 110 lb, she was a small girl. Her shoulder-length hair resembled the style of the time: parted to one side and curled inward at the ends. With her family, she attended the First Baptist Church in Everman. Here, Edna, known to everyone as 'Louise', volunteered to help in the nursery. Around June or early July 1966, she started dating Robert Brand, who hailed from Alvarado, Mexico.

Robert was a handsome young man who loved music. He worked at various jobs, which paid for his guitar, and he played with a group of friends at clubs for teenagers. That summer his younger cousin from California, Marcus Dunnam, was staying with the Brand family in Alvarado. Marcus liked to play the drums and he, too, performed in informal teenage groups. He wanted to be a machinist in the Navy.

At about 7pm on Saturday, 6 August 1996, Louise left her Everman home with Robert and Marcus. Some time during the evening, probably while parked at a secluded baseball park in Robert's 1955 Ford, Kenneth Allen McDuff crept up to the youngsters and told them to get out or he would shoot them. After taking what money they had, he ordered them into the trunk of the Ford. With Dale Green driving and McDuff leading the way in his Dodge, they rode into the countryside near the Tarrant and Johnson County line near Burleson, Texas. They crossed a highway – probably US81 – and proceeded down gravel roads to a cow pasture. Here McDuff stopped, looked around, and then pronounced: 'This isn't a good place.' They backed out and drove to another more isolated field.

McDuff had learned from the mistakes that had put him in prison after his burglaries only a year earlier. On this night, and for the rest of his criminal career, he was as sophisticated and evidence-conscious as any criminal could be. During this event he took extraordinary care in deciding where he would commit these killings. He brought Roy Dale Green and his teenage captives to a tiny farm-to-market road numbered FM 1017. Mr and Mrs Raymond McAlister lived only 400 yards away. Mrs McAlister later testified that she saw two vehicles pull off the road and into a field at about 10.30pm. When another car passed by, the lights of the first two vehicles were switched off. As this was a spot used by courting youngsters, the farmer's wife was too tired to bother herself. She didn't hear any gunshots nor did she hear any of Louise's agonising screams.

The following morning, Bill Saunders of Burleson was driving west along FM 1017. He intended to go fishing when he spotted a 1955 Ford parked up against a fence. Thinking it unusual to see an unattended, parked car with the trunk opened, he stopped to check it out and was the first to witness the grisly scene. Tarrant County Sheriff Lon Evans later said that it 'looked like an execution'.

The next day, Monday, 8 August, over 2,000 people assisted in a search using helicopters, horses and motorcycles. The search, however, did not conclude until Roy Dale Green arrived to point out where Louise's body had been dumped. Overcome with fear, his conscience had got the better of him and he had confessed to being involved in the triple homicides with McDuff.

> 'Killing her was like squashing a cockroach.'
> – Kenneth McDuff, on killing
> Edna Louise Sullivan, to the author

In 1968, Kenneth McDuff received three death sentences, while Roy Dale Green was sentenced to 25 years. In 1976, after hearing voices and seeing visions that kept him awake at night, Green was transferred to Rusk State Hospital, Texas. He spent three years there before being released on parole in 1979. In all he served just 13 years for his part in the 'Broomstick Murders', so named because McDuff snapped Louise's neck using a broomstick, as described earlier.

In a damning indictment of the judicial process inmate #EX 485 McDuff walked to the electric chair twice before last-minute stays were granted. Thereafter, his sentence was commuted to life and, on Wednesday, 11 October 1989, with the Texas prison population bursting because of overcrowding, he applied for parole. Applications were rushed through without being read properly, so he became just another number among thousands to become one of the twenty former Death Row inmates and 127 murderers to be released. He was considered 'unlikely to kill again', set free and paroled to Milam County, having served 23 years in jail. Three days later, he killed again.

Sarafia Parker was a black female prostitute in her twenties. She stood at five-foot-six and weighed about 115–120 lb. A pedestrian walking along the 1500 block of East Avenue N.

CASE STUDY – PSYCHOPATH: KENNETH ALLEN MCDUFF

in Temple – a small city 48 miles due south of Waco – spotted Sarafia's corpse lying in a grassy field. She had been beaten and strangled no more than twenty-four hours before she was discovered.

Texas Ranger John Aycock later found a witness who thought he could place Ms Parker in a pick-up truck driven by Kenneth McDuff, on or around 12 October. On that day, McDuff had reported to his parole officer, whose office was in Temple, but that was all the cops had on him. The case remained unsolved until he confessed shortly before his execution on 17 November 1998..

> 'I don't know why people got so excited, I was just standing there with my knife.'
>
> — Kenneth McDuff

In July 1990, McDuff was returned to prison for violating his parole after making death threats against a black youth three days earlier. Although he used the services of black hookers, he was a virulent racist and, on 11 July, Kenneth and his nephew had gone into Rosebud. Outside a store on 301 Main Street, he sat on the sidewalk to listen to band practice. One of the band members, Robert McBee, stepped outside during a break (he had met McDuff for the first time the evening before). As the men sat on the kerb, four young black males walked by. McDuff greeted them with, 'Hey, nigger, I bet you don't like white boys any more than white boys like you.'

'No, I don't,' replied one of the lads.

After a heated exchange, McDuff retrieved a switchblade knife from his car and approached the most vocal of the young men: a sixteen-year-old high-school student who then ran into an alley bordering the building and grabbed two bricks with which to defend himself. Realising he was outnumbered, McDuff backtracked and returned to his car, humiliated in front of his friends because he thought that blacks were inferior to whites. He regarded himself as one of the few whites who had the courage to confront blacks, a skill he had learned in prison. In his car he carried what most people would call a 'tyre-thumper', which is long piece of round wood with a metal cap on one end and a leather wrist-strap at the other. McDuff, however, called it his 'nigger-thumper'. He also carried a hunting knife under the seat of his car.

'Yes, I bribed anyone who wanted to lock up my Kenneth. They all took my money including Larry Pamplin.' Addie McDuff, to the author at interview in 1997.

Later on during the evening of the racial confrontation, the black teenagers who had been accosted by McDuff, accompanied by one of their fathers, contacted the Justice of the Peace, Judge Ellen Roberts, and a complaint was drawn up. Never a man to turn down a bribe – especially from the wealthy McDuff family – the next day Sheriff Larry Pamplin called the judge, asking her if she might drop her complaint in favour of a lesser County Court Complaint and Warrant. However, McDuff was arrested on 18 July and held in the Bell County Jail pending a hearing then a trial. Just two days beforehand, he had wrecked yet another car, causing injuries to his sixteen-year-old nephew.

'McDuff is probably the most extraordinary violent criminal to set foot in Falls County, Texas.'
– Falls County District Attorney Thomas Sehon –
September 1990 letter to the Texas Department of
Criminal Justice

CASE STUDY – PSYCHOPATH: KENNETH ALLEN MCDUFF

On 11 September 1990, an 'Administrative Release Revocation Hearing' took place at the Bell County Jail and this psychopathic criminal did precisely what Ted Bundy had insisted on doing (see also page 116) – testifying on his own behalf. The official record of his testimony read as follows:

> RELEASEE [McDuff] essentially testified to being in Rosebud, Texas on the night of the alleged incident. RELEASEE was at the building where the band practices listening. RELEASEE walked out of the building and bumped into a black male. The black male stated to the RELEASEE "Watch where your [*sic*] going peckerwood." RELEASEE said the same back to the black male. RELEASEE went to his car and returned to the building where he listened to the band some more. RELEASEE walked out of the building at the intermission. A black male with a white woman came by and spoke to the RELEASEE. There were no threats exchanged. While outside a black kid came jitterbugging by speaking in slang. After passing by RELEASEE the black kid was some distance away when turned and assumed a fighting position. RELEASEE walked to the edge of the building where two black males were waiting with large pieces of debris in their hands. RELEASEE turned and went to the car where RELEASEE retrieved a knife. With the knife at his side RELEASEE asked the two men what they had in mind.

Had McDuff stopped there, his testimony might have worked in his favour. As this was more of a civil matter, Sheriff Pamplin was not required to turn up to give his evidence. The four men who had made the complaint failed to materialise. The only evidence came from Robert McBee and his was hearsay at best. For a few moments it seemed like McDuff would beat the rap and walk free but he could not shut up. He had to pontificate, in the process revealing the depths of his racism, and in so doing dug his own grave: 'Everywhere people go, blacks intimidate whites,' he raged.

At this point in the testimony, McDuff's attorney had to shout at his client in order to stop him testifying, but he refused and went on to make more wild assertions as to how different racial groups react in social situations and how he was intimidated by black people.

The hearing ended at 1.10pm and McDuff – now tagged inmate #227123 – returned to the state prison system, exactly one year after he had been released. Two months later, on Tuesday, 18 December, he was out on parole, yet again.

The year 1991 found the ever-mobile forty-five-year-old McDuff frequently changing work and his locations. At the start of the year, under the initial supervision of his Temple parole officer, he was assigned to the Dallas District because he had found employment as a warehouse forklift operator in that area. Two weeks later, he was fired.

McDuff returned to Temple, where he tried to move back in with his parents, but they would have none of it. However, they did fund his stay in the Jean Motel. Then McDuff cottoned on to another wheeze: he discovered that he could have access to a private room, eat three square meals a day in a cafeteria, receive money for subsistence – even during the holidays – and receive an education. All he had to do was enroll at college under Project RIO (Re-integration of Offenders), a course intended to turn untrained, uneducated ex-convicts into employable workers. He started this programme at the Texas State Technical Institute (TSTI), Waco, on Monday, 21 January 1991.

CASE STUDY – PSYCHOPATH: KENNETH ALLEN MCDUFF

Now McDuff was in his element. On a campus where women outnumbered men by nearly four to one, it was the ideal set-up: a nearly maintenance-free room, someone to cook for him, access to young men, some of whom were mightily impressed, or afraid of his 250-lb frame, plenty of vulnerable and gullible women, the opportunity to deal in drugs and the location being remote, all of which suited him perfectly.

Living in room #118 at Sabine Hall, he entertained a string of prostitutes, planned heists and burglaries, threatened other students, attacked people on and off the college grounds and stole anything not nailed down. It got to the point where none of the residents wanted anything more to do with him; they hid when he was around. He was dangerous, downright crazy, yet it seemed no one had the courage to alert the authorities to the madman living on the campus.

At five-foot-five and weighing a mere 115 lb, Brenda Kay Thompson, aged thirty-seven, looking more like fifty, was a two-star hooker living on Delano Street in Waco. She plied her nocturnal trade on 'The Cut' and 'The Strip' (Highway 77 or the 'Old Dallas Highway'). Not exactly Miss Apple Pie, emaciated Brenda, with her missing teeth and a birthmark on the back of her neck, had more tattoos than a fairground worker and a criminal rap sheet as long as time itself. There were bench warrants out for her failure to answer bail for perjury. She had a federal record for taking stolen autos across a state line. There was larceny, violence, moving traffic violations, trespassing charges and numerous counts of forgery. If the US Marshals didn't seize her soon, she'd kick up dust and disappear. Like cheap guinea perfume Brenda had 'Interstate Flight' plastered all over her worn-out face.

At 11.10pm on Friday, 6 September 1991, Brenda had been

arrested on 'The Strip' for offering sex to an undercover vice cop and she was taken to the McLennan County Jail. Within hours she was bailed; five weeks later, she climbed into McDuff's red pickup truck in Waco.

Records show that on Wednesday, 9 October 1991, Waco Police had set up a drivers' licence and insurance checkpoint near the junction of Miller Street and Faulkner Lane. But the cops had another ploy in mind: to discourage 'Johns' (punters looking for prostitutes) from visiting 'The Cut'. At 9.30pm, officers stopped a car in which Brenda, wearing red polyester pants, was a passenger. She was arrested and at 12.32am, booked into the jail, only to secure her release eight minutes later through a bail-bond service. Immediately she returned to 'The Cut', where she agreed terms with McDuff and they took a ride – straight to the junction where the cops were positioned, so they tried to flag him down.

With the red-and-blue strobes lighting up his cab, he stopped some fifty feet from the barrier. An officer walked towards the truck, shining a flashlight into McDuff's face. Suddenly, Brenda began screaming and kicking. To the cop it appeared that she had her hands tied behind her back. She lay back and started kicking out the windscreen with such force it shattered the glass, and she continued to kick and struggle.

Almost immediately, McDuff floored the accelerator. He drove straight at the officers, who moved quickly to get out of the way. Scrambling to their cars, they sped after him south down Miller Street towards Waco Drive, where he turned off his lights to disappear into the darkness, taking Brenda Thompson with him. Using skills developed decades earlier when outrunning Sheriff Larry Pamplin, he eluded police by going the wrong way along one-way streets. He turned west on US84 towards Gatesville, then north on Gholson Road for eight miles until he arrived at a wooded area. Knowing what a terrible temper McDuff had, and in the knowledge that his prey had wrecked his windscreen, Brenda undoubtedly suffered a tortuous and excruciating death.

Just a month before his execution, McDuff told police where to find the body. It was discovered near Gholson Road on Saturday, 3 October 1998.

Although much younger and more reckless than Brenda Thompson, Regenia 'Gina' DeAnne Moore was certainly cut from the same cloth. Aged twenty-one, she was even smaller, at five-foot-four in height, weighing a mere 110 lb. She already had three children, who had been adopted by relatives. Like Brenda, tattooed Gina had a crack habit. She was also a heavy drinker with a history of forgery and would steal money from her clients in a dangerous practice known as 'clipping'. However, while her teeth were perfect, her blonde hair streaked with red and well-kempt, already it was apparent that she was physically somewhat decrepit and her face bore testimony to this. Her blue eyes sparkled, but like Thompson's, they were sunken into sockets surrounded by bags and she had a ruddy complexion that seemed to be the mark of working the streets, where booze, drugs, beatings, venereal disease and a poor diet all took their toll.

Somewhat coincidentally, Gina's last arrest had taken place on the same night that Brenda was pulled in – 9 October – by the very same police who would later chase McDuff in his red pickup. She was found to be in possession of rocks of cocaine. Taken to the McLennan County Jail, she too was quickly bailed only to return to 'The Cut'.

Gina was last seen alive and apparently arguing with McDuff at around 11.30pm on Tuesday, 15 October 1991. She was sitting in his truck at the corner of Faulkner and US 77, within sight of a fast-food joint called the Chicken Shack and the Inn 7 Motel before they drove off. Her body (as has been described at the start of this chapter) was discovered on Wednesday, 29 September 1998, shortly before McDuff's execution.

'It was like McDuff saying; "Okay, Regenia's gone – Big Deal".'

– ATF Special Agent Charles Meyer

Regenia's mother, Barbara, had become convinced that McDuff was responsible for her daughter's disappearance, even more so because it was now the talk of 'The Cut'. But the courageous mother persisted in tackling him. Visiting him at Sabine Hall, on 19 October, she accused him of killing her daughter. He reacted, shouting: 'I dropped the bitch off, I didn't even fuck her!' When she asked him about his cracked windscreen, he blandly claimed: 'So fuckin' what? I parked it in the wrong neighbourhood!'

The day after Barbara met with McDuff, five Waco police officers called on him too. He ran rings around them. One of the cops actually recognised him as being the driver who had tried to run him down. Outside, in the parking lot, another Waco officer who'd been at the checkpoint spotted McDuff's red pickup truck with the smashed windscreen, which had been kicked from the inside out and shattered. However, the inside of the vehicle had been washed clean. McDuff claimed that he had picked Gina up at the corner of Faulkner and the Loop. He agreed that he picked up prostitutes regularly down at 'The Cut' and stated that after they had done 'the business', he had dropped her off. Eight days later, on 28 October, despite the fact that they knew he was a former Death Row inmate who had killed three times previously, that he had a history of extreme violence against young men and women, and that he was a hardened criminal, the police dropped the matter of aggravated assault against McDuff because other hookers had not been 'placed in fear of their lives'.

Life went on at 'The Cut' as if nothing had ever happened to Regenia Moore and Brenda Thompson and the police's attitude was one of: 'The girls behaved in a way that almost invited death,' as a US Marshal explained to me during my time in Waco. He went on to say: 'They boozed up, used drugs, had every venereal disease under the sun, even AIDS. Some get beat up, others killed. Catching a virus is the least of their problems. Maybe Gina and Brenda ran off and married billionaires and rode around in expensive cars. Nobody really gave a fuck.' Nor did McDuff, it seemed.

Sometime around early November, Kenneth returned the red pickup truck to his father. JA didn't even question him about the smashed windscreen. Even more remarkably, although the WPD had run the licence tag back to JA, they had not even bothered to visit McDuff Sr. Without wheels, the over-confident Kenneth McDuff came up with yet another scam – he borrowed a 1985 two-door Ford Thunderbird from one of his sisters. The powerful, mid-sized car, with over 100,000 miles on the clock, was perfect and soon he was tearing up the dirt roads of Texas, thieving, drug dealing and attacking people all over again.

In Austin, way back in 1990/91, a drive-thru car wash existed on the corner of West Lynn and West Fifth Street and here, on Sunday, 29 December 1991, twenty-eight-year-old Colleen Reed met Kenneth Allen McDuff for the first and last time. Standing at five-foot-three and weighing 115 lb, with dark brown hair and brown eyes, she was petite, hardworking and a scrupulously honest woman.

Although plenty of photographs exist of Colleen, for us the most important were two black-and-white shots taken at precisely at 8.45pm at an ATM machine outside a popular Austin grocery store called Whole Foods, situated on 914 North Lamar Boulevard. Here, she deposited $200 – a Christmas gift from her father (the transaction number was 7967). In the store she bought a gallon of milk and a bottle of vitamins. She paid the $3.12 bill in cash and left the premises to get into her Miata car at 8.59pm – the car needed a wash.

The car-wash address on Google Maps will show the reader the exact location. What the map will not portray – and the police photos will – is that the stalls were painted various shades of brown, covered in parts with sheet metal and with white cinder block walls. In those days it was a ramshackle joint; on the periphery were oak trees that still stand witness today. Across the street were the offices of the Travis County Democratic Party. To the west, across the street from West Lynn, was Don's Depot – a piano bar and saloon with an outside stoop, with two old railroad cars out back. Colleen parked her car in the third stall.

McDuff, along with a thirty-four-year-old convict called Alva Frank Worley, had already been drinking from a six-pack as they cruised around Austin before they spotted Colleen with a wet sponge in her hand. She was wearing gold-rimmed glasses, blue jeans, a T-shirt and a black-and-white Nike jacket. Seconds later, witnesses heard a short scream, a car door being slammed shut, and they watched in amazement as a light-coloured car screeched away along Powell Street, leaving a cloud of exhaust smoke in its wake.

CASE STUDY – PSYCHOPATH: KENNETH ALLEN MCDUFF

'I heard an all-out serious scream. I'm from New York
and I know what a real scream sounds like.'
– Mike Goins, witness to Colleen Reed's abduction

What follows is an horrific account of abduction, torture, rape
and murder most foul. It is no Stephen King invention either, for
it illustrates how a sado-sexual psychopath's mind truly works
and this is how the tragic events unfolded as related to police
– and this sequence was confirmed to me when I interviewed
McDuff on Death Row, after which he finally gave up and told
of the place where Colleen took her last, precious breath.

After his arrest, according to Alva Frank Worley, McDuff had
picked him up in the Thunderbird at around, as he said, 'Six or
seven that night.'

'We went to Love's Truck Stop, near temple, where he got
gas. I understood that we were going to get some speed or coke,
whatever we could find,' Worley told police. 'We stopped at a
Conoco truck stop on Interstate 35, on the northbound side
of the highway, past Jarrell. I bought a six-pack of Budweiser
Longnecks. We had already drunk a six-pack, or better,
before that.'

'Big Mac' then drove on to Austin, onto Sixth Street,
where they bought hamburgers at a Dairy Queen, after which
McDuff spotted Colleen Reed in the car wash. Within minutes
he had the young woman by the throat. According to Worley,
McDuff dragged her towards his car. 'She was shouting like
hell,' he later told Tim Steglich, of the Bell County Sheriff's
Department, adding, 'She was screaming, "Not me, not me!
Please let me go."'

While you can read those words, can you even imagine her
terror? Begging for her life, Colleen was subjected to what can
only be described as a ride into Hell as the threesome headed

north along Interstate 35 towards Round Rock, near the Old Chisholm Trail, where they stopped. Climbing into the rear seat with Colleen, McDuff ordered Worley to drive some more. The raping before the torture and the killing had only just started. He taunted her, hit her, beat her around the face and demanded oral sex. 'He forced her down onto him and she gagged,' Worley told Investigator Steglich.

Colleen Reed met her dreadful end on an old abandoned road within scream-shot of JA and Addie's ranch on the corner of 317 and Cedar Creek Road, a track almost overgrown with bushes, trees bordering both sides. I visited this place with Tim Steglich and a TV film crew. As Tim recounted the murder, he said on camera: 'You know, Chris, I often drive past this track. I always remember that poor girl,' and he had tears in his eyes, adding: 'What a terrible place to die!'

I spent some time with my TV crew talking to Tim Steglich at the very spot where Colleen was repeatedly raped, while Worley, allegedly, sat passively in the driver's seat of the Thunderbird to watch McDuff burn the young woman with lighted cigarettes. 'By that time,' Worley explained, 'she was passive. Just sobbing, which made Mac madder than hell, before he snapped her neck. He threw her like a sack of potatoes into the trunk of his car.'

> 'You want a body, you want Coleen's body. That's gonna cost you $500.'
> – Kenneth McDuff, filmed interview with the author:
> Death Row, Ellis Unit, Texas

Worley was later charged with rape and murder after he confessed to a relative. A manhunt for McDuff was launched but not before he had killed twice more. The body of Colleen Reed was recovered shortly before his execution.

CASE STUDY – PSYCHOPATH: KENNETH ALLEN MCDUFF

'Kay was a street person, but a sweet woman who loved children.'
— McLennan County Deputy Sheriff Richard Stroup
referring to Valencia Kay Joshua

Twenty-two-year-old part-time prostitute Valencia Kay Joshua had a troubled life as a juvenile, a criminal record as an adult, and she was on probation too. A thin, black female, about five-foot-seven, it is believed she had only been in Waco a couple of weeks before a witness saw her for the last time on 24 February 1992. Joshua had been looking for Kenneth McDuff in his dorm room at TSI. She was wearing a dark windbreaker, tight blue jeans and had an ornate barrette in her hair.

On Sunday, 15 March 1992, walkers found a human skull that had been exposed by animals behind the James Connally Municipal Golf Course and close to McDuff's college. Police were called, and nearby, in this mosquito-infested place, they uncovered a naked body buried in soft, moist clay, along with a cloisonné hair comb. The inlaid pattern depicted an orange butterfly amid green leaves and red flowers. This had been Valencia's proudest possession. She was identified by means of fingerprints. At her autopsy it was determined that she died as the result of strangulation.

McDuff hinted at his involvement in this, his penultimate murder, for the first time during my interviews with him on Death Row. 'Yeah, I recall a black bitch knocking on my door around that time. That's all you're gonna get,' he said, wearing a smug grin.

And that is how McDuff played me in his brief correspondence and during interviews. Smug, cocky, overconfident, whining about his current ill health, he was the manipulating psychopath if ever there was one, but I had his measure. However, I needed to find the deposition site of Regenia Moore's body, so I bit my tongue. Regenia's mother, Barbara, had begged me to ask McDuff where her daughter was. She wanted to give the girl a decent burial, just as Addie McDuff would wish for her son. Once I had that information, and only then, would I come down hard on Kenneth Allen McDuff and wipe the smile off his face. When I did, I came down on him like a ton of bricks to the extent that he went berserk. As a result of my actions, this monster had to be electronically stunned by guards before being dragged back to his cell.

'We had a feeling that this is bad, this can't wait.'
– Bill Johnston, United States Attorney on the initial
disappearance of Melissa Northrop

It was 4 July 1995. The Americans love to celebrate Independence Day so as a special treat, US Marshals Mike and Parnell McNamara took me to dinner in Waco. Along with Assistant US Attorney Bill Johnston, I tucked in to the largest slab of beef I'd ever seen accompanied by ranch fries and gravy, while the McNamara brothers went for the crocodile. I was soon to meet the formidable Addie McDuff on her isolated ranch but first they wanted to tell me all about Kenneth's final victim, twenty-two-year-old Melissa Northrop, who went missing from her place of work, at the Quik Pak #8 store, off New Road, alongside Interstate 35.

During the early morning of Monday, 1 March 1992, the two-and-half months' pregnant Melissa was working the early shift in Quik Pak when McDuff strolled in. He had parked his Thunderbird close by. Ironically, he had briefly worked at Quik Pak and had actually met Melissa's husband, Aaron, so he knew the layout of the store. McDuff's intention now was to rob the place and then abduct, rape and murder Melissa.

Described as four-foot-eleven and weighing 100 lb, she lived with her husband, Aaron, at 3014 Pioneer Circle, Waco, and when she did not return home and failed to answer his many calls, Aaron jumped into his father's Ford Taurus and raced 15 miles to the store. When he arrived at around 4.20am he found a bewildered customer waiting to pay for his purchases. When asked where Melissa was, the man gestured as if to say he didn't know. Aaron immediately jumped over the sales counter, hit the 'No Sale' button and opened the register: all of the money was gone. He saw his wife's purse under the counter, where she always put it, and a notepad full of prospective names for the baby that was still in her womb. Rushing outside, he frantically searched the entire area but her heavily-used orange Buick Regal with a white top, licence tag TX LP287 XHV, was not there. At precisely 4.47am, he dialled 911.

Police arrived on the scene within minutes and reckoned that $250 had gone missing from the register. The cops then woke up several drivers who were sleeping in their cars nearby. No one had seen or heard anything. Nobody had witnessed Melissa's abduction at all, or had they?

Richard Bannister and his wife Ollie were staying at The New Road Inn. They had been at a bar called Misty's until it closed at 2am. After putting his heavily intoxicated wife to bed, Richard decided to take in some fresh air and walk his cocker spaniel, which had been locked in their motel room for several hours. Out in the gravel-covered lot, Bannister saw a man answering McDuff's description trying to 'nudge-start' (jump start) a burnt-orange Buick Regal with a Ford Thunderbird. He offered to help but the man yelled: 'Nope, I got it!' Giving a further description to police, the witness recalled the man was wearing a short-sleeved shirt and that one of the sleeves was dirty; he also had a cut under his right eye. Bannister had not seen a woman, but someone else had.

Louis Bailey, who was on his route delivering issues of the *Dallas Morning News*, drove past Quik Pak when he spotted a car parked across the access road. The driver's side door was open and the interior light was on. He looked towards Quik Pak but saw no one.

Then another witness came forward after seeing the Quik Pak store swarming with cops. A local man, who knew Melissa, saw her car heading north on Interstate 35 at around 4.15am. She was in the front passenger seat and looked frightened.

But what of McDuff's Thunderbird? Police soon located the locked car parked close up to a truck in the lot. After moving it to Big Boys Wrecker Service in Robinson, two FBI agents watched the inventory being taken down by the local cops, who found numerous documents with McDuff's name all over them: a wallet holding his driver's licence, a Goodyear Tire Protection Plan, a crumpled-up, white cowboy hat and a receipt for petrol purchase at the Quik Pak dated 29 February 1992 – a date when McDuff had worked at the store.

Within hours McDuff's details were placed on the US 'Most Wanted' list, his full details including a description of him being plastered over newspaper articles and on television.

Mark Davis, a former college student pal of McDuff's, came forward to say that on an earlier occasion, 'Big Mac' had tried to enlist him to rob the Quik Pak store. Indeed, Bray went even further. He said that 'Big Mac' had boasted that the easiest way to get rid of a body was to slit open the abdomen and throw the body into water. Hookers and boozers, students and local villains, indeed almost everyone who had been robbed, threatened or beaten half-senseless by McDuff, called the police offering information. Yet, despite all of this, when the cops knocked on Addie McDuff's door, she claimed to know nothing, adding: 'You're here to hurt my boy. My gate is right down there. Close it on your way out!'

But what of Melissa Northrop? Although the precise details of her journey into Hell will never be known, we do know that McDuff drove her some one hundred miles north on Interstate highway 35 to an area southeast of Dallas County, near a small rural farming community called Combine. On the morning of 1 March 1992, he turned left from Bilingsday Road onto an unmarked dirt track called 'James Road', whereupon Melissa's car became bogged down in mud. McDuff then death-marched the terrified woman one and a half miles across open fields, over five-strand wire fences to a gravel pit just off Bois D'Arc Road.

As the US Marshal brothers told me: 'Undoubtedly Melissa begged McDuff to let her live. Like his other victims, she could not have known that such pleas only fuelled his lust for brutality and torture. He took off her socks and laces from her tennis shoes and made ligatures to tie her feet and her hands behind her back. This motherfucker not only killed the poor girl but the baby growing inside her womb.'

Except for his only male victims, Robert Brand and Mark Dunnam (who were shot to death at point-blank range), all of McDuff's victims died slow, agonising deaths. But, unlike as he did with most of his other female victims, McDuff did not bury Melissa. 'After I used her up,' he told me, 'I threw her into the flooded gravel pit. To me she was just trash.'

On Friday, 6 March 1992, Melissa's car was found abandoned by patrolwoman Aletha Jesettes of the Dallas County Sheriff's Office. She called it in and now the search for the missing woman focused on the immediate area. Her body was discovered at 6.00pm on Sunday, 26 April by Jeffery Heard – his uncle,

Henry 'Red' Heard, leased the gravel pits from the Forge Gravel Company for fishing. Jeff had put his boat into the water and after a short while he noticed something strange floating in the pit: it was the body of Melissa. She had been there since the day McDuff had killed her.

At the time of recovery she was floating in about four feet of water, about five feet from the shore and about one and a half miles from where her car had been discovered by Officer Aletha Jesettes. The corpse was in an advanced state of decomposition. Time, water and small animals had ravaged her. Had she not been found on 26 April, or soon afterwards, she might not have been discovered at all. Her hands had been tied behind her back by shoestrings and a jacket pulled down over her arms as if to immobilise her. Her ankles had been tied together at one time; remnants of black shoestrings were found around each ankle. Part of the lower torso was missing.

Deputy Parker recalled that: 'She may have been weighted down for a while. I guess that gas brought her to the surface. Her bra was still in place, but there was no clothing from the waist down.'

Nearby, someone spotted a black, high-top tennis shoe bobbing in the water. It was a size six shoe with no laces belonging to Melissa Northrop.

> 'Holy fuckin' shit! This guy is a ringer for Richie Fowler [Kenneth McDuff]. He's been in my fuckin' truck!'
> – Gary Smithee, employee of the Longview Trash Disposal Systems

McDuff's days were now numbered – eight days, to be precise. While he ate his supper, a dumpster driver called Gary Smithee would soon collect the $5,000 reward for locating the monster after watching a video recording of *America's Most Wanted* on TV. Only the day before, 'Big Mac' had been in Smithee's truck.

Thirty-six-year-old Smithee arrived home on Friday, 1 May 1992 and settled down to watch a recording of *America's Most Wanted*. Within moments he put down his beer and peered closely, then even closer towards the screen. The man he saw as being one of the most wanted killers in the US was looking right back at him. Gary knew him as 'Richard Dale Fowler' – a very recently employed co-worker, a braggart who, from the outset, constantly boasted about his sexual prowess, particularly with young women.

> 'We went looking to run down dirt and we knew just where to find it – on a trash site!'
> – US Marshal Parnell McNamara on arresting Kenneth McDuff – to the author

Smithee thought long and hard about pointing an accusatory finger at McDuff. First, he talked to a colleague before telephoning the Kansas City PD. Sergeant Johnson took the call and immediately ran a search through their computer for the name 'Richard Fowler'. Back came a description that matched both Fowler and McDuff. A man giving the name of Richard Fowler had been arrested during a prostitution sting and charged with soliciting an undercover cop. Running a further search, the detective noted that Fowler's fingerprint record card matched those of McDuff's. ATF agents would later interview the real Fowler, who was from Louisiana. He had last seen his tattered Social Security card when he visited a pool hall and left it with an attendant to check out a cue stick. Although law enforcement had their suspicions, how the card went from the attendant's hand to McDuff's back pocket is anyone's guess.

What is now known, however, is that on Tuesday, 10 March 1992, McDuff stayed at a Salvation Army shelter in Tulsa, Oklahoma. He booked in using Fowler's identity card. At about 6.00pm on Sunday, 15 March, McDuff/Fowler walked into the Kansas City Rescue Mission, Kansas City, Missouri. He stayed at the shelter from the 15–18 March free of charge. Men wishing to stay more than five days at the mission had to pay $1.00 per night, or they could join a work detail to pay for their keep.

On 19 March, he signed on with a job-finder agency called Dixie Temporaries, who found him part-time employment working a garbage collection service for $190 per week. For the next few weeks, he never missed a day of work and was always on time. McDuff then acquired a flat at Clyde Manor Apartments, in Kansas City. He shared the place with a fellow sanitation worker called Francis and, by all accounts, both men, who were of equal size and weight, got on very well, 'although he talked a lot of bullshit,' Francis later told the police.

Following Gary Smithee's telephone call in anticipation of collecting the $5,000 reward on the fugitive's head, time was now running out for McDuff. Sergeant Johnson learned from Longview Trash Disposal Systems which vehicle he would be driving in and determined the route it would take on Monday, 4 May. It was going to a landfill site on 85th Street and Hickman Mills, south of Kansas City, between 1.00pm and 2.00pm. The police set up a seven-man surveillance team working under the guise of a commercial vehicle stop at 85th and Prospect.

'We wanted to make sure the location we picked was isolated in the event of trouble,' Sgt Johnson explained to me. 'McDuff was reported to be armed and dangerous. The site we picked was the type where some vehicles were routinely stopped, and there were no people around.'

To lend further authenticity to their plans, the police borrowed a car that Kansas City Engineers used for their routine truck inspections. When the vehicle (No. 103), in which McDuff was riding, approached at 1.32pm, a lone officer waved it to the checkpoint. Instantly smelling a rat, McDuff attempted to get out and make a run for it, but with sawn-off shotgun muzzles rammed into each ear, one officer screamed: 'Move and you're FUCKIN' dead in stereo!' so McDuff stopped dead in his tracks and immediately clammed up, like a captured crocodile with its jaw tied shut.

My initial interest in Kenneth Allen McDuff sprang from a meeting with two FBI agents in Oregon. They suggested that if I wanted to get to grips with a savage homicidal psychopath then I should travel south and hook up with the McNamara brothers, two legendary US Marshals based in Waco. They mentioned McDuff; that he was, without doubt, the worst of his kind in the Lone Star State's history, and that they could make a call and smooth the way for me.

Arriving, first in Dallas Fort Worth, then staying at motels around Texas, I networked town, county, state and federal law enforcement to meet some of the toughest, and sometimes the dumbest cops, one can imagine. And this networking also enabled me to interview another heinous killer, the infamous Henry Lee Lucas, who, at that time, was also on Texas's Death Row at Ellis 1 Unit (now closed).

Getting to interview Kenneth McDuff was the easy part for me. As he was a psychopath, I knew that he would have a massive ego and would want to talk to a guy, and a British film crew, who had come all the way across 'The Pond' to see him. I would be a 'mug' he could manipulate. This would be his brief moment; one where he could bathe in the limelight, and, as the camera rolled, all he could do was complain that he had been wrongly convicted and unjustly treated. 'I am seriously ill. I need medication and I can't pay for it,' he moaned. 'I can tell you a lot more,' he added, 'and $US500 would get me the medication I need here.'

So, I allowed him to have his say, with the occasional nod of phoney sympathetic agreement from me. However, for my part, I now had a more serious task in mind: to try and help Regenia Moore's mother, Barbara, get closure and be able to find her dead daughter and give her a decent burial.

I explained to McDuff that perhaps I could raise the money he needed, but in doing so there would have to be a trade-off. 'You know, Ken,' I said, 'but I'm looking at Regenia Moore. Maybe we can work on that?'

On my second visit to Ellis 1 Unit, McDuff was a little more aggressive towards me, but I now had his measure. I could see right inside his head and I could see this criminal's mind working – perhaps better than he knew himself. 'Ken, you are a dead cert for the murder of Melissa Northrop because I have been through the evidence against you with a fine toothcomb. I have met most of the cops involved and that murder is down to you,' I said, all matter-of-fact. 'I have seen the forensics, Ken. Your hairs were found in Melissa's car. I have been through your history and leaving aside all of the other stuff, if you want the $US500, it's in my back pocket right now.' And I flashed the bills, the bait.

McDuff's expression was one of descending blackness: he stared right through me. My very mention that I had been talking with cops, lots of cops, including Sheriff Larry Pamplin, along with Roy Dale Green and his other weak-willed cohort, Worley, was infuriating him, for he realised that he no longer had control.

People like the McDuffs of this world are cowards. I had

learned that when he was faced-up to by a male of equal size, or by a group of black men – whom he hated with a passion – he always backed down. He was a sadistic bully who preyed on petite, vulnerable women. A braggart and a pathological liar, he was used to always getting his own way. I also knew that he would sell someone out for the price of a case of beer. To him the $500 handout was worth giving up the final resting place of Regenia Moore – she meant nothing more to him than that.

> 'I can't take the cash from you in here. Visit my Mom, give it to her. If you can bring me a signed receipt from her showing she's got the money, I'll give you that bitch, Moore. Mom can then put the money in my account here.'
> — Kenneth McDuff, to the author at Ellis 1 Unit

This statement from Kenneth McDuff was the first admission to anyone that he had abducted, then murdered Regenia Moore. All I had to do now was confront the 'Pistol Packin' Momma': a woman who kept two vicious Rottweilers on her isolated ranch that even police feared, and I would have to get her to play ball with me. Here was a mother who once told police: 'Junior ain't never done anything wrong in all his life.'

And I had to walk up her long driveway, alone!

Addie (now deceased) was a protective mother, despite her son's evil deeds. She gave me an hour of her time, during which she rooted through boxes, digging out old photos and other material that might have interested me. I mentioned Kenneth's request for $US500, and would she accept it on his behalf and give me a note as a receipt? She refused the money but signed a receipt anyway. Bless her! We had both conned McDuff but he didn't know it – just yet.

Later, I asked McDuff why he had not settled down and started some form of meaningful relationship with a woman. 'I feel very old and tired, Chris,' he replied, looking extremely sorry for himself. 'Once I wanted a wife and a family, just like other people do. Right now I am like a man in the desert that is thousands of miles from the nearest water, with no possibility of reaching water, but keeps walking anyway. I don't know why I keep walking. Is it some inter-instinct [*sic*] to strive on?'

Changing his theme in a heartbeat, he said, 'Now, let talk about money. You showed me the receipt and I've told the cops where Regenia is. Well, on this one, I'm like the man in the desert that struck gold, and can only carry out what he can carry. I only have need for a few thousand dollars, like for burial expenses, and to maintain myself while I live. I will charge whomever $US700 per [outstanding] body. An international money order of postal orders will do. Have it sent to my inmate's trust fund in my name. That way, I don't get shafted, you know.'

Ever the sneering, manipulative psychopath to the end, McDuff must have thought that I also lived in his world, where elephants flew, lead balls bounce and fairies reign supreme. He didn't need a cent for burial expenses, which are provided gratis to executed men and women in 'The Lone Star State'. He didn't even need to pay for a plot. Peckerwood Cemetery, in Huntsville, is the final resting place for hundreds of killers who have crossed the line.

McDuff never received a dollar from me or anyone else. However, shortly before he was executed, he did lead police to several other body deposition sites where human remains were found.

After refusing a last meal, at 5.44pm on Tuesday, 17 November 1998, he looked scared as the witness viewing room curtains were drawn back. Warden Jim Willett asked him if he had any last words to say into the microphone above his head. McDuff simply replied, 'I'm ready to be released. Release me.'

US Marshal Parnell McNamara gently placed his hand on the shoulder of seventy-four-year-old Jack Brand.

'I've been waiting for this for thirty-two years,' said the father of Robert Brand, who was murdered by McDuff in 1966.

'Are you all right?' Parnell asked quietly.

'I feel like thirty-two years have been lifted from my life,' the old man said before he broke down in tears.

But I want to leave this chapter on a high note and it is all about 'Don't Mess with Texas'. This was something my TV producer, Frazer Ashford, whom I mentioned earlier, realised when he sat down in the blistering Texas heat on a Fire Ant hill in Denton County – can you imagine the pain? I call it payback time for him telling everyone that I was often a pain in his ass!

In dusty, tumbleweed Wichita Falls, Sheriff 'Hound Dog' Conway showed me the old courthouse, the gallows still there, as was the hanging tree in the town square with a rusty calaboose out back. We had coffee in a café – a former bank. There, still evident, were bullet holes in the outside walls – a legacy of Bonnie & Clyde.

I met with Wise County Sheriff Phil Ryan and Denton County Sheriff Weldon Lucas – the latter being the man who arrested the serial killer Henry Lee Lucas, whom I also interviewed, and I saw the chain gangs toiling the highways and byways.

Actually, I love Texas to bits!

CASE STUDY: SAVAGE
John 'JR' Robinson

'Robinson? I wouldn't leave him alone in my yard to
wash my truck. That sumbitch would steal the truck, the
hose, the faucet [tap], and carry away as much fuckin'
water as he could.'

> – Jeff Tietz, former Kansas City police officer,
> to the author

Consider the case of Mr J. R. Robinson. Is it possible to imagine
none of the doctors, high-flying businessmen and women, his
previous employers, didn't cotton onto this man's true nature
before being taken to the cleaners? The list even includes
Harvard Medical School-educated Dr Wallace Graham, former
Brigadier General of the US Air Force and the personal White
House physician to none other than President Harry S. Truman
and his wife Elizabeth.

Surely one would imagine that someone among this legion
of decent citizens – and this may have included you and me
– would have had just a teeny-weeny inkling that JR was a

thoroughly evil man. But, you see, we didn't spot Dr Shipman either, did we?

So, here we are again, this time with family in tow. Let's imagine walking slowly around Mr Robinson, standing motionless on his plinth. Reading the pamphlet on the table next to him, we learn that JR was born on Monday, 27 December 1943 in Cicero, Illinois, a working-class suburb of Chicago. He was one of five children to devout Roman Catholics, and you are about to say: 'WOW! Hey dearest, look at this! When JR was thirteen, he became an Eagle Scout. Gosh, he was chosen as the leader of 120 Scouts, who flew to London to appear before Queen Elizabeth II and the Duke of Edinburgh, at a Royal Command Performance at the London Palladium! Umm, yes, on 18 November 1957. Wow, he even chatted backstage to Judy Garland and told actress Gracie Fields that he planned to study for the priesthood!'

Taking a few steps back we can see that JR looks every inch an average, honest businessman; certainly no different to the thousands of well-suited gents who pour through London's train station turnstiles morning, noon and night. Precisely five-foot-nine he weighs 167 lb, with green eyes and is balding with partially grey hair. He wears gold-rimmed spectacles and is so perfectly normal in every other respect you wouldn't take notice if he sat down next to you on a bus.

Ah, I see that you are now reading through JR's curriculum vitae, richly embroidered as it is in merit and distinction. A freshman at Quigley Preparatory Seminary, in downtown Chicago, he married Nancy Jo Lynch in 1964. 'We were together for 41 years,' says he. 'I shared some of the best days of my life. She loved me and we were always a happy couple.'

Moving down the first page of JR's CV, we learn that he attended a trade school in Kansas City, Missouri. Here, he learned the radiology profession, earning numerous diplomas. He was just twenty-one at this time. Nancy gave birth to a daughter [name deleted to protect her identity] and JR applied for a job as a lab technician and office manager. Indeed, the aforementioned Dr Graham later recalled that he had been impressed with Robinson's credentials as an Eagle Scout and his 'extensive credentials', him having a university degree in radiology.

Around 1970, JR's CV shows that he changed jobs to become the manager of a TV rental company and he did very well because in 1977 he bought a large, waterfront house. It was set in four acres of prime real estate at Pleasant Valley Farms, an affluent and prosperous neighbourhood of Johnson County, Kansas. By now, he and Nancy had four children and it was here, in picturesque, rural surroundings, that JR formed a company called Hydro-Gro Inc. According to him, the firm dealt in hydroponics, a method of growing plants using mineral solutions, heat and, instead of soil, a hell of a lot of water.

In the CV folder you'll see a glossy, 64-page brochure promoting Hydro-Gro Inc. It states that John is a 'sought-after lecturer', 'author' and 'pioneer in hydroponics'. Indeed, he truly was appointed to the board of governors of a workshop for disabled people to be awarded the distinction of becoming 'Man of the Year' for his work with the handicapped. Indeed, as the press cuttings prove, amid the glare of much publicity, the *Kansas City Times* proclaimed Robinson's virtues and, at a special dinner and presentation ceremony, he was given a grandiose gesture of approbation in the form of a certificate signed by the mayor *and* the Missouri State senator.

We also learn from his CV that in 1980, JR was given the position of director of personnel with the Mobil Corporation, then he moved on to add yet another firm, Equi-Plus, to his impressive portfolio. This newcomer to the Robinson stable specialised in 'management consultancy' and was very soon engaged by Back Care Systems Inc., a well-respected company that ran seminars on the treatment of back pain. And did he give them a pain in the back? Did he ever!

We can see from JR's CV that he was now an established Kansas City high-roller, who had no problems attracting investors for his next venture, Equi-II – an Overland Park corporation. He was presently describing himself as a 'consultant in medical, agricultural and charitable ventures'. Indeed, so impressed were they with JR, that local companies and organisations were literally begging him to join them. The Truman Medical Center, in Independence, a small city in Montgomery County, approached him. The doctors and medical hierarchy were so impressed with JR that he was invited to speak to their social workers, telling them that he, together with some other local businessmen, had formed Kansas City Outreach. This, he explained while talking patronisingly over the top of his spectacles, was a charitable organisation, which would provide young unmarried mothers with housing and career training, along with a baby-sitting service. At the same time, JR, using the Truman Medical Center's credentials, was also pitching the same project to Birthright, a set-up giving help to young pregnant women, who, in turn, pointed him in the direction of Hope House, a refuge for single mums.

JR was now considered a Patron Saint of Lost Causes, so much so that this Saint Jude was affirming that Kansas City Outreach was likely to receive 'funding from Xerox, IBM, and other major corporations', and he provided the correspondence to prove it.

So there we have the CV, which John Robinson has in a folder next to him, standing on his plinth:

CASE STUDY – SAVAGE: JOHN 'JR' ROBINSON

- The Eagle Scout who entertained a British Queen and rubbed shoulders with famous entertainers.
- Well-educated with a degree in radiography.
- Happily married for forty-one years with four adoring children.
- Lab technician and office manager to none other than a brigadier general who had been US President Harry Truman and his wife's personal physician.
- Manager of a TV rental company.
- Founder and CEO of Hydro-Gro Inc. – 'sought-after lecturer and author'.
- Kansas City 'Man of the Year'.
- Director of Personnel with the Mobil Corporation.
- Founder and CEO of Equi-Plus – consultants to Back Care Systems Inc.
- Founder and CEO of Equi-Plus II – 'consultants in medical, agricultural and charitable ventures'.
- Consultant to the Truman Medical Center.
- Fundraiser for Birthright and Hope House to help pregnant mothers with a refuge, education, work placement and baby-sitting, with funding from Xerox, IBM and major corporations.

The problem was that all this was nonsense. And no one, NOT ANYONE, suspected that JR was a sexual deviant and soon-to-be savage sado-sexual serial killer from start to finish.

So, having walked around JR and read the CV he wants you to believe – and even today he still demands you believe he has a gilt-edged reputation – let's take off his mask of alleged normalcy and see precisely what was going on inside this wicked man's head.

BEGINNING WITH JR'S
SCHOOLING

JR was an Eagle Scout and that's as good as it gets. His record at Quigley Prep Seminary shows that he was a 'lacklustre student and a discipline problem', so much so that he didn't return for his second year of study. He was denied admission as a sophomore due to his 'academic and behavioral shortcomings'.

HIS MARRIAGE

Indeed, so happy was his wife Nancy that after forty-one years of domestic purgatory, and now aware of his philandering ways after his arrest for multiple homicide (another of her husband's notable shortcomings), she said that JR had never done an honest day's work in his life. Added to which was the not indelicate issue of her suddenly learning of him having murdered at least seven women and stuffed their remains into steel barrels, where they were left to decompose in their own fluids. Oh, yes, and Nancy was none too pleased to learn that he had also stolen the baby of one of his murder victims and sold the tot to his unwitting brother Don and wife Helen, the childless couple being anxious to adopt. For this service, JR generously discounted the cash price to $3,000 for the adoption certificate, which was signed by a notary, two lawyers and a judge (the entire document being phoney).

Previous to JR's arrest for murder, Nancy, just like Sonia Sutcliffe and Primrose Shipman, had not suspected that her husband was a savage sado-sexual serial killer any more than anyone else had.

CASE STUDY – SAVAGE: JOHN 'JR' ROBINSON

DR GRAHAM

It *is* true that JR secured a job with this distinguished gentleman, but only after he'd provided phoney credentials in the form of fake certificates that he himself had manufactured. And let's get this straight for Dr Graham was nobody's fool. This man was a former boxer with an interest in botany, who featured in *The New York Times Magazine* in 1964. What's more, he was a hero. In the spring of 1944, as a member of the First Hospital Unit of the First Army, Captain Graham had waded ashore at 'Easy Red' Omaha Beach, four days after D-Day. With the battle still raging just a few miles ahead, he treated the wounded in the thick of battle and, by nightfall, his tents, with 400 beds, had taken in close to 900 of the wounded and dying. Moving across France and Belgium, then into Germany, his unit saw some of the war's bitterest engagements, including the Battle of the Bulge, where he was wounded. He was awarded the Bronze Star among other decorations, as well as medals from France, Britain, the Netherlands and Belgium.

So how did JR repay Dr Graham? He embezzled $US33,000 from the then fifty-seven-year-old, engaged in sexual liaisons with both office staff and patients – persuading one patient in the X-ray lab to have sex with him by pretending his wife Nancy was terminally ill and unable to satisfy him sexually.

Just six months after he was taken on at the medical practice, JR was able to buy a new house. He had drained the practice's bank account to such an extent that a bewildered and intractably confused Dr Graham was unable to pay Christmas bonuses to his staff.

In 1969, Robinson was convicted of this theft. Because it was his first offence and, pledging restitution, a Jackson County judge exercised leniency, sentencing JR to three years' probation. Dr Graham never saw a cent of the money that JR had stolen from him and died a highly disillusioned man. A brigadier general (later a major general of the US Air Force), who was also a medical doctor and clearly exceptional in terms of intelligence, decency, honour, ability and experience of life, was defenceless against JR's cunning.

TV SALESMAN

It is true that JR next found employment with a TV rental company. He soon 'tuned in' to stealing merchandise from this employer too. When his crime was eventually exposed, the firm did not prosecute, but sack him they most certainly did. His boss later said: 'He gave a very good impression, well-dressed, nice-looking, seemed to know a lot, very glib and a good speaker. You know he went on to defraud tens of thousands of dollars from various companies to help him on his way.'

HYDRO-GRO INC.

Giving credit where credit is due, if JR was anything he was persistent and remarkably evasive. For the next 20 years he bounced from job to job, managing to evade custodial sentences by crossing his fingers and jurisdictional boundaries, at the same time convincing employers not to press charges whenever he was found out.

Claiming to be a 'sought-after lecturer, author and pioneer in hydroponics', the latter assertion would have certainly come as a surprise to the ancients, as the Hanging Gardens of Babylon, the Aztec's Floating Gardens of Mexico and those of the Chinese are far earlier examples of hydroponic culture than JR could have 'pioneered'. Indeed, Egyptian hieroglyphic records, dating back several hundred years BC, describe the growing of plants in water, so hydroponics is hardly a new method of growing plants. But by the 1970s, it wasn't just scientists and analysts – many of whom worked for NASA – who were involved. The many virtues of this method of plant production also began to attract traditional farmers and eager hobbyists, but John E. Robinson, the self-proclaimed pioneer in hydroponics – and this will come as no surprise – was not listed among them.

Hydro-Gro Inc was, of course, a bogus set-up, and in its development JR swindled a close friend out of $25,000. The man had been duped into investing because he hoped to get better investment returns to pay for his dying wife's medical care.

THE *KANSAS CITY TIMES*

Here we celebrate not only the gullibility of the reporters who covered JR's elevation to 'Man of the Year' award, but also the crass stupidity of scores more sensible business people right up to City Hall, the mayor and the State Governor, for now we find JR using his remarkable skill in deception to run rings around the lot of them. I mean you could not make this up if you tried for not a single person took the trouble to check the veracity of JR's phoney credentials, least of all if he had ever been in trouble with the police or the judicial system, which he most certainly had.

JR did, however, come unstuck. A short time after receiving his 'Man of the Year' award, which, according to him came as a 'complete surprise', and telling me in a letter that, 'I had no idea that the City would be honoring me', it turned out this meritorious award had been obtained fraudulently. It transpired that it had been granted as a result of fake letters of commendation received at City Hall, all written by none other than the 'Man of the Year' himself – John E Robinson Sr.

Things now went from bad to worse for JR when the city fathers, whose names had been forged on the letters of recommendation, read about the event in the local press. One man was outraged because on his alleged letter supporting Robinson, his name had even been spelt incorrectly. The *Kansas City Times*, stung by the scam, took its revenge by exposing JR as a fraud. His children were ridiculed at school and his wife was reluctant to show her face in public. But how did JR react? One might have thought that if he had possessed the right moral ingredients then he would have concocted a potion to make himself invisible. The truth, however, was that JR, a fake who was as genuine as a hooker's smile, couldn't have cared less and continued to sail on regardless.

DIRECTOR OF PERSONNEL AT THE MOBIL CORPORATION

'He [JR] had no real employment, unless you consider figuring out ways of scamming people out of their money to be real employment.'
– District Attorney Paul Morrison – Robinson's murder 2002 trial

When JR worked for Mobil, he soon honed in, like a heat-seeking missile, on the company's chequebook to divert the not insubstantial sum of $40,000, plus $300.00 in postage stamps into PSA, a paper company that he owned. Once again he found himself on probation, this time for five years.

Between 1969 and 1991, John Robinson was convicted four

times for embezzlement and theft, earning himself another notable distinction: that of being barred for life by the Securities and Exchange Commission from engaging in any kind of involvement in business. So did this bring an end to this man's criminal versatility? Not a chance!

EQUI-PLUS

'Christopher, you ask me to describe Mr John Robinson. In hindsight, I don't think that we carried out due diligence very well when we took on Equi-Plus. Actually, we did meet with John Osborn [JR's alias] from time-to-time, and we were very satisfied with the credentials Equi-Plus provided. We were conned. He took us for something like $40,000.'

– Former CEO of Back Care Systems,
to the author in 2012

Avoiding financial castration by the skin of his teeth and using a whole raft of aliases to include 'John Osborne', JR soldiered on, unfettered and undeterred, to start up Equi-Plus. Engaged by Back Care Systems, an honourable company that ran seminars on the treatment of back pain, he would soon give the firm a pain in the backside, while Robinson was in his element.

To keep this brief, Equi-Plus, owned by John Robinson, aka 'John Osborne', was awarded a lucrative contract to prepare a package that included a marketing plan, printed publicity material and promotional videos advising the public on how to successfully resolve back pain. However, what Equi-Plus actually provided was a string of inflated, in most cases bogus, invoices and very little else.

Once again, a criminal investigation was started into the

business activities of the energetic JR, who responded by producing a series of faked affidavits, all of which attested to the legitimacy of the invoices submitted to Back Care Systems.

EQUI-II

While the aforementioned investigation continued, this slippery eel founded Equi-II, a corporation in which he described himself as a 'consultant in medical, agricultural and charitable ventures'. Using some of the money embezzled out of Back Care Systems, he acquired an apartment in Olathe, a city south of Kansas City. Here, in this most agreeable of extra-marital climates, he was able to enjoy numerous sexual affairs with women, one of whom is quoted as saying: 'John kind of swept me off my feet [echoes of John Cannan here]. He treated me like a queen and always had money to take me to nice restaurants and hotels.'

Well done, John, but there's no such thing as a free lunch. Retribution loomed on the horizon for the thieving and libidinous Robinson. The theft of the money from Back Care Systems resulted in him being convicted and, given his previous criminal record, this time he faced a possible prison sentence of seven years. However, there was not much chance of JR doing seven years behind bars, for he spent just a couple of months in jail while he assisted the warden in keeping better financial records before being placed on probation, this time for five years.

THE KILLINGS

Sadly, I am obliged to explain to the reader of this book that my allocated 75,000 word count for *Talking with Psychopaths and Savages* is all but expired at this point, and please understand why this restriction prevents me from detailing JR's murders in any detail, for this book is about getting inside the heads of these evil men and women, not so much about the intricate and disgusting details of their crimes. As I mentioned right from the get-go, I have thousands of official documents, scenes-of-crime photographs, countless upon countless letters from psychopaths in my library – material never published before, let alone not having seen the light of day. Some of this invaluable research material has been copied, and sent gratis, to the FBI and other law enforcement agencies and institutions with a professional interest in the study of psychopathy.

My book, *Dead Men Walking: True Stories of the Most Evil Men and Women on Death Row*, also published by John Blake, does have a chapter dedicated to John Robinson. This contains much fuller details of JR's murders. He murdered Lisa Stasi after entrapping her during one of his outreach projects. After killing her, he sold her baby to his brother.

While serving a much longer prison term for fraud in the Western Missouri Correction Facility, he befriended, of all people, the facility's doctor, one William Bonner. And, while incarcerated, JR developed an extra-curricular relationship with Dr Bonner's vivacious forty-nine-year-old wife, Beverly.

With echoes of John Cannan's relationship with solicitor Annabel Rose in mind, it's interesting to note that Beverly was the prison librarian and JR soon inveigled his way into a job looking after her in every sense, to include caring for her financially. After his release from prison, he employed the utterly besotted, and now divorced Beverly, as a director of Hydro-Gro, then he murdered her, continuing to claiming her alimony payments, which were directed to a post office box number used by him.

No one would ever have guessed that Beverly Jean Bonner

(who upon inquiries from her husband was told by JR that she gone to Australia) was now rotting inside a steel barrel in Locker No. (E2), next to two other 55-gallon barrels containing the remains of Sheila Dale Faith and her handicapped daughter, Debbie, whose government cheques also continued to supplement Robinson's income.

No one could ever have imagined in a million years that former 'Man of the Year' JR was, indeed, the 'Slave Master' who combed through the darkest corners of the World Wide Web and its BDSM sites, trawling for victims whom he could lure into his own lethal web, to savagely rape, abuse, treat like trash, torture, kill and dump in barrels, too. Did any of these women ever consider doing what I have suggested previously in this book and in *Murder.com*? Namely, to take a step back, walk around the person who currently charms you, entrances you, and at least use a little commonsense before jumping in? No!

This book is about talking with psychopaths and savages – at least this is the brief from my publisher, John Blake. Professor Leigh (name and date omitted changed to protect her identity) and I decided that we would both approach John Robinson, each using our own particular skills. For her part, she would entice him with the pretty female fisherman's lure of BDSM. Some of how he responded to her is published exclusively in *Dead Man Talking*. Shocking stuff, believe me. The remainder, of course, is not for our eyes as this is FBI-generated material.

While Leigh would use sex as a lure, for my part, I would approach avaricious Mr Robinson using the bait of financial gain and as a result, all of his overblown vanity would be turned upside down. Effectively, to get the ever-manipulative John Robinson to thoroughly expose the man behind the mask,

CASE STUDY – SAVAGE: JOHN 'JR' ROBINSON

Professor Leigh and I would collectively use 'Mind Control' and when we had what we needed, we would pull his plug.

To begin with, JR demanded $500 from me for details of his Eagle Scout appearance at the 1957 Royal Command Performance in front of HM Queen Elizabeth II. Notwithstanding this information can be readily found on the Internet, John wrote to me, saying:

> I have never discussed this with anyone before, and I will not discuss it with you now. This is very valuable information to me. Your British readers would be very interested in my appearing before the Queen. If you send me $500.00 I will give you the exclusive story, which you can sell to the media and make a lot of money.

I then wrote to him, saying that I wanted to write a fair and honest account of his life and of the fix he now found himself in. That perhaps the media had it about right, that he *was* addicted to sexual exploitation. His reply of 4 March 2008 was:

> Your unwarranted accusation of attempted manipulation and flim-flam (as written) much says it all. Don't blow smoke. I don't have time for meaningless delays. I don't have the funds to play games.

At once readily immersing himself in sexual BDSM fantasies with Leigh, JR then demanded that myself and a TV production company should 'dig deeper' and should follow his every whim because he is also a totally innocent man (bearing in mind he had already pleaded guilty to avoid the death sentence). He then had this to say:

TALKING WITH PSYCHOPATHS AND SAVAGES

I was represented by a court-appointed attorney who did NO INVESTIGATION, hired no experts, tested nothing and admitted in court a day prior to my trial they had not read discovery.

> — John E. Robinson, letter to the author,
> 14 January 2008

This was an untrue statement because the case against JR was so overwhelming that his attorney advised his client that he should either plead guilty and receive a natural life term or face the death sentence. Robinson opted for the former but now, sensing the international acclaim he had always sought was within reach, JR continued with:

> Next we will proceed to the expert phase. First to examine and evaluate documents, photos and testing. Then to complete the necessary testing that has never been done before. Each step of the way, we will evaluate and adjust our investigation or approach as required.
>
> The proposed budget is fairly simple at this point but may have to be adjusted depending on need:

Database::£100,000.00

Investigators::$150.00

Travel::$20.00

Experts::$60,000.00

Attorney::$50,000.00

Communication, copies, supplies @ $10.00

Equipment::$8.00

Misc::$2,000.00

With this proviso that my attorney would control all information and distribution of funds. Nothing will begin until there is a form written agreement in place.

In short order, JR followed this up with:

> My letter to you was clear about the possibilities available to you. Yet you responded with a request for information about my formative years, assuming it would be no threat to my present and future legal status. Unfortunately, that is not the case. When I win a new trial, it will be necessary to prepare a 'mitigation case' containing the very information you now seek. My attorneys did not provide or provide any mitigation evidence at my first trial [for murder].
>
> I did offer you a smidgen of palpable research material right there in England. In November of 1957, I was a 13-year-old Boy Scout who traveled to London to appear in the Command Performance for the Queen. No one has yet recovered the newspaper articles of that trip. [Oh yes, we have, John!]. As you see, everything is tied together.

John went on to say:

> Christopher, I offered you to do a real life true crime book and documentary. One that would expose blatant police and prosecutorial misconduct, fairly present the real evidence including complete details of the lives of the victims, and perhaps unveil the real killer. You could of course simply go for titillating, sensationalized products based on fiction already out there. That decision, of course, is yours.

JR rambled on and on to me (despite the fact that he was also writing about extreme S&M practices which included 'Slave Contracts', bondage, beating, mutually acceptable rape, another use for bananas, extracurricular activities called 'SKAT' and 'Golden Rain', and total submission to 'The Master', to my colleague Annabel Leigh). He wrote to me with:

> Determined to either prove my innocence or die before trying I began writing letters to anyone and everyone I could think of for both the UK portion of my case as well as those who might possible [*sic*] help on this side of the pond. I wrote to Alan Hayling – head of documentaries at the BBC, in March 2007, and received not even a courtesy reply. I recently wrote to Mr Felix Dennis, owner of *Maxim* magazine, who lives in Stratford-upon-Avon, and have no word yet.
>
> My basic offer has been very simple. If they would provide funding [the previous $400,000] for the investigation and testing, and the equipment necessary, I would give them access to the results no matter the outcome as long as everyone agrees that nothing would be made public until my attorney authorized release.

Nevertheless, moving up a gear from second to third, JR put his boot to the metal. Working up lather with hardly a breath in between, he wrote:

> The cost of putting all discovery information onto a searchable interactive data base, investigating, testing, travel and equipment will be about $400K and will require at least twelve months to complete. The investigator will need some specialized equipment – video and digital

recorders capable of two concurrent recordings. All funds would be disbursed to my attorney. I would receive nothing but an allocation to cover supplies and postage. As a bonus for you, I have lots of criminology students who write to me and we can add them to our research team for a small cost to cover their expenses.

He then added:

We are starting from scratch with a thorough methodical investigation of everything. I have studied the several book covers you sent to me. One of your books is published by Virgin. In fact, I have already written to Richard Branson and I am anticipating a favorable reply so maybe you and Mr Branson can work together. Every document, every photo, every video, every witness, testing every item and utilizing acknowledged experts to evaluate to calculate every person or object. As written.

As the reader may now imagine, I was rapidly losing the will to live with all this drivel pouring through my letterbox. Even my 'Postman Pat' – ever the discreet sort of guy who wears Royal Mail issue shorts in the most inclement weather – remarked: 'And here you are, sir. Another lot of crap from Mr Robinson today!'

'We started removing bodies from the front [of Locker E2]. After less than 10 minutes there was a very foul odor that with my past experience I associated with a dead body.'
    – Douglas Borchering, Overland PF officer shortly after Robinson's arrest on Friday, 2 June 2000.

'Ah, yes, John,' I replied. 'That sounds just fine. But what about the five decomposing bodies found in barrels on your property and in your unit at the storage unit? If you could provide me with the name, address and zip code of your attorney I can contact him.'

Completely ignoring my questions, Robinson replied:

> To facilitate this investigation we [the non-existent attorney] have obtained every page of material connected to my case, some 300,000 more or less. Here is how we anticipate proceedings:
>
> A) A database will be designed with unlimited search capabilities. All documents will be scanned, cross-referenced with new documents added as developed.
>
> B) A full-time investigator will be hired under the supervision of my attorney. He/she will complete the legwork required to secure records and documents previously ignored, and conduct video interviews with all witnesses. My attorney has taken on a very able researcher called Miss — — [name supplied]. Her fees will be negotiable and all financial transactions between Miss Leigh will be conducted through me, personally. I think that $5,000 per week will be acceptable to her and my attorney.
>
> John...

> I may be able to up the ante for you. For several years I have been in contact with a person who befriended Dennis Rader, the confessed BTK killer of 10. This person visited him in jail and corresponded with him regularly. This individual claims to have details and information never before revealed and has been

working on a book. This person has information, wants to do a book but has no industry name like you. The two of you should be able to do a great 'insider' true crime book and a documentary about BTK. You and your publisher could end up getting two for the price of one. I will await word from you.

For God's sake JR, what about the five bodies [in the barrels]?

For the record, I will explain exactly how the Kansas Department of Correction mail system works. When a letter is received it is automatically date stamped on the outside of the envelope. Then the letter is opened by the censors, date and time stamped, read and all letters to the inmates in segregation copied.

And so he goes on and on, and for ten more pages of excruciating drivel, so it was at this point that I decided to pull the plug on JR.

By now I had seen a copy of the 'Slave Contract' he ordered Annabel Leigh to download from the Internet (you can find these contracts if you have a mind to) and she signed it for him. However, what a 'Slave Contract' basically entails is that the 'Slave Master' (in this case, JR) completely controls and dominates his slave (in this case, Annabel Leigh) forever and a day. The slave will submit herself/himself to any form of extreme BDSM practices to include: waiting hand–on–foot, bondage, whipping, thrashing and other forms of humiliation that my publishers *absolutely forbid* me from detailing here for fear of upsetting readers of a more delicate disposition. And, if this is not entirely sufficient, the 'Slave Master' often demands control of all of the slave's finances, too.

TALKING WITH PSYCHOPATHS AND SAVAGES

What truly shocked me is the fact that several of JR's murder victims actually signed 'Slave Contracts' with him and ended up in barrels.

When he learned, from myself, and Annabel Leigh, that he, this homicidal 'Del Boy', had been stitched up and conned.

'You, Berry-Dee, have wasted my valuable time,' he fumed from his Special Housing Unit cell, where he lives in solitary confinement (like Kenneth Bianchi) because the other inmates would kill him. 'I have never asked you for $400,000. I didn't say I was going to use students, and if you print this I might sue you. This is what he wrote. I fucking told you that I never used the Internet, and I was never into BDSM, and I was never into kinky sex. FUCK OFF!'

> 'This is all classic John Robinson. The guy was and is a gamesman to the end.'
> — District Attorney, speaking to the *Kansas City Star* after Robinson's trial

> 'JR loved mirrors. He spent half of his life admiring himself and polishing his act in front of mirrors. And could this man talk, he never stopped yapping on and on. I guess he had to, Chris, because he wasn't exactly a fine figure of a man and he had a waddle to his walk. I now tell my colleagues that if it walks like a duck, preens its feather like a duck and screeches like a duck, then it's a Robinson.'
> — Stephen Haymes, former probation office to John Robinson to the author at interview in 2012.

And, that was it, end of story. Clearly, I'd pissed JR off. If John

CASE STUDY – SAVAGE: JOHN 'JR' ROBINSON

Robinson wasn't such a deadly dangerous man, one could read his letters and have a damned good rib-tickling laugh.

But was this really the end of my work with JR? I am mindful that he has not revealed the body deposition sites of three victims of whose murders he was convicted – Paula Godfrey, Lisa Stasi and Catherine Clampitt – –thereby denying closure to their families. Therefore, Professor Leigh and I set John Robinson up, with Ms Leigh using her cleverly designed 'honey trap' and me offering the lure of untold riches. We effectively turned the tables on this man who has, for decades, been turning the tables on just about everyone he came into contact with. The results were disturbing, and when JR reads this book, he will flip again.

For me, and Professor Leigh – who for decades has been covertly working with serial killers and has had many remarkable successes and contributed immensely to the FBI's offender profiling database – this was something of a pyrrhic victory.. John Robinson, in this respect, still remains in control, a 'Slave Master General' and 'Master Manipulator' to the end.

Tailpiece: Could You Have Spotted These?

PAEDOPHILES

For decades the now-deceased psychopathic and self-obsessed paedophile Sir James Wilson Vincent 'Jimmy' Savile, OBE, KCSG (31 October 1926–29 October 2001, aged eighty-four) was feted by the British media. He hosted the BBC television show *Jim'll Fix It* (1975–94) and was the first and last presenter of the long-running BBC music chart series *Top of the Pops*. According to his Wikipedia entry, he raised approximately £40 million for charities.

Did any of the scores of psychiatrists (who *must* have read an edition of the *Diagnostic and Statistical Manual of Mental Disorders* or Professor Hare's Checklist), child welfare workers, plus senior NHS management staff who gave Mr Savile complete and unfettered access to the children's wards at Stoke Mandeville Hospital in Aylesbury, Leeds General Infirmary and Broadmoor Hospital in Berkshire (as well as other places), suspect for one moment that he was a predatory psychopath? Absolutely not!

During his lifetime there had been allegations that he was abusing children, but they were dismissed, with the accusers ignored or disbelieved – some of whom he took legal action against. Fourteen police forces across the UK now believe that Savile was one of Britain's worst sex offenders with some 300 victims, among them staff and patients from various institutions aged between five and seventy-five, throughout several decades.

NOT PSYCHOPATHS OR SAVAGES, BUT MONSTERS

The former radio and television presenter for the BBC, James Stuart Hall (b. 25 December 1929), spent most of his career parading himself across our television screens, becoming known nationally for presenting *It's a Knockout* and *Jeux Sans Frontières* (1965–99). In December 2012 and January 2013, aged eighty-three, he was charged with multiple sex offences. He was sent to prison and was released on licence in December 2015. Did the millions of viewers who heard this monster reporting on football matches, or his wife of fifty-seven years, ever consider him a pervert? No!

In my former capacity as a freelance investigative journalist, I knew the London-based publicist, Maxwell Frank 'Max Clifford' (b. 6 April 1943). We met in his office, and it wasn't a plush place either. Did I suspect that this happily married man was a sexual beast? Not at all and nor, it seemed, did the scores of newspaper people and the millions of readers who bought his most often controversial 'Red Top', Kiss-and-Tell stories. Indeed, I met his ailing wife, Elizabeth, who passed away in 2003. She doted on Max, and he on her. He married Jo Westwood in 2010. She rapidly divorced him in 2014 after he was sentenced to eight years imprisonment when found guilty of eight indecent assaults on four girls and young women aged between fourteen and nineteen. At the time of writing, he is behind bars at HM Prison Littlehey in Perry, Cambridgeshire. During his long and successful career did Elizabeth, later his second wife Jo, suspect that Clifford was a sociopath? Absolutely not!

Then there is the convicted paedophile Rolf Harris CBE (b. 30 March 1930). Adored by millions since childhood, now we learn after so many Christmases have passed that this once famous showbiz star and cartoonist, who rubbed shoulders with royalty, a Pope and who knows who else, most often had his didgeridoo in one hand and a hapless youngster in the other.

I'll give him 'Tie Me Kangaroo Down, Sport', for in my opinion this disgusting man should have been horsewhipped within an inch of his life.

Those of us – especially people of around my age – will recall Harris presenting shows such as *Rolf's Cartoon Club* and *Animal Hospital*. In 2005 he was commissioned to paint an official portrait of Queen Elizabeth I. As I understand it, anyone even coming close to 'Her Mage' must undergo a strict vetting process, let alone share her company while she sits for a portrait (which in Harris's case was not a very complimentary portrait at all). Of course, no one at the Palace, nor his wife, Alwen Hughes, nor anyone else involved in the arrangements had an inkling that the manipulative, amoral Aussie from Bassendean, Perth, would be jailed in 2014, aged eighty-four, on 12 counts of indecent assault on four female victims, then aged between eighteen and nineteen. This displeased Her Majesty; so much so that she stripped him of the many honours awarded him. My sources tell me that the portrait painted by Mr Harris has since been destroyed.

Harris is presently serving a prison term of five years and nine months at HM Prison Stafford, where he teaches his fellow inmates to paint.

Conclusions

'Christopher. I have to tell you that it was after reading your book, *Talking with Serial Killers*, that I decided to study criminology and go for a degree. Thank you so much.'

– Jake, now studying criminology,
Hampshire, UK, 2016

There, I think that I have arrived at the end of my journey with you on this brief visit to the almost unfathomable mindsets of psychopaths and savages, and I await the wrath of psychiatrists from almost any place in so doing. But this is not a book intended for such an illustrious, professional readership because I am sure the experts will all know better than me (or maybe not), or they will sit on the fence, as they so often do, yet this is *my* book, so I am up for criticism if it comes my way.

While I am full of admiration for those who do concern themselves with trying to unravel the psychopathic mind, after reading through Professor Hare's world-recognised PCL-R Checklist, which writer Jon Ronson alludes to in *The Psychopath Test*, I conclude that it is designed for people such as psychiatrists, prison officers, welfare workers and the like. I would imagine that a qualified psychiatrist – who ought to have studied *DSM-IVTR* (or any previous edition) would, or should, know what constitutes a psychopathic personality in the first place.

I have talked with many correctional officers charged with looking after the welfare of convicted psychopathic killers and other savages and, quite frankly, whether or not a felon is a psychopath matters little in the performance of their daily duties. Whether an inmate is a mass murderer, or a persistent shoplifter, a sociopathic bent lawyer, judge, showbiz star, sports person, rip-off banker or expense-fiddling MP, they are all treated the same way within the correctional system and this is a good thing. Serial killer Michael Ross learned and taught Braille while on 'The Green Mile'. Rolf Harris teaches cons to draw and paint. Once that prison gate slams shut, they simply become a 'number' within the correctional system and that is a fact.

As for welfare workers studying Professor Hare's Checklist? Well, these offenders only come to the attention of welfare workers once the criminal deeds have been done and, as the Professor himself says, psychopathy is incurable in any event – so what's the point

The subtitle of Jon Ronson's book is: *A Journey Through the Madness Industry* and, whoopee, has he got it right on this score, with this suggestion. One can use all of the psychopath tests ever invented but one *cannot* spot a psychopath until – most especially in the cases of *homicidal* psychopaths – it is far too late.

I could have cited hundreds of cases where this dread scenario applies. One has only to research the thousands of cases going back decades where – like the aforementioned sexual predator Neville Heath (see also pages 58–9) – men, women and oft-times children have fallen prey to such killers without a clue that their lives were about to be snuffed out in an instant. And the reason why we do not suspect that evil may be coming our way is because we live in a 'Bubble World'. The furthest thing from our minds (even *my* mind) is to refer to some form of psychopathic checklist before we date someone, employ someone, or indeed are treated by a doctor such as Harold Shipman, who can be listed among the scores of doctors, psychiatrists, nurses and surgeons who have committed homicide over the decades.

Yet so many thousands of gullible men and women *do* indeed fall foul of such predators lurking in the darkest places on the Internet, or in dating agencies. In doing so they may be offering themselves up on a plate to be conned, robbed, raped or even murdered, as was the case with John Robinson. Using the Internet, JR lured several of his female victims to their deaths by phoney offers of well-paid employment. This form of deadly entrapment has been going on for decades using newspaper 'Want Ads', more recently 'Craig's List' and the 'Lonely Hearts' columns. I could write yet another book detailing cases running back a hundred years on this subject alone.

History confirms that psychopaths are incurable and savages cannot be tamed. A narcissistic personality is easier to spot within an interpersonal relationship where red flags pop up that underneath this narcissism – especially involving threats of violence, unreasonable control, unfounded jealousy and blatant lying – there exists a metamorphosing psychopathy of sorts, therefore any further relationship should be avoided at all costs. We all want to see goodness reciprocated in others, but beware of the mask that hides the intentions of those not so inclined –

and the psychopath and bullying narcissist are, at best, weak and lonely folk, for they have only one thing in mind: themselves.

So, can you imagine having a twisted, corrupt mentality? One that offers only glibness and superficial charm; a grandiose sense of self-worth; a need for stimulation and that you are constantly prone to boredom? Being a pathological liar, cunning and manipulative, with no feelings of remorse or guilt? Can you picture yourself as one who is shallow, harbouring a callous lack of empathy; living from day to day a parasite upon your fellow man, unable to control your behaviour or to form a meaningful relationship with a partner, colleagues and real friends (of which you'll have none), all topped by a complete lack of realistic, long-term goals? Remember, this is the world that the psychopath inhabits – and beware, for savages lurk everywhere.

> The naïve person believes every word but the shrewd one ponders each step.
> The wise one is cautious and turns away from evil but the stupid one is reckless and over-confident.
>
> Proverbs 14: v. 15–16

For fear of seeming Evangelical, this dark world is truly not a good place to be except for the fact that psychopaths are, indeed, few on the ground and the majority of us live healthy, decent and honest lives. My book *Murder.com* was an early morning wakeup call to all who seek love on the Internet for in Cyberspace there are countless human predators waiting to entrap you, rob you, rape you or maybe kill you as happened with many of JR Robinson's victims. So, *Talking to Psychopaths and Savages* attempts to reinforce the writing on these two dark literary walls.

CONCLUSIONS

If you even sniff that someone is an overt narcissist or has the self-serving egotistical traits of a psychopathic person, or has moments when a savage nature peeks from behind a placid mask avoid them like the plague for your life and the lives of those close to you will be a lot safer and more enjoyable for it!

I stated at the beginning of this book that the world of psychopaths and savages is not a nice place to be, but I want to end on a much lighter note; one that I truly hope will bring a smile to your face, and this is a true anecdote indeed.

Quite recently I had cause to visit a friend who had suffered a breakdown and been placed under Section 3 of the Mental Health Act in St James Hospital, Portsmouth.

Upon leaving I was confronted by a doctor. What follows is our somewhat disturbing conversation:

Doctor: Where are you going?
CBD: Home.
Dr: What's your name?
CBD: Chris Berry-Dee. I am a true-crime writer and TV documentary maker.
Dr: Oh, *really*!
CBD: Yes. I am visiting a patient. I've been chatting to a psychiatrist.
Dr: Everyone in here talks to a psychiatrist. You are not going anywhere.

By now I was not only getting annoyed but becoming somewhat concerned, with echoes of the 1975 movie *One Flew Over the Cuckoo's Nest* rapidly creeping into my mind.

CBD: Look. Don't mess me about. I am not in the mood for it. I consult for law-enforcement agencies on serial homicide. I'm not Napoleon...

Dr: I can see that, because you are not wearing his hat.

I am *not* going back!

Sweet dreams.